ACE

Foreign Language Education

Introduction To BTM: Babble Training Method

All inquiries should be addressed to:

Book Domain LLC.
543 E Louise Dr Phoenix, Az 85050

Ordering Information:
Amount Deals. Special rebates are accessible on the amount bought by corporations, associations, and others. For points of interest, contact the distributor at the address above.

Printed in the United States of America.

ISBN-13   Paperback   978-1-964100-44-9
           eBook   978-1-964100-45-6

Library of Congress Control Number: 2025902467

ACE

Foreign Language Education

Introduction To BTM: Babble Training Method

Revised 2025

CHEOL BEOM LEE

BOOK DOMAIN LLC
Publish to Perfection

CONTENTS

PREFACE

After I published the first version of this book, *Thoughts on Foreign Language Education,* in 2009, had no meaningful responses from anyone. I took it as karma for this book. Yet, I was just happy that I at least did what I had to do: Reveal the undisputable truth for successful foreign language education for someone who would find this book later.

Now, about one and a half decade later, I received some meaningful response, and I revised the first book to add the strength to the one and only truth for successful FLE: BTM.

We know that piano skills cannot be acquired through rule studying, reading, writing, memorizing, listening, watching, and/or playing music with others. We know one can play music only after he/she acquires the required skills.

The history of foreign language education has proven that foreign languages cannot be acquired through rule studying, reading, writing, memorizing, listening, watching, and/or conversation. Few of us know conversation is possible only after he/she acquires the required skills.

It's very unfortunate that absolute majority of us including the leaders of foreign language education still have a blind faith in that foreign languages can be acquired through rule studying, reading, writing, memorizing, listening, watching, and/or conversation.

There is one and only method for one to be good at playing the piano. We know what it is. Likewise, there is one and only method for one to be good at speaking a foreign language. Yet, many of us, especially the leaders of foreign language education, still don't recognize it.

Over a decade has passed since this book was published. No meaningful changes have happened in the paradigm of foreign language education. I hope BTM will serve as a corner stone to set up a new normal paradigm for foreign language education.

From Flat Iron City
Boulder, Colorado
2025

ABOUT ACE FOREIGN LANGUAGE EDUCATION

Ace Foreign Language Education offers clear and easy solutions for the all-time unsolved dilemma with language programs: Never acquired oral proficiency. Lee claims that acquisition of oral proficiency is an easiest challenge compared to the acquisition of grammar, reading, writing, and listening skills. Lee further claims that the traditional methods have been completely wrong for the past century just like the geocentrism had been completely wrong until mid 19th century.

Lee claims that language is a skill of the speech organ to be acquired. The one and only way to acquire such skill is to follow the secret of natural language acquisition: Babbling. According to Lee's working hypothesis, three acquisition factors of physical capacity, linguistic intuition, and linguistic resources can be acquired at the same time only through intensive babble training over sufficient amount of real input to survive. Languages have been rather easily acquired with babbling only without acquisition of grammar, reading, writing, and/or listening comprehension skills. Yet, no languages have been acquired without babbling.

As a metaphor, Lee compares language programs to piano programs which contrast drastically to each other. Lee emphasizes that language teachers and students should follow the models of piano teachers and students.

In *Ace Foreign Language Education,* Lee introduces a revolutionary one-and-only universal approach called Babble Training Method

(BTM) to assure successful language acquisition. Lee also pinpoints the exact reasons for the all-time failure of the popular language programs. BTM is a comprehensive oral proficiency-oriented foreign language education method. It serves as a road map for teachers and students who are engaged into teaching or learning foreign languages.

In *Ace Foreign Language Education*, Lee takes readers on a transformative journey through the art of learning and mastering new languages. Drawing on decades of experience as a polyglot, a language teacher, and a linguistics expert, Lee provides a comprehensive, step-by-step guide that is accessible to anyone—from beginners to advanced learners—seeking to acquire a foreign language with confidence.

Unlike traditional language pedagogy books that focus purely on grammar and reading, *Ace Foreign Language Education* emphasizes a holistic, practical approach to language acquisition through intensive drills to talk over real input just like how a native language is acquired in a real world. The book breaks down common barriers that often prevent learners from reaching oral proficiency, such as blinded belief in grammar, extensive reading, listening, watching TV or movies and the overwhelm of memorizing endless vocabulary lists. Lee introduces readers to the concept of language immersion techniques, mental conditioning, and learning through real input, offering strategies that mimic natural language acquisition methods.

Through engaging exercises, real-world examples, and detailed explanations, *Ace Foreign Language Education* shows that learning a new language doesn't have to be daunting—it can be an exciting, rewarding experience. Lee's personal anecdotes and insights into how language learning shapes one's worldview and connects cultures provide an inspiring backdrop to the book.

Whether you're learning for travel, business, or personal growth, *Ace Foreign Language Education* is the ultimate resource to help you achieve fluency and unlock the power of communication across cultures.

Summary: BTM Hypothesis

1. Working Hypothesis on Language Acquisition

Language acquisition requires babbling[1] over due amount of real input[2] and time[3] to acquire the following three acquisition factors[4] simultaneously: (1) Linguistic intuition, (2) Physical capacity, (3) Linguistic resources.

2. Working Hypothesis on Input and Output

    (1)   There is no mutation between input and output.

---

[1] I use the term 'Babble' or 'Babbling' to mean the learner's repeated acts of mimicking, copying, talking to oneself, memorizing, practicing, and using Real Input with a purpose of acquiring language, especially oral proficiency. However, in a broad sense, I also use the term to mean the learner's repeated practice acts of listening, reading and writing after Real Input with a purpose of acquiring respective skills.

[2] This is a term I use as a reference to the realistic input that learners can acquire and actually use in his/her real life environment. Depending on intended outputs, real input can be specified as real input to learn talking, reading, listening, writing, and grammar respectively. Input which lacks the features like usability, story, conversation, vocabulary, voice, and grammar, which are required to facilitate the acquisition of the intended output, is not qualified as effective and efficient real input for the respective intended outputs. In a narrow sense, real input means practical expressions with native speakers voice which students can use for oral communication in their daily environments.

[3] Due amount of real input and time varies depending on individual's linguistic resistance against TL and degree of mental immersion to learn TL. Concrete discussion will be introduced later.

[4] See the article under the title of 'Working Hypothesis on Language Acquisition'.

(2) No input produces no output.

(3) There is individual linguistic resistance[5] to be overcome for meaningful transition from input to output.

(4) The input the most real, simple, and well understood to learner produces the most effective output.

(5) The proficiency level of the outputs depends on the quality, quantity, and the reality of the inputs retained in learner's linguistic resource pool.

(6) The input is most effectively retained in the linguistic resource pool by being repeatedly performed on regular basis with the constant and strong level of mental immersion.

(7) There is a certain sequence and combination of input categories which is most effective to acquire and develop oral proficiency as an output.

3. Practice Model of BTM

BTM takes as its practice model the process of the natural language acquisition and skill improvement as shown in the typical process for children to acquire and develop language skills of mother tongue.

---

[5]   The linguistic resistance is the degree of one's physical and cognitive unfitness to process the input, which deters the production of output. The linguistic resistance is mainly caused by the linguistic distance from one's MT to TL, and by one's age. One's age shows the degree of the firmness of the physical and cognitive adhesiveness to the linguistic features of one's MT. In addition, the linguistic resistance can be increased by any kinds of individual unfitness to process the input. The linguistic resistance explains why different languages are less or more challenging for students with different MT backgrounds to acquire them compared to other languages. It also explains why children in general can acquire a foreign language relatively faster than adults.

4. Appearance of BTM

BTM (Babble Training Method) is a comprehensive oral proficiency-oriented foreign language education method. It serves as a road map for teachers who are engaged into teaching foreign language to students, or for those learners who want to learn a language by themselves. BTM offers the ideas and methods of teaching foreign languages based on a systematic education process which covers from the acquisition of the speaking skills to the development of oral proficiency. Also, BTM answers the biggest question, with respect to foreign language education, of 'Why does it not work?' Further, BTM offers detail answers to the concrete questions of 'when?', 'where?', 'what?', 'how?', and 'how much?'.

The fact that there are hundreds of different languages does not mean that different methods of education are required for each language. This can be understood from the fact that all the mother languages have been successfully acquired through exactly the same manner. Accordingly, BTM claims to be the universal method for learning languages.

The appearance of BTM has been triggered by the following issues which the conventional Foreign Language Education ("FLE") methods commonly shared:

First, the conventional FLE methods so far have been focused on acquiring a particular area of language skills. That is, they are heavily restricted to developing a particular language skill instead of developing the comprehensive language skills of speaking, reading, writing, and listening. Some methods would solely focus on practicing intensive listening while some other methods would focus on practicing intensive reading, grammar, or speaking. To resolve this issue, BTM offers systematic step-by-step FLE process for learners to acquire comprehensive language skills as well as for developing oral proficiency.

Second, the currently prevailing methods take only the visible activities like speaking, listening, reading, and writing as the targets of language education. As they are restricted solely to the surface phenomena of the general linguistic activities, they overlook the important process based on the underlying phenomena of language acquisition. Accordingly, they are not designed to build the underlying skills for learners to acquire the comprehensive language skills. Instead, they are built to demonstrate the surface phenomena of TL activities to the learners who are not ready, leaving learners at no place to acquire TL. BTM recognizes that there are must-do Babble Training in the underlying process of acquiring language skills. Based on such recognition, BTM offers systematic Babble Training for learners to develop the underlying skills to acquire respective language skills as well as to improve oral proficiency.

Third, as new technology based methods have appeared with no fundamental changes from the traditional practice, both FL teachers and learners get easily dazzled and lost. This is not to say that all the technology based methods are wrong. The fact that a method or material has been developed with the most modern technology does not necessarily mean that it should take the priority to be applied to FLE. Also, any most recent method or material does not mean it must be the best method. Each of them may fit very well in certain steps of FLE process. However, certainly, not all of them should be the number one step to start with in FLE, or be considered as the best without being tested for their effectiveness. The FLE industry is not a fish industry where most fresh fish is always considered the best. BTM applies the FLE methods to effectively build the underlying skills.

Fourth, the traditional methods do not offer ideas and methods of how to teach particular skills of TL effectively. Effective or not, new foreign language studying methods and ideas are introduced every time. However, the actual teaching methods have not changed for generations. BTM, based on many theories, observations on language acquisition and teaching, and logical analysis for the acquisition of language skills and the development of oral proficiency of TL, offers systematic process of teaching or learning foreign languages.

Fifth, the birth of BTM was triggered the most by the prevailing pre-modern unconscious recognition of the FLE process. The most prevailing recognition of FLE process for long time is in the grammar→reading→writing→listening→speaking order with minor differences of opinions for some parts of such order, but not with drastic or fundamental differences. This kind of process has not been set by particular thoughtful proposals. Rather, it has been naturally set like that in accordance with the required foreign language skills at different times through out the industrial history. BTM, again based on the underlying phenomena of acquiring and developing oral proficiency, and the observation of the most natural, effective process for people to acquire languages, introduces systematic and effective FL teaching process and ideas.

CHAPTER 1

Background of Foreign Language Education

As FL teachers, how many fluent speakers have we produced in our own teaching?

As FLE experts, what have we done to help FL learners to pick up TL?

Have we been on the right tracks?

Why do people wander around the world to learn FL?

Why can't they pick up the language at home?

1

We have AI. Why Do We Learn Foreign Language?

Language is a tool for the communication of the human being. Without language, human beings would have to suffer a lot to understand each other. Or, the life of human beings without such sophisticated languages that we have been using may not be so much different from that of Chimpanzees.

We use language primarily to share, deliver, and/or collect information to support our judgment process. In other words, language is a media through which people convey their status of recognition, thoughts, and needs. Language, as a communication media between people, therefore, is the very one that everybody should have a good command of.

The story of Babel Tower in the Bible is quite symbolic in that it shows the power of language when shared by everybody. Language brings the power of unity among the people within the language, which makes things become possible that are impossible among people of different languages. As language reflects the culture, value, philosophy, spiritual world, and subconscious world of the people, the fundamental tie for unity is made through commanding the same language.

Unfortunately, whether it is God's will or not, it seems very unlikely that the world would be able to show the true power of the human world as it would be not realistic for the people in the world to share one particular language.

Now that it is very unrealistic for every body in the world to use one common language, which would allow the miracle of reaching the heaven to happen, what should we do to maximize our individual potential values in this world of competition? I suggest one should grab the power of at least one language other than the mother tongue. If mother tongue is to swim in the river for the daily life of where one was born, foreign language ("FL") is to reach out to the sea to expand one's life for success.

It is very obvious that having solid bilingual or multilingual skills bring about priceless value to an individual. Acquiring languages is just like attaining the skills of different skills on top of one's major profession. Depending on the levels of one's bilingual skills, it brings one the senses of confidence, leisure, freedom, relaxation, security, privacy, connection to a different world, control, achievement, pride, and so on. It surely could lead one to the world of more opportunities. It does not require a lot of explanation and testimonials to help people understand the significance of the benefits that a solid bilingual person gets in the real world of competition where only the best survives.

If a computer engineer would acquire the skills of building a house, the engineer could enjoy utilizing the skills to take good care of his house whenever maintenance is required. The engineer also could customize the house to his own tastes for himself. The engineer could control the time, cost, materials, designs, and further feel proud of himself for doing it by himself. The engineer also has the luxury of an option to change his profession to a different field if he wishes so. The engineer could enjoy the communication with people from the world of construction. Of course, one can do these things without necessarily having to acquire the skills of house building. Money can make a horse go.

However, there are things that bilingual skills can bring to one's life that other skills or money cannot: The privacy and the ability to process the information directly from the people speaking different languages. No matter how much money one would pay to hire a bilingual person, one could not get the linguistic sense and feelings reflecting the unique cultures and philosophies.

A monolingual person in terms of communication skills is just like a computer with a Z80 CPU, one of the earliest generation CPUs of the computer industry. What was wrong with the Z80 CPU computer? Nothing. Nothing was wrong at least mechanically with the later processor generations of the 286, 386, 486, and many processors which were introduced sequentially. However, they have been laid off one after another just because they cannot process the bombarding 3 dimensional levels of commands, information, and demands in such manner as the users would expect them to. They simply did not have the capacity to effectively process the every-day-evolving high levels of information presented to them. Yet, we still expect the processors to be continuously evolved. Upgrading a computer system does not happen by simply purchasing very expensive peripheral devices.

With the era of information war, the world requires us to be able to process the multi dimensional bombarding information in various forms of languages from all over the world. Those who, in addition to one's expertise, can fluently process the information are always strongly wanted by the governments and companies. The demand for solid bilingual skills will continue to increase. As a matter of fact, monolingual people will be the ones among others who would be most vulnerable in every time of poor economy.

Now, with the arrival of AI era, people believe that the walls of communication barrier in the global stage have been lowered significantly. In the language service industry, AI already has exceeded human. It generally can provide faster and less expensive language services as long as one knows how to use the AI devices. It can repeat translating documents with hundreds of pages in a matter of seconds for no extra charges other than the purchase price which can be very nominal compared to the rates charged by professional translators.

As a retired professional translator, I have seen many critical errors AI made. I have seen many cases where the message translated by AI would be totally the opposite to the intended original message. This issue can be overcome with the advanced capacity of AI. Yet, one may not want to completely rely on AI's language services.

However, it is still true that AI will bring huge benefits to human being in that it can translate enormous amount of industrial information into the languages of choice instantaneously.

I would say that AI is more industrial language oriented than personal language because personal language is much more complicated than the industrial language is. AI may never be perfect with translating personal language as human can never be perfect with understanding personal language either.

Yet, human can understand personal language better than AI can. Unlike human, AI cannot understand the meaning degrees of such words as "Okay", "Yes", "No", "I love you", or other daily common expressions said with the combination of those non-linguistic features like intonations, volume of sound, the atmosphere of conversation, body gestures, facial expressions, eye directions, time delay, cultural specificity, and/or reluctant, lovely or disappointed voice tones, and etc.

No matter how advanced AI would be, it would be quite unrealistic to share love, friendship, emotion, trust, partnership, feelings, spiritual world, and warm heart through AI between parties. Only through personal language, can one build a close, friendly, harmonious relationship, which is characterized by mutual understanding, empathy, agreement, and easy communication, not through AI language.

So, let AI be what it can be the best. One still need to be bilingual or multilingual to build rapport with the global people to succeed in achieving what one wants.

2

Goals and Nature of Foreign Language Education

I am writing this book with an emphasis that the primary as well as the ultimate goals of foreign language education ("FLE") should be to help the learners to acquire and develop the oral proficiency of TL.

People would largely agree with me on the goals of FLE. However, many of them would not agree with me when I clarify that my point here is to exclude all of the traditional methods which teach students the systematic rule based reading and writing of TL, which most of the people, including the FLE experts, teachers, and learners, so surely believe to be the primary methods of FLE. Most of them think this way because they have been brain washed by the traditional FLE methods in believing that acquiring such rule based reading and writing skills is the only bridge, which every body must pass through in order to reach to the beginning of developing the oral language skills. Therefore they develop and follow the FLE methods based on such thorough belief on the knowledge of the rules as the ultimate solution of learning FL. I believe that such belief by the people is based on insufficient understanding of the natures of language and language acquisition.

To acquire TL means to be able to command the language in the same way as one would command one's own mother tongue ("MT"). Even though the proficiency level of one's TL may vary from that of one's MT depending on the levels of experiences using the language, the ways one commands TL should be the same way as one does it with the mother tongue.

So, the standards for evaluating anyone's FL skills should be the verbal communication skills. Regardless of one's ability to understand a language through reading, writing, and listening, one cannot be said to have obtained the language without being able to command the language freely through verbal communication. No matter how poor one's reading, writing, and listening comprehension of a language may be, one still can be classified as having conquered the language as long as one can fluently command the language verbally.

There are countless people in the world who still cannot read and write their own mother tongues, but can naturally command their languages verbally very well without difficulties. Looking into the human history, more human beings so far have lived in the world without letters than with letters.

Accordingly, I believe that the most fundamental aspect of language acquisition is to be able to carry out verbal communications in the language. The skill to perform verbal communications in a given language is the most basic skill required to command a language. Believe or not, I am sure that the verbal communication skill is also the easiest skill, compared to the skills of reading, writing, and grammar, to develop. Also, that is the skill, once developed, which helps one build other skills such as reading, writing, and understanding the grammar easily. In fact, once one can command the verbal form of TL fluently, it is a simple matter of being able to recognizing the written words for one to read and write in TL.

Therefore, I emphasize that the primary goal of FLE should be to help the learners to build the verbal communication skills to fluent level by teaching the oral language from the beginning. We all know people acquire foreign languages by learning directly the oral languages of TL in a couple of years. Also, we all know that people do not pick up foreign languages by learning the rule based reading and writing. This is why teaching oral language from the beginning is very important.

Once this primary goal is met, FLE should focus on the ultimate goal of developing the oral proficiency into higher levels through a lot of trainings for talking, reading, listening, and writing. By achieving the primary and advanced goals, one will conquer TL just like one's own mother tongue.

I am also writing with an emphasis that language by nature, whether it may be a mother tongue or FL, is not of a science subject to be studied or researched for understanding, but of skills to be acquired. Genius or not, only those who babble days and nights in TL could command the language fluently. Accordingly, FLE should not be focused on breaking down the atoms of TL for learners to understand the providence of how it works, but on consistent and continuous efforts of teaching for learners to acquire the skills.

In other words, the nature of language is just like that of any musical instruments or sports such as basketball and soccer. Thus, the nature of FLE should be just like that of teaching the piano or the sports. The skills of playing the piano can be built only through numerously repeated exercises of various types of piano music until one obtains the semi-instinctive piano skills. It cannot be built through scientific approaches. The skills of commanding language can be developed only through numerously repeated babbles of various types of daily life expressions until one obtains the linguistic instinct of TL.

Various FLE methods are developed by individual FLE experts based on one's own understanding about the nature of language. With different understandings on the nature of language performance, it is very natural that many different methods are to be developed. If one would see the nature of language as of only vocabulary matter, one might naturally focus on developing FLE methods for learners to obtain as many vocabularies as possible from the beginning.

Most of the FLE experts and non-experts believe that FL is to be studied for understanding before anything else. They argue that picking up FL is different from picking up a mother tongue because typically one would have quite well developed brain by the time one receives FLE from school. With a quite well developed brain, one has the power of understanding and reasoning to figure out how TL is to be processed. They believe that once the human brain could parse TL, one will get to command the language. For this reason, they naturally focus on figuring out all the rules for the learners to realize the providence of TL.

However, let alone the effectiveness, such atom rule and theory based teaching has many problems. First of all, not many people know all the secrets of TL. Second, as it takes years of repeated classes for them to teach the rules, they would not have enough time to reveal all the secrets of TL. Even they learn the rules and theories mostly afterwards through the process of teaching classes in repetition. Once they learned the secrets of TL by repeated teaching experiences, they tend to think that the secrets are easy enough for learners to tackle and digest. They easily forget that they had such hard time to study the secrets when they were young in school. It is as if a frog does not remember when it was a tadpole. In addition, learners also do not have enough time to overcome the difficulties of the rules and understand all of them.

On the other hand, some of FLE experts believe that FL is to be learned through directly acting in the language. Therefore, they would use TL only in the class from the beginning and heavily focus on forcing learners to speak TL right away. Not knowing the effective methods to act in TL, the learners would try to dig TL deep and deep to find the secret of atoms and to see how they work together.

Once they find some of the logic of secrete, they would apply it once to act in the language and be satisfied with the performance. Some of the eager learners would try very hard to gain more secretes so that they could use it next time in similar scenarios. This is how the learners become so fluent only in the theories of TL.

So far, I have tried to show the goals and nature of FLE which I am very certain of. I also tried to point out the very important message that different goals and understanding of the nature of FLE would result in totally different approaches to FLE. As FLE is a rather multi year commitment, misleading approach to FLE would mean tremendous waste of resources, including very precious time for young people which cannot be recovered at all. We could not knowingly afford any misleading or wasteful methods of FLE.

Before reading any further, one should definitely review ones own understanding on the goals and the nature of FLE.

3

Methods of Foreign Language Education

Before I talk about why the oral proficiency of FL is not learned from the school, let me briefly introduce the summaries on the different types of FLE methods that have been known to us. The following summaries are quoted from an internet source. It will help us understand the different aspects of FLE methods.

Grammar Translation: The Grammar Translation method started around the time of Erasmus (1466-1536). Its primary focus is on memorization of verb paradigms, grammar rules, and vocabulary. Application of this knowledge was directed on translation of literary texts--focusing of developing students' appreciation of TL's literature as well as teaching the language. Activities utilized in today's classrooms include: questions that follow a reading passage; translating literary passages from one language to another; memorizing grammar rules; memorizing native-language equivalents of target language vocabulary.

Direct Method: The Direct Method was introduced by the German educator Wilhelm Viëtor in the early 1800's. Focusing on oral language, it requires that all instruction be conducted in TL with no recourse to translation. Reading and writing are taught from

the beginning, although speaking and listening skills are empha-
sized--grammar is learned inductively. It has a balanced, four-skill
emphasis.

The Silent Way: The teacher is active in setting up classroom
situations while the students do most of the talking and interaction
among themselves. All four skills (listening, speaking, reading &
writing) are taught from the beginning. Student errors are expected
as a normal part of learning; the teacher's silence helps to foster
self-reliance and student initiative.

Suggestopedia: The learning environment is relaxed, sub-
dued, with low lighting and soft music playing in the background.
Students choose a name and character in TL and imagine being
that person. Students relax and listen while dialogues are presented
accompanied by music. Students later practice dialogues during an
"activation" phase.

Community Language Learning: Teachers recognize that learning can be threatening and by understanding and accepting students' fears, they help their students feel secure and overcome their
fears of language learning--ultimately providing students with posi-
tive energy directed at language learning. Students choose what they
want to learn in the class and the syllabus is learner-generated.

Natural Approach: Introduced by Gottlieb Henese and Dr. L.
Sauveur in Boston around 1866. The Natural Approach is similar
to the Direct Method, concentrating on active demonstrations to
convey meaning by associating words and phrases with objects and
actions. Associations are achieved via mime, paraphrase and the
use of manipulatives. Terrell (1977) focused on the principles of
meaningful communication, comprehension before production,
and indirect error correction. Krashen's (1980) input hypothesis is
applied in the Natural Approach.

Reading Method: The reading method was prominent in the
U.S. following the Committee of Twelve in 1900 and following
the Modern Foreign Language Study in 1928. The earlier method

was similar to the traditional Grammar/Translation method and emphasized the transference of linguistic understanding to English. Presently, the reading method focuses more on silent reading for comprehension purposes.

ASTP and the Audiolingual Method: This approach is based on the behaviorist belief that language learning is the acquisition of a set of correct language habits. The learner repeats patterns and phrases in the language laboratory until able to reproduce them spontaneously. ASTP (Army Specialized Training Program) was an intensive, specialized approach to language instruction used in during the 1940's. In the postwar years, the civilian version of ASTP and the audiolingual method featured memorization of dialogues, pattern drills, and emphasis on pronunciation.

Technological Approaches: This approach has been utilized since the 1920's in FL classrooms. Access to audio visual equipment and materials such as records, short-wave radio, motion pictures and films, wire recorders, video tape recorders and computers enhance instruction as well as provide student opportunities for authentic exposure and interaction in TL(s).

Cognitive Methods: Cognitive methods of language teaching are based on meaningful acquisition of grammar structures followed by meaningful practice.

Communicative Methods: The goal of communicative language approaches is to create a realistic context for language acquisition in the classroom. The focus is on functional language usage and the ability to learners to express their own ideas, feelings, attitudes, desires and needs. Open ended questioning and problem-solving activities and exchanges of personal information are utilized as the primary means of communication. Students usually work with authentic materials in small groups on communication activities, during which they receive practice in negotiating meaning.

Total Physical Response Method: This approach to second language ("second language") teaching is based on the belief that listening comprehension should be fully developed before any active oral participation from students is expected (just as it is with children when they are learning their native language).

Total Physical Response Storytelling Method: This approach was modeled after the TPR method but provides the critical vehicle–storytelling–to utilize and expand acquired vocabulary by contextualizing it in high-interest stories which students can hear, see, act out, retell, revise and rewrite.

Lexical Approach: Based on the idea that an important part of language acquisition is the ability to comprehend and produce lexical phrases as unanalyzed wholes, or "chunks," and that these chunks become the raw data by which learners perceive patterns of language traditionally thought of as grammar--that language production is the piecing together of ready-made units appropriate for a particular situation--the Lexical Approach concentrates on developing learners' proficiency with lexis, or words and word combinations. This method proposes that it isn't grammar but lexis that is the basis of language and that the mastery of the grammatical system is not a prerequisite for effective communication.

Focus-On-Form Approach: The Focus-On-Form Approach considers grammar to be heterogeneous, meaning that some grammar points are easy to explain and easy to apply, and other points are difficult if not impossible to apply. This method proposes that the real problem is that grammar instruction in both approaches is limited to a small set of pedagogical practices. A Focus-On-Form pedagogy profitably mixes explicit and implicit skills depending on the grammar item and the communicative task.

Content-Based Method: In content-based instruction (CBI), the curriculum organizing principle is subject matter, not language. CBI can be focused around regular academic courses such as history and science taught in TL or organized around a series of selected themes drawn from the regular curriculum.

Cortina Method: This method was developed by R. D. Cortina in late 19th century. It focuses on brief introduction of TL's linguistic features to start with, and on conversational interactions during the class. Teachers are required to carry on the class only in TL unless there should be an absolute necessity for the teacher to use the common language to answer, or in giving any explanations that might be required during the first lessons. Students are required to be well prepared before coming to class, so that the whole of the time may be devoted to conversation.

According to above types and summaries of various FLE methods, it seems that the worldwide traditional FLE methods, especially for the secondary and above schools, have been mainly of Grammar Translation method and Reading method. I could also see some of the methods such as Audiolingual and Technological Approach methods have been applied in college laboratories.

4

The History of Traditional FLE Methods

As English has been the world most popular language for the past century, the major TL for the prevailing FLE worldwide has been English. Also, compared to the education of other languages, English education seems to have been developed most actively in terms of the education programs, textbooks and study reference materials introduced by individuals as well as education related entities. Even in many English speaking countries like the USA, Canada, England, Australia, and Philippines, the English education for foreign students has been very popular, intensive and systematic. For example, the university ESL schools in English speaking countries offer 4-5 hour daily English classes to the foreigners for months or even years. As far as I know, except for some organizations or institutes with specialized goals, not many schools or colleges in general in the USA provides so intensive FLE to the students.

Therefore, I will take the trends of the English education as an FLE to review the transitions in terms of the traditional FLE methods. Among many other countries where English education has been very systematic and intensive, I will take the TESL situations in Korea as I am more familiar with the Korean TESL in general than in any other countries.

Even though different countries might have been deployed different FLE methods, I assume that the transition of the English education methods in Korea is not too much different from that of in other countries except for the English education in some countries where English has been appointed as an official 2nd language. Such an assumption is based on my findings from the testimonies of many people I met from many different countries who agreed and confirmed my such assumption to be correct. Also it is based on the fact that the English education of the non-English speaking countries have been aimed at such general English evaluation methods as written tests for college entrance exam, TOEFL, and TOEIC.

The traditional English education in Korea starts as one advances into a middle school. The school offers English class every day and starts to teach basic English grammar. On top of that, many of the students would go to private English institutes every day after school to learn English. The three year middle school English classes are mostly spent on studying the basic English grammars. All class materials and textbooks are designed to illustrate the grammars. English dialogues in each chapter would be easily ignored, and the English texts are also used mainly to find and explain the grammar points applied in the texts.

The English education in high schools is still based on Grammar Translation Method. In high school, more sophisticated aspects of the English grammar are taught. The English textbooks would include 2-3 page long texts in each chapter for the students to read and comprehend by applying the grammar components they learned. Through the three years of high school education, the amount of English texts for the students to read would be about 150 pages at most. However, I don't mean to say that the reading amount is the most important issue in learning English.

As the national college entrance English exam started testing one's listening comprehension skills from several years ago, the high schools in Korea started adopting Technological Approaches on top of Grammar Translation Method. Obviously, such an addition of Technological Approach is based on the concept of Total Physical Response Method, which is based on the belief that listening comprehension should be fully developed before any active oral participation from students is expected.

With the intensive Grammar Translation Method for middle school and high school, and with the Technological Approaches during the high school, only few of the hundreds of the high school graduates still can introduce one's family members in English.

As one gets into a college, one would receive one more year of English education as it is required. The typical English education in colleges is a mixture of Grammar Translation Method and Reading Method. It would lead the students to read a lot more than the students read in high school, and still expect the students to find out and understand the grammar components applied in each sentence. To be able to understand the meanings of the articles without being able to explain the grammars used in each sentence would be considered as having not strong foundation of English.

Outside of the English classes offered in the college, most of the college students study English very hard because the English test score is considered to be one of the most important factors to decide one's competitiveness. Accordingly, they would spend at least 2-3 hours every day studying English during college. Many college students would spend over 10 hours a day studying English for one to two years to get high scores in TOEFL or TOEIC.

The methods they would mostly adopt during such very intensive self teaching period in the college are Grammar Translation Method, Reading Method, Lexical Approach method, and the Technological Approach method to improve their listening comprehension skills. In other words, they would study the English grammar, reading, and listening comprehension all together by assigning couple of hours every day for each of the study areas.

Over all, so many people in Korea would spend close to 10 years of very intensive efforts based on such English education methods as stated above. This way, yet not many college students would succeed in earning very high scores from TOEFL and TOEIC.

However, even those people who have been successful with the tests yet have not conquered the English language, and do not command English very well. They may be able to introduce their family members with severe mumbling, but their business performances in English are speechlessly poor. It is very frustrating that the students can't speak even the basic level English well enough after so many years of heavily focused efforts on following many different methods.

As people could not pick up English yet, people started looking for new methods. To them, there was only one method that they haven't tried: Immersion Method, which I define as a method of immersing the students into TL community. As they have found that all the methods they have tried very seriously so far have turned out to be failures, they believed that one should be mingled with TL community to pick up the language. As a way of mingling in TL community, thousands of college students would fly every year to the English speaking countries all over the world to learn English. They take the advantages of taking ESL classes from the ESL schools and, also at the same time, being immersed into the English community. I would use ESL & Immersion Method for this type of method.

The college ESL schools and private English schools in the countries of English language, like the USA, England, Australia, and etc. for example, have welcomed the students who flew in from all over the world to be immersed in the English community.

Most of the ESL schools in the English speaking countries adopt the same methods as the schools in Korea have been doing: Mostly, they run the ESL programs based on the Grammar Translation Method and the Reading Method. However, the differences are that the classes are performed by English only speaking teachers, and that the English classes in ESL are much more intensive. On top of such traditional FLE methods, the ESL schools add a couple of more methods such as Direct Method and Content-Based Instruction (CBI) Method by offering some classes like English culture class in English.

Most of the Korean ESL students would stay for one year or less in abroad to learn English. After one year of immersion into English community and ESL classes, the students get to manage their daily life matters in English such as ordering food at a restaurant, renting a car, greeting people, asking directions, and etc. This is a quite productive result compared to the results of about 10 years of English education in Korea. However, that is the limit of their English skills. Most of them still don't acquire the English language well enough to handle business matters.

One of the problems of ESL & Immersion Method is that the students do not really get immersed into English community. They mostly get along with the people who came from foreign countries to learn English like themselves. They are not native English speakers. Only the teachers are native English speakers. Consequently, most of the ESL students do not get immersed into English community.

As it has turned out that the one year ESL & Immersion Method is not so much effective for the college students to acquire fluent English, many rich parents in Korea started sending their children to the elementary or middle schools in the English speaking countries for longer period. They think that college student age is too old to acquire a foreign language, and one year in local community is not enough.

The children would stay in the country for three to four years, or until they graduate from a high school, or even enter a college. For this, the family members would have to be separate for many years as the mother would need to stay with the children and the father would stay in Korea to maintain the work income to support the family away. In reference to this kind of families, new Korean words are created depending on the level of richness of the families.

Eagle Family refers to the rich family who could afford the expenses and time to fly back and forth to visit each other whenever they want to; Goose Family refers to the mediocre rich family members who could afford the expenses and time to visit each other by the season; and Penguin Family refers to the less rich family members who could not afford the expenses and time to visit each other for many years. I will use the term of Goose Family Method for this type of FLE.

It is yet too early to evaluate whether Goose Family Method is successful or not. In terms of English acquisition only, it seems that Goose Family Method is working. The young children of goose and penguin families around me do pick up English after about 3 years. However, many broken goose and penguin families have been reported to the newspapers for reasons which one could easily imagine. The sufferings of the unbroken families are also beyond imagination.

In the view of English acquisition, Goose Family Method seems to be quite effective for almost any young child if the family could support the child for over three years. Also, even though the students could not pick up English very well, the about one year long ESL & Immersion Method seems to be somewhat effective compared to the traditional English education in Korea. However, one of the problems with these methods is that it cost too much and can be available only for rich people. Therefore, it cannot be a method for public education.

Recently, many colleges in Korea have adopted CBI Method to improve the students' English skills. For this purpose, many colleges strongly recommend the professors to lecture in English only. However, it is yet to be waited and seen if the CBI Method in a college would boost up the students English skills, which unfortunately I doubt.

Another very popular trend in Korea is constructing English Village, where students could visit and build experiences of being immersed into English life for weeks and months. Again, considering the results of the ESL and Immersion methods in the English countries for one to two years, chances are that the idea of English Village could be just superficial.

So far, I have introduced in detail the transitions of various TESL methods in Korea. Based on the information I have collected from many friends of other non-English speaking countries, I believe that the transitions of TESL in other countries are quite similar with very minor differences coming from the characteristics of the school systems.

Further more, I believe that FLE methods for different languages other than English in different countries basically do not differ a lot from the TESL methods applied in Korea.

I have shown that the traditional FLE mainly based on Grammar Translation Method and Reading Method for multiple years has failed to help students pick up TL. In addition, I tried to show that ESL & Immersion Method for the students with Grammar and Reading methods background is not so effective either.

I showed how the students, for example, in Korea, who have been very successful with the past generation English tests such as TOEFL and TOEIC, have failed to speak fluent English. Consequently, it is proven that none of these methods really help the students to acquire the English language.

The point I am trying to convey to the readers by introducing the specific transitions of TESL methods in Korea is that, regardless of some differences in the trends of FLE methods for particular language, FLE methods applied without serious thoughts on the goals and the nature of foreign language education are meaningless and could cause interferences with one's serious efforts to learn TL.

5

Problems With the FLE Methods

In the previous article, I introduced different types of FLE methods. Most of the methods have been introduced to us at least for multiple decades. Also, among them, the grammar translation method seems to be a prevailing method, which has been adopted worldwide for the last century. Regardless of so many kinds of methods introduced to us, the history of FLE shows that few of them have been successful in producing fluent TL speakers.

To judge a method to be successful or not is of course very difficult. One of the reasons for this is that the successful achievement of FLE would be the results of the combined effects of the methods, teachers, and students as well. Regardless of how good a method would be, it would not be successful without the effective efforts of the teachers and the students. For the same token, regardless of how hard the teachers and students together would work, it would be meaningless if the method does not really lead them to the language itself. I cannot get rid of a strong belief that the major reason for the failure of FLE so far is because of the latter case.

Actually, in judging the effects of FLE methods, it is not impossible or too difficult to find the efforts of the teachers and the commitments of the students to learn to the maximum level of their capacities if one would consider the desperate efforts exerted by both the teachers and students to tackle English as a second language in many none English speaking languages. One can easily find that the English learners in those countries desperately endeavor to learn English. They would mostly start with the grammar translation method, and move on, without systematic order, to different methods such as lexical approach, reading method, listening method, and so on. The teachers both in schools and private institutes would also commit themselves to teach the students English through unsystematic various types of teaching methods.

Yet, as far as I know, majority people agree that the worldwide English education has failed to produce fluent English speakers. This is especially true in those non Indo-European language countries. I believe there is a reason for this, which can be explained by the concept of linguistic distance, which is introduced in a later chapter.

One thing I found from the methods above is that they are heavily focused on teaching the linguistic features and non-verbal communicative skills of TL instead of developing the intuitive linguistic skills for oral proficiency. In other words, none of the methods seem to really focus on building the very basic linguistic skills for the students to develop the verbal communicative skills. Every body agrees that it is very important for students to build strong basic skills to acquire a foreign language.

Therefore, all teachers and programs have focused on offering FLE for students to build up so-called strong basic skills for significant time to begin with. Yet, after years of FLE, most of the students are easily found to be lacking of the basic linguistic skills such as producing correct sounds and phrases which are very crucial to make meaningful expression in TL.

This, after all, tells us that we have misunderstood about the concept of the very basic linguistic skills and about how to help students develop such linguistic skills. Then, what are the basic skills to be acquired to learn a language? I propose the linguistic intuition and physical capacity to be the basic skills which students should build to acquire language.

I define the term, linguistic intuition, as one's semi-instinctive understanding and performance on the sounds, structures of words and sentences, interpretation of meanings, and usage of linguistic resource such as sets of expressions, morphemes, words, idioms, and other useful expressions of a language. Then, the physical capacity means the physical ability to listen and articulate the sounds of TL fluently.

Some of the methods seem to be more real and effective than other methods in terms of developing the verbal communicative skills. The Cortina method, for example, seems to focus on the practical practice of the students for verbal communication. It also briefly introduces basic linguistic features to the students in the beginning. Yet, it seems to heavily focus on leading the students to communicate in TL from the beginning, leaving the students to figure out how to acquire and maintain the basic language skills, which is a big issue to the students because students are not familiar with the idea of how to acquire and maintain such skills.

This method may work more effectively for students who learn TL with very short linguistic distance or a very close family language. For closely related languages, like between English and Italian, for example, it would take much less efforts for students, based on their linguistic intuition and skills for their mother tongue, to build the basic linguistic skills like producing the sounds and acquiring the linguistic intuition.

Therefore, students, who's TL is one of the family languages of their mother tongue, could easily participate in the class where Cortina method is being applied without suffering from so much difficulties coming from the linguistic distance. The concept of linguistic distance is of the degree of the differences between two languages, and will be introduced in a later chapter.

However, for languages with quite far linguistic distance from each other, like between Korean and English or between Japanese and English, it would not be practical to lead the class in TL only, leaving the students to do the work of building the basic linguistic skills by themselves as a homework. Not only that, this method is not practical to many countries where not many FL teachers can lead the classes in TL only.

As the methods do not lead students to build the basic linguistic skills of TL, the students are the ones who have to acquire TL by themselves to the performing level of TL. None of the methods really show how to teach students to acquire the linguistic intuition instead of linguistic knowledge of TL to reach to the level of performing in TL. It is not practical to assume that students, who do not know what and how to do as well as how much to do, could acquire TL by themselves at home to the level of oral performance regardless of what is being taught in class.

As a metaphorical expression, I would say that the methods above are of teaching brand new babies how to play in a soccer game. In the view point of soccer, those methods are of rules, strategies, techniques of shooting, dribbling, or passing, watching others playing, and of physically playing the game. When the babies cannot even stand, walk, or run yet, all of the methods could not be effective. The babies need to be taught from the very 'basic skills' such as how to sit, stand, work, run, and control the ball, all of which require tremendous amounts of repeated practices, very well before they are educated for such 'high level' techniques. I don't see any of the methods are seriously designed for developing such basic skills of learning a language.

For this purpose, I am presenting a five level **Babble Training Method** ("BTM") to cover the most important stages of learning language. In acquiring language, Babble Training to learn talking ("**Babble Training**")[6] is the most critical requirement for any body

---

[6] In this book, I use the term "Babble Training" generally to mean students' repeated practice in a duly manner as suggested by BTM to learn talking. However, I also use

to be fluent. Without a successful conquest of Babble Training, no one actually could acquire language.

Another thing I found missing from the methods is that no one method above introduces systematic steps of teaching TL for students to acquire TL from the beginning to the proficiency levels. Each of the methods could be useful only if they are applied correctly to a certain proper stage of language acquisition process.

Hence, the methods need to be arranged in a systematic structure for learners to acquire TL in a most effective way. Right now, the teachers and learners of foreign languages are faced with numerous methods unstructured. Consequently, not understanding the appropriate process of language acquisition, they are left with uneducated choices to be made. Consequently, they would play by the ear in choosing the methods one after another depending on what they listen to.

I also want to point out that some of the methods could be quite dangerous. If FLE teachers and learners would be stuck with some of the methods for long time, it would not be easy for the learners to be able to recover the damages incurred to them.

To me, the most dangerous method is the grammar translation method. It has been proven through the long FLE history in the world that the method at best could only produce monitors not speakers. It has been proven by the hundred of thousands of students who were heavily educated with this method. The deeper one would dig into the grammar, the more professional monitor one would be. They could easily point out grammatical mistakes from other people's speech based on their limited understanding of the grammar, but they really cannot verbally communicate in TL.

---

the term to mean students' repeated practice in a duly manner as suggested by BTM to learn reading, listening, speaking, and writing when used in respective contexts.

By nature, grammar is not a part of language but a systemic description of language. Therefore, conquering the grammar of a language has nothing to do with the language skills. It is just like conquering the rules of the soccer has nothing to do with the soccer skills as a player.

Listening method has been also proven to cause damages. Many of my readers who claimed to have spent two to three years of heavily focused time on listening to study English offered testimonials to me on this. They listened to professionally produced audios, or watched TV for many years according to the listening method. However, they get so upset with what they have got ultimately: they can listen to a little degree but cannot say an expression of their own for survival.

I would like to warn the FLE teachers and learners that they should first clearly understand what it really takes for a human being to be a fluent speaker of a language. To be a fluent speaker of a foreign language should not be too much different from to be such a speaker of a language. What it takes all for a person to be a fluent commander of a language is a systematic or ideally structured Babble Training. That is all what it takes.

Again, to approve or disapprove certain FLE methods is not easy. To prove certain methods to be effective or ineffective is even more difficult because scientific approach to language acquisition is yet too far. However, we should take a position with respect to the FLE methods introduced so far as it clearly has not been productive or successful in producing fluent bilingual speakers. We should explain why we have been failing for centuries in FLE. One criterion that I am applying to explain the failure of the methods is from the natural language acquisition process (NLAP) of human being.

Comparing the major aspects of the FLE methods and those of NLAP, we can easily find that there is one big difference. In NLAP, there is a very significant amount of time unconditionally spent on Babble Training. Meanwhile, the FLE methods do not focus on

Babble Training so much. They do not mention the fundamental role of Babble Training in learning foreign languages. This probably is because that they are not aware of such fundamental role of Babble Training in language acquisition. All of them focus on teaching the surface factors of language learning.

In the life of a frog, there are three separate sequential stages: Tadpole stage, frog stage, and growing stage. Likewise, in the life of language acquisition, there are also three separate sequential stages: Babbling stage to learn talking, acquisition stage, and improving stage.

Therefore, to save the time, efforts, and tremendous amount of resources, I will present structured ideas of how to acquire and develop oral proficiency based on my direct experiences of learning and teaching foreign languages as well as based on the valuable inputs from others who are involved in FLE, and who have shown great interests in FLE.

6

Why Is Oral Proficiency Not Learned From School?

As far as FLE in the school is concerned, I cannot avoid thinking that it has been failing so far. I am not aware of any public or private school language programs that produce solid bilingual speakers by their own merits. I am quite sure that the majority of the school language education programs have been failing to produce solid bilingual speakers. If there are any public or private schools which have been very successful in producing such bilingual speakers, I would love to take them as exceptional.

Some people may well point out that the job of finding school language programs as a success or failure is a very subjective issue; and that the focus of the evaluations should vary depending on the goals of the language programs. I don't deny the one, but I don't agree with the other because no language programs should have any other primary goals than making the students speak the language to begin with.

Of course, I find that every body agrees that the ultimate goal of language programs is to make the students speak the language very well. Accordingly, the success or failure of all language programs should be judged based on the students' speaking capabilities of TL. For this, I believe that the traditional and contemporary FL programs of the schools in the USA as well as other countries have been failing.

It seems that the results of the FL learning through such social environment as with family members, friends, relatives, and community members who speak FL to the learners dramatically contrast, in terms of the oral proficiency of FL, with that through the school environment with apparently very well organized and systematic language programs. Namely, students pick up FL more effectively through the social environment than through the school environment.

I want to emphasize here that in referring to the types of FL learning environments, I am using the term of the 'school environment' to specifically mean only the traditional or contemporary mainstream school environments. I consider any school language programs that do not put the heavily weighted focus, from the beginning, on teaching students how to speak TL as belonging to the traditional or contemporary language education. I do not intend to include in it any particular exceptional school environments for teaching FL, nor want to categorize all the future school environments ever evolving as being the same as the traditional or contemporary school environment. It is because I do not want to deny the future possibilities of FLE in school environments outmatching the social environments. In fact, I strongly believe that there is a way for the school to surpass the social environment in terms of teaching FL to the students. For that reason, I am writing this to share my vision with the readers.

I admit that the comparison here for the results of FL learning through the two environments is not based on a conclusion of a scientific research. To do scientific researches on this subject, it would require a lot of observations, experiments, and data analysis based on various types of such respective factors as student ages, period of study, daily hours of study, teaching methods, areas of subjects being taught, backgrounds of one's linguistic relationship to FL, linguistic distances between one's mother tongue and FL, and etc.

Without presentation of any scientific conclusions, so far, I have not met anybody who denied the argument that FL learning through the social environment is more effective than through the school environment. Everybody seemed to take it granted without hesitation that FL learning can be done most effectively through the social environment.

I asked people about what make them believe that FL learning is most effective in the social environment. Most people responded to me that it is because students are forced to be immersed into FL when surrounded by the social environment. They further believe that students, on the other hand, cannot be immersed so much into FL when studying FL in the school environment. Some other kinds of responses to the question are students don't get to talk to each other in FL in the school environment. Other group of people responded saying that, in school environment, students don't get the motivation to speak FL while, in the social environment, students are strongly required to speak FL for survival or at least to get along. Well, all sound like good answers.

Yet, I have a feeling that they lack understanding of some very fundamental facts. Don't the school language teachers strongly induce the students to be immersed into what is being taught at school? The school language teachers always squeeze ideas for students to be immersed into what they teach not only at school but also at home after school. They always give home works, quizzes, exams, and project assignments to the students. This is same in every school: middle schools, high schools, and in colleges. I really doubt that the immersion level in the school environment is significantly less serious than in the social environment.

Let me take an example of college students for the forced immersion level. The language programs at my department of the University of Colorado at Boulder offer 5 credit Asian language courses such as Arabic, Chinese, Hindi, Japanese, and Korean. Each course has 5 class hours per week. One can easily figure out that the students who take one of the language courses need to review and prepare for the classes every day; and, on top of that, they need to work for homework, frequent quizzes, midterms, finals, and projects. This would easily lead the students into a quite intensive and active immersion into FL at least 2-3 hours for normal weekdays, and much more during the period of tests and projects.

Another interesting example of forced immersion into FL is the ESL programs. Based on the information I have collected from many essays, mails, and articles that are uploaded by many ESL students all over the world, I have found that the ESL programs over the world countries are all same or quite similar to each other. It is also true that quite a number of the ESL programs that I know of are actually very same or at least similar to each other.

The ESL program students in the University of Colorado at Boulder are from all over the countries in the world whose languages are not English. The ESL program offers 4-5 English classes every day Monday through Thursday or Friday. It is heavily intensive English language program. Students from all over the countries are forced to be immersed into English literally all day long during the school and after school as they live in the USA. Compared to FL program of my department at the University of Colorado at Boulder, the degree of forced immersion for the ESL students are much more intensive.

To understand the real issues of the immersion idea better, let's look more deeply into the backgrounds of how the ESL students studied English prior to coming to the ESL school in their own countries. Let me first restrict myself to the immersion of students in Korea as I was grown up and lived for about 28 years there before I came to the USA. As I have been constantly in contact with what is going on in Korea mostly through news media, I would say that I am still quite familiar with the school environments of Korea.

To make a long story short, the students of the middle schools and above in Korea are forced to be immersed into what are taught from the English class at least two hours a day. Most of them endeavor very hard to be further immersed into English by spending a lot more hours every day for studying English in and out of the school. Most of the college students in Korea would immerse themselves into studying English many hours a day: even over five very intensive hours a day. They are strongly committed to challenge and pick up English for their life. After all, the students in Korea would be heavily immersed into English over 6 to 10 years of period. Many of them come to the ESL programs in the USA or in other English speaking countries to further immerse themselves into English for one or two years.

Many people from Japan and China that I know volunteered to confirm that that is quite the same situation in their countries also. Compared to the immersion-into-English situation of the students in Korea, Japan, and China, the USA students' immersion-into-FL situation does not seem to be even close for matching. One American would say, "No wonder, we are true American". However, it is not my point. My point is that, regardless of such school-driven heavy willingly committed immersions into FL (primarily English) by the peoples of Korea, Japan, and China, they still remain as true Korean, Japanese, and Chinese without being solid bilingual speakers.

After all, I took the above example to show that the forced immersion level in learning FL from the school environment is not less serious as the immersion level coming from the social environment, if not more. I can also show plenty of factual bases that the school environments do stimulate the students to speak FL; and that they emphasize the importance of being able to speak the language fluently.

Now, let me get to the point of what I think as missing in the school environment for teaching FL. Missing in FLE by the school environment is the oral language training. This is exactly what I see as missing from FL classes in the school. There is not much oral language to be picked up in the school language class. This is the reason I am sure why the oral proficiency of FL is not learned from school.

The only difference between the school environment and the social environment for FLE is the clear fact that, in one environment, students learn every thing but the oral language, and, in the other environment, they learn nothing but the oral language.

So far, I don't think that the schools have taught the oral language itself enough to the students during the language classes. Or, at least, the oral language training itself has been completely ignored or buried by the education. I understand that nobody intended to do so. It happened under the belief that they were teaching the best methods for the students to learn the language. I truly believe that the teaching methods they have applied in the school so far just simply did not work. Therefore, it is not surprising at all that schools have not produced solid bilingual speakers through the language classes.

When there is such a dramatic difference between the two environments, it is not an issue any more of who are better teachers between the members of the social environment and the language teachers of the school. Regardless of who are teaching, students are to fail in one environment and to succeed in the other environment.

What do I mean by saying that the oral language is missing from the school language education? What do I mean by saying that the schools have taught every thing but the oral language itself to the students? Let's talk about it.

7

Because We Have Not Taught Babble Training

So, what do they have been teaching in the school language classes?

Traditionally, there are five main subjects of the school FLE: grammar, reading, writing, listening, and speaking. Then, people believe that they should follow a certain sequence or combination among those five subjects to tackle the language. That is, whether it is right or wrong, there is a logical chain in people's mind, which connects each of those subjects in a particular set of sequence.

Somehow, among such different subjects, most of the people, in old time as well as nowadays, who are involved in FLE consider grammar as the most fundamental subject in studying FL. Therefore, they start teaching the grammar to students before anything else. They would use hundreds of unfamiliar grammar terms without explaining clearly what they mean and how they are supposed to work.

They would also quote various texts to analyze the sentences and find the grammar components in them. They would sometimes try to have students say some expressions to demonstrate how the rules apply in saying the language. After spending years of teaching the grammar like that, they would direct the students to start and focus on reading in FL.

As grammar is such difficult and evolving every day, the teachers would need to spend years to teach parts of the grammar repeatedly to help the students understand them. Understanding the grammar of a language, which one cannot speak, is very difficult. Even understanding the grammar of one's own language is not easy. Then, it gets over soon before they really get it: Students graduate from the school.

After all, in the school FL class, most of the time given to the teachers and to the students to teach and learn TL is spent on the very complicated grammar. As a result, the students even do not get many chances to read in TL. Even if they do, they would only find out how difficult it is to read and understand based on their incomplete grammar skills. As a result, students are back to square one in terms of FL skills again upon getting out of the school. Only thing that remains to the students is the memory of having intensive grammar classes in the school.

Even though the teachers would intend to support the students up to the levels of reading, writing, and speaking in TL, they cannot get into the higher levels because they don't have enough time even to complete a thorough grammar education. Eventually, very few people get out of the school with very limited TL skills in general, let alone the oral proficiency. Only few number of people at the end of the school can really read TL very well, let alone speaking the language, after so many years of investing all kinds of personal, school, and government resources. That is why I call it as a total loss.

Traditionally, the goals of FLE in schools have been to teach students to acquire the perceptive skills of TL, mostly of written language. This is because, I believe, until the mid 20th century, people didn't have to cope with the situations where instantaneous verbal interactions with foreigners are required. The old time communications with foreigners is of document based communication mode rather than simultaneous verbal communication mode. So, at that time, it should be satisfactory for the learners to be just able to read documents and write in reply to the correspondences from foreign partners.

Hence, it is not a surprise to see that the traditional FLE in secondary and post secondary schools heavily focuses on teaching the grammar of TL. Apart from the aspect of the time and cost effective issue, it is true that grammar helps one to analyze and understand the meanings of sentences in TL. Accordingly, with good knowledge and skills in the grammar, one could do it without having to acquire TL. For this reason, every body pursues the same track. However, many people do not seem to know of how hard, ineffective, unproductive, destructive, and detrimental it is to tackle a language from the grammar side.

Such a trend of offering the grammar based teaching is especially true for the schools of many non-English speaking countries, where most of the FL teachers are not native speakers of TL or do not speak TL. It is also true for most of the ESL schools in the USA. Likewise, in Asian countries like Korea, China, and Japan, where English is considered as one of the most important second language for the students to learn, FLE in schools traditionally offers very intensive English grammar classes for many years.

To realize that there is not much of real input to learn talking being taught in the school language classes requires very careful understanding of about the nature of human language, and how the language skill is acquired. Human language in nature is an intuitive vocal communication tool. To command the language fluently requires unconscious semi-instinctive movements of the speech organs of our body. Such kind of semi-instinctive physical movements of the speech organs could be acquired only through repeated exercises until the body builds up the semi-instincts to react semi-instinctively with the idea coming from the brain.

The fact that better-than-native-speaker level excellent knowledge of TL does not let one speak the language fluently has been proven by millions of people through out the world who studied, for example, the English grammar for many years, and yet can't even order a meal at a restaurant in English.

The fact that excellent skills of reading and writing TL on top of the outstanding grammar knowledge do not let one be fluent speaker of the language has also been proven by millions of our ancestors and contemporary people right around us. They could read and write, for example, English very well to the level of receiving very high scores in the English tests. Yet, most of them could not order a meal at a restaurant in English either.

Those people who exerted their own efforts so hard beyond the levels of what teachers taught in school, such as grammar, reading, and writing, to be able to listen and understand FL very well have also failed to develop advanced level of the oral proficiency. They have succeeded in getting very high scores in FL tests, like PBT or CBT TOEFL, or TOEIC tests for example. Yet, very few of them can make a simple business phone call in TL.

After all, in most of the worldwide countries, it is well known that schools spend around six years or so in teaching mostly grammars, reading, and writing based on the traditional FLE agenda during the middle and high school periods. Then, very hard working students spend about another 4 years or so studying TL in colleges. Not only that, many people still continue studying TL even after the college. This is especially so for the people studying English in Korea, for example. I know the people in many other countries have exactly the same situation as the Korean people do. Yet, the over-ten years of FLE has brought almost nothing to the students as long as the students' FL performance is concerned. In other words, all the efforts for such a long time end in vain.

Most of all, it is not simply lost of the time and resources. It means much more than that. With such 10 years of time spent on studying the grammar, reading, writing, and listening to TL, most of the students would miss a lot of opportunities and the best physical conditions to learn the oral language to the professional level because their muscles and nerves on the speech organs have already aged. We all know what aging means to our capacity to learn FL. Lost of the opportunities and physical adaptability for excellent performance, because of the aged body, could be the biggest suffering from such kind of absent minded education.

The above facts should be enough grounds to show that the traditional and contemporary FLE with heavy foci on the subjects of grammar, reading, writing, and even listening comprehension has proven itself to be unproductive in terms of achieving the goal of oral proficiency. The fundamental reason for such unproductiveness is that none of the subjects are the language by themselves. Language by nature is to be of oral communication tool. None of the above is related to the skills of oral communication. The skills of oral communication can only be developed through the intensive trainings for oral communication.

Therefore, no matter how great a teacher would be, no matter what procedures or sequences of teaching would be based on in teaching the subjects, the traditional and contemporary FLE has not much chance of producing students with the oral language skills. It is very unfortunate that the majority of FL teachers around the world either with or without own choices still stick to the traditional FL teaching methods.

As such traditional and contemporary FLE turns out to be unproductive, we started offering TL education to limited students through short or long term immersion into the TL community. We actually did not teach them. It is rather that some rich parents sent their children to the TL community, where the children pick up the language. Richer people could send the children away to the TL community longer for better acquisition of the language. Or, the whole family even moves to the country of TL for the children to pick up the language. The children who would be immersed only for short time on the other hand would pick up the strong stimulation and challenge to study the language.

While the few selected students are away from school being immersed into TL with or without their family, most of the FL teachers taught the remaining majority students with the traditional methods knowing that it would not work, and believing in that more and more students should leave schools to live in TL countries.

In general, the public schools seem to be the ones who are most reluctant to change. They rather refuse to change. On the other hand, the private schools, and the private language institutes are more responsive in realizing issues and adapting adjustments in their teaching methods.

Therefore, some FL teachers in private education groups have realized that what we taught so far are not productive, and have been trying to teach the language in its true sense to the students through conversation or one to one instruction. Or, some other native speaker teachers led the students using the direct methods. However, it does not seem to be that such teachers have been teaching what makes students pick up TL.

Now, let's review the issues once again. What makes students pick up TL when immersed into TL community? Why students do not pick up TL from FL classes? People have a lot of different answers to these questions. Majority people attribute the cause to the 'lack of grammar skills', first, and 'lack of reading skills', second, and argue for more FLE on grammar and reading. Many others blame the 'lack of vocabulary skills' of the students.

So, we have taught more grammar, reading, and vocabularies, yet in vain. Others claim that listening skills should be taught, which many students did for themselves, yet in vain. Then, people seem to have realized the real problem when they say 'we need to teach speaking the language'.

However, looking into the deep side of what they do, it does not seem that they really teach students what make the students pick up the language yet. In other words, they are teaching the speaking skills in the surface level. They don't seem to realize that there are a lot of preparations to be done under the surface level to spit out one expression to the surface level.

Basically, we have taught every thing possible in the surface level to our students. Whatever self-or-other appointed FLE expert people have said, we taught them to the students.

However, all of those methods have a common fundamental problem in that they only focused on those areas of the linguistic system and phenomena which can easily be seen above the surface level. The thorough observations to find and develop what sustain such phenomena of language acquisition and development under the surface level have been totally missing. Based on what we can see from the ducks freely floating on the water, we have developed a lot of methods for students to float on the water.

Consequently, none of our students were successful floating on the water. Instead, to develop failure free methods, we should have observed very carefully what is happening under the water for the ducks to appear so freely floating around.

There is something under the surface level that is most needed, most real, and most critical, which would make students pick up TL no matter where they study TL. If they don't get it, they would not pick up the language no matter how deeply they would be immersed into the TL community. If we do not teach it to the students, they would not pick up TL. Without it, nothing on the surface level is meaningful. This is what I mean by that we have not taught in the school language class. I call it Babble Training.

8

Wrong Answers on Language Acquisition

Over the past century, the language programs have failed time after time and added a new track each time, ending up with a long list of tracks. Included in the long list of tracks are grammar, vocabulary, reading, listening, conversation, writing, native speaker teachers, language village, language training abroad, and etc. It seems that there are no more tracks to added.

It typically takes over 10 years for students to complete this long list of tracks. Yet, literally no one has picked up meaningful level of oral proficiency. Consequently, all of those tracks individually or collectively have been proven as non-effective tracks for acquisition of oral proficiency.

Accordingly, the questions of 'what to do?' and 'how to do?' to acquire oral proficiency has never stopped. Yet, it has been very frustrating that many linguists and language teachers still offer some of the tracks from the list as creative and prosperous answers to the questions.

Some offer an i+1 or optimal input theory based reading track as if it would assure a success. All kinds of reading tracks already have been heavily done by numerous students and proven to be a failure to acquire oral proficiency. I don't understand why they are so stuck with the reading track.

Some others offer the listening track emphasizing that one should be able to listen and comprehend first before one can speak. They further emphasize that one cannot speak language without listening and comprehension skills. Which is absolutely not true. Thus, they emphasize the don't-ask listening to TVs, dramas, or movies. How come they can't see the proven fact that countless students who received excellent scores in the listening and comprehension tests have failed to acquire oral proficiency?

Many language education professors and teachers also say that students need experiences to meet and try native speakers. This track of get-along-experience with native speakers is not only non-realistic for most of the students but also does not bring acquisition of oral proficiency either. No native speakers except for kids would love to spend time to mingle with foreigners who don't speak and understand their language. Occasional mingling with native speakers don't help at all.

Furthermore, even though they don't count anyway because none of them are new ideas but from the old long list of the tracks which has been proven to be failures, all such answers tend to be confusing, vague, and self-contradictory.

Listening to various answers by so-called professional language teachers or linguists, I always felt something terribly stuck in my stomach. First, I know that none of the answers are cool. Second, even though they are wrong answers, they are so abstract without detailed directions. None of the answers tell students where to start at and what to start with. They are vague and so self-contradictory: How a student who cannot speak the language can build an experience of talking to a native speaker? How students can watch TVs, dramas, and movies when they cannot understand the language?

Here is a very clear reason for students having to spend many years of lifetime and tons of money only to fail: The language professors and teachers not only have led or pushed them into wrong tracks but also given them very wrong, vague, confusing, abstract answers to their questions.

As the one and only way to successful acquisition of oral proficiency, I have developed and introduced Babble Training Method ("BTM"). The practice model of BTM is the way kids acquire language. The simplest way to follow the model is to adopt the way they teach piano. We all know the one and only way piano teachers teach, and what students do to learn the piano.

It's a universally proven fact that kids acquire language in about 30 months so fluently. The fact that babies can acquire language in about 30 months is not a miracle. It simply means that the way babies acquire language is the easiest and simplest method of language acquisition.

BTM guarantees any students to acquire language at a level corresponding to the amount of real input they acquired and retained; just like the piano students acquire piano skills at a level corresponding to the amount of music they acquired and retained. The more they acquire, the higher their proficiency goes. Real input in a narrow sense means practical expressions with native speaker's voice[7] which students can use for oral communication in their daily environment.

Also, I have authored, edited and published a series of four books called *BTM Real English* as exemplary real input textbooks for English teachers and students.

---

[7] This is a term I use as a reference to the realistic input that learners can acquire and actually use in his/her real life environment. Depending on intended outputs, real input can be specified as real input to learn talking, reading, listening, writing, and grammar respectively. Input which lacks the features like usability, story, conversation, vocabulary, voice, and grammar, which are required to facilitate the acquisition of the intended output, is not qualified as effective and efficient real input for the respective intended outputs. In a narrow sense, real input means practical expressions with native speakers voice which students can use for oral communication in their daily environments.

To acquire language, BTM suggests that, depending on learners, a minimum 1,000 ~ 3,000 real input should be acquired and retained for 2~3 years. Once a language is acquired it requires continued babble training to acquire more real input not only to maintain the acquired language but also to improve oral proficiency, just like what native speakers do.

In the beginning part of the paragraphs, I boldly stated, "It typically takes over 10 years for students to complete this long list of tracks. Yet, literally no one has picked up meaningful level of oral proficiency."

I stated as such with assurance because, based on BTM Input and Output hypothesis, I know that no one can acquire oral proficiency without meaningful amount of real input acquired and retained enough to speak the language. It's just like no one can play the piano without meaningful amount of music acquired and retained enough to play the piano.

None of the tracks of the traditional methods of language education have driven student into intensive babble training over real input. Accordingly, no students could have acquired and retained meaningful amount real input, therefore, it is a natural conclusion that none of them could have acquired meaningful level of oral proficiency.

CHAPTER 2

Problems of Stephen Krashen vs. BTM

The truth is that language is acquired only through Babble Training. This is the only needed and sufficient condition for acquisition. Therefore, one cannot talk without learning to talk first.

Krashen said that natural acquisition takes place after **silent period** when comprehensible input is constantly provided. Had he observed it correctly, he would have said that natural acquisition takes place after successful **Babble Training**.

Krashen has offered variations of inputs, but he offered no inputs for Babble Training. Talking cannot be acquired through inputs for reading, listening, writing, speaking or grammar.

All the inputs Krashen has introduced are inputs for reading and listening, not to learn talking.

That is why Krashen's theories have failed just like all the traditional methods have.

Talking about various types of inputs is meaningless when there is no program designed for students to learn talking first.

1

Problems With Krashen's Input Theories:

Input Hypothesis (i+1), Comprehensible Input, and Optimal Input

1. History of Krashen's Input Hypotheses

A prominent linguist and seemingly most popular influencer on language education, Stephen Krashen, has introduced a number of theories and guides on language acquisition. In his early time, Krashen believed in grammar and ran grammar based language education programs for long time at the University of Southern California.

Then, he confessed that grammar does not help students to acquire language, and turned away from the grammar theories to jump into the input theories. He has introduced multiple 'input' theories including Input Hypothesis (i+1), Comprehensible Input Hypothesis, and Optimal Input Hypothesis. He seems to believe that the failure of language acquisition so far has been fundamentally caused by not effective inputs including grammar.

He continued realizing problems with his input theories and introduced one input theory after another. However, to me, none of them seem to make any significant differences in the real world of language education industry anyway. Unfortunately, his theories seem to have added more confusion and unstable concept of language education to the learners and teachers.

We don't know when he would stop introducing a new input theory. Further, the inputs he has introduced so far as effective for language acquisition are, I believe, nothing new but the ones which have been tried by hundreds of millions of people in the world and proven as failure by the history of language education.

I know as a matter of fact that there are hundreds of thousands of people in Korea who have tried all different kinds of inputs available in the bookstores, movies, dramas, magazines, and storybooks for well over 10 years or even 20 years, but failed to be fluent in English. I know as a matter of fact that the Korean people are not the only people who are so eager to acquire English as a second language.

2. We All Acquire Language The Same Way

Krashen answers to the most important question on language acquisition "How do we acquire language?" with the Comprehensible Input Hypothesis that "We acquire language in one way and only one way when we get comprehensible input in a low anxiety environment." He also declared, "we all acquire language the same way". Further, he stated that natural acquisition will take place after silent period when comprehensible input is constantly provided to students and it's an inevitable phenomenon.

Krashen's comprehensible input surprisingly contradicts one of his old hypotheses: Language Acquisition-Learning hypothesis where he argued that acquisition (conversation) contributes to the fluency, and on the other hand learning (grammar) contributes to the accuracy. Based on this theory, he, a very typical grammarian linguist, insisted that conversation based acquisition program and systematic grammar based learning program should be pursued together. However, he didn't hesitate to turn down his own theory when he learned that both fluency and accuracy are achieved through acquisition only. He also claimed that systematic grammar education does not work in language education.

Krashen's input theories presume the language acquisition device (LAD)[8]. That is, he seems to believe, when those inputs are constantly provided to students, the LAD will work for acquisition. He also seems to believe that acquisition must take place when inputs are constantly provided.

I absolutely agree with Krashen that we acquire language in one way and only one way. However, I don't agree with his comprehensible input theory to be really the one way and only one way to acquire language because the history has proven that the 'comprehensible input in a low anxiety environment' has failed countless students.

To me, we acquire language in one way and only one way. Intensive Babble Training over real input for extended time period is the one and only way for all of us to acquire language.

3. Problems With Krashen's Theories

3.1. Input Theory

Krashen's input hypotheses, whether i+1, comprehensible, or optimal input, contain a problem in itself that the definitions of those inputs are very vague and not concrete. In a lecture, he explained

---

[8]   LAD (Language Acquisition Device) is a virtual concept introduced by Chomsky that all men are borne with language acquisition device somewhere in the brain, which processes and acquires the linguistic inputs.

what is a comprehensible input. He took an example of describing human face naming and pointing eyes, nose, mouth, ears... It seemed that the comprehensible input means an input comprehensible to students based on the context. This would limit the FL teaching mostly to natural immersion environments, or to programs having to utilize visuals, which would raise a lot of barriers, restrictions, and difficulties in most of FL programs.

In many lectures, Krashen emphasized reading for students to learn language. This clearly shows that Krashen recommends reading as a way of taking comprehensible input. What about writing?

However, the history of language education clearly shows very few cases where students have acquired language through reading. Further, the history clearly has proven that few students have acquired language with listening either.

To me, the input theories are to fail because those comprehensible or optimal inputs to read are not designed for effective and efficient Babble Training for acquisition.

3.2. Affective Filter Theory

To enhance acquisition, Krashen proposed Affective Filter theory that student's acquisition level may vary depending on motivation, self esteem, and anxiety. It seems to make sense that a student with low motivation, low self esteem and high anxiety would not acquire language. However, the Affective Filter theory has failed to explain the contrary fact that numerous students with high motivation, high self esteem and low anxiety still have failed to acquire language after endless efforts to tackle comprehensible input provided to them.

If the history clearly shows that acquisition of excellent reading and listening skills through a lot of reading and listening have failed learners to acquire language, what's the use of talking about effective input from reading and listening, or even writing?

So far, I have pointed out the problems with Krashen's Comprehensible Input and Affective Filter theories. I like he pointed out that grammar does not count anymore in language acquisition; and that we acquire language in one way and only one way.

However, I don't agree with the comprehensible input to be the only condition because Krashen misses a fundamental requirement to acquire language: Babble Training.

As a matter of fact, I refuse to admit the comprehensible input theory as an effective way of language acquisition. It's not much different from those traditional methods which have misled and failed the students.

3.3. Optimal Input Theory

Krashen's Optimal Input hypothesis is fundamentally not much different from the Comprehensible Input hypothesis. He seems to have simply created a concept of optimal input to include 'compelling', 'rich', 'quality', and 'quantity' inputs on top of the 'comprehensible' input. He argues that the optimal input would be the most effective input for language acquisition. Also, he argues that story listening and guided reading are the best method to get the optimal input.

Krashen argues that acquisition happens through the optimal input. That is, students will acquire language when provided with the optimal input containing the five characteristics of 'comprehensible', 'compelling', 'rich', 'quality', and 'quantity' through listening and reading.

However, in real world, reading a lot of books will help students only with improving reading skills. Likewise, story listening or other types of listening will help students only with improving listening skills. This has been proven as a truth matter especially for strange languages[9] through the history of language education.

For example, it's not a secret at all that students with high scores of listening and reading skills in TOEFL or TOEIC surely have high level of listening and reading skills, but no fluent level of speaking skills at all. This history proven real world indicates that Krashen's comprehensible input and optimal input theories do not entail acquisition of oral proficiency.

I believe that language acquisition cannot be expected when the input is not designed for effective and efficient Babble Training regardless of whether any input would be optimal for reading and listening, or not.

[9]   I use this term in reference to those languages totally unrelated to each other bearing extremely different linguistic features as well as cultural features like between Korean and English or Japanese and English. On the other hand, languages like English, Spanish, and German show relatively minimum level of differences linguistically and culturally. I call these languages as cousin languages, which are relatively much less challenging to acquire.

2

Fundamental Reasons for Failure of Krashen's Theories

The fact that Krashen's input theory has been complemented and developed into various versions show that the input theory series, if successful, do not guarantee acquisition. It means that the input defined by the theories, and the required acts of taking the input, if successful, do not satisfy the requirements for acquisition.

I can see why the input theories cannot bring successful acquisition. I will explain the reasons with BTM's working hypotheses.

1) There Is No Mutation Between Input And Output

One of BTM's input-output working hypotheses stipulates that no input can produce an output of different category. That is, comprehensible input for reading will produce acquisition of reading skill only as output. Likewise, optimal input for listening will produce acquisition of listening skill only as output. So, the outcome of writing as input will be acquisition of writing skill. Grammar as input will produce knowledge on grammar only. This is why grammar does not contribute to acquisition as Krashen said.

Based on my own experience of language teaching and my observations, I believe this is a universal phenomenon. Some people would dispute this hypothesis by saying that there are people who picked up some degree of speaking skill through input for listening. Such phenomenon does not prove the hypothesis is wrong. It simply means that there was some degree of Babble Training (repeated efforts to remember and say) by the student over the given input for listening. If someone picked up some extent of speaking skill through input for reading, it also simply means that there was some extent of Babble Training by the student over the given input for reading.

The types of inputs Krashen introduced through his input theories are inputs for reading and listening. So, only expected output from those inputs will be acquisition of reading and listening skills.

2) No Input Produces No Output

BTM's another working hypothesis on input output is that 'no input produces no output.' The failure of Kreshan's input theories to acquire verbal fluency comes from the fact that the theories do not offer the real input to learn talking except for immersion case.

Krashen argues that the optimal input would be the most effective input for language acquisition. His optimal input carries the five characteristics of 'comprehensible', 'compelling', 'rich', and 'quantity'. Also, he argues that story listening and guided reading are the best method to get the optimal input.

However, the optimal input through the guided reading and story listening are hardly effective real input[10] because they are

---

[10] This is a term I use as a reference to the realistic input that learners can acquire and actually use in his/her real life environment. Depending on intended outputs, real input can be specified as real input to learn talking, reading, listening, writing, and

designed to be optimal for reading and listening, not for Babble Training.

Consequently, as the input from the optimal input method lacks the features required to be real input, no meaningful output for acquisition of oral proficiency can be expected. It does not matter whether i+1 input, comprehensible input, or optimal input is offered. They are not qualified to be real input for Babble Training, consequently, students will fail to acquire talking skill.

3) No Babble, No Acquisition

BTM's another working hypothesis on language acquisition is 'No Babble, No Acquisition.' This self explanatory hypothesis claims that no acquisition can occur without the babble[11] activities. According to this hypothesis, the three acquisition factors: linguistic intuition, physical capacity, and linguistic resources can be achieved simultaneously only through Babble Training.

If any one of the three acquisition factors would be zero, one cannot perform any linguistic activities like talking, listening, reading, and writing. [12] Also, intensive Babble Training helps learner to over-

---

grammar respectively. Input which lacks the features like usability, story, conversation, vocabulary, voice, and grammar, which are required to facilitate the acquisition of the intended output, is not qualified as effective and efficient real input for the respective intended outputs.

11 I use the term 'Babble' or 'Babbling' to mean the learner's repeated acts of mimicking, copying, imitating, or practicing linguistic input with a purpose of acquiring language, especially speaking skills. However, in a broad sense, I also use the term to mean the learner's repeated practice acts of listening, reading and writing after linguistic input with a purpose of acquiring respective skills.

12 See the article under the title of 'Working Hypothesis on Language Acquisition'.

come the linguistic resistance[13] learner has against TL. Accordingly, Babble Training is a must-do activity to acquire language.

The fact that Krashen's input theories do not offer the real input required for acquisition of verbal fluency is one of the two fundamental causes for the failure of the optimal input theory based programs.

The other fundamental cause for the failure of the optimal theory based programs is the fact that Krashen has not applied the very crucial factor of Babble Training in acquisition to his input models. Krashen does not seem to consider Babble Training as a crucial factor of acquisition. He does not seem to acknowledge the crucial role of Babble Training in language acquisition.

In natural language acquisition, family members, especially mother, play most of the role of offering real input and leading the baby to babble. So, after certain amount of real input and time of Babble Training, the mother language is acquired. No babies acquire language without babbling to learn talking. Likewise, no learners can acquire language without tenacious Babble Training over real input.

---

[13] The linguistic resistance is the degree of one's physical and cognitive unfitness to process the input, which deters the production of output. The linguistic resistance is mainly caused by the linguistic distance from one's MT to TL, and by one's age. One's age shows the degree of the firmness of the physical and cognitive adhesiveness to the linguistic features of one's MT. In addition, the linguistic resistance can be increased by any kinds of individual unfitness to process the input. The linguistic resistance explains why different languages are less or more challenging for students with different MT backgrounds to acquire them compared to other languages. It also explains why children in general can acquire a foreign language relatively faster than adults.

3

BTM In Real World

I personally have an experience of failing in English acquisition. I also have an experience of successfully acquiring English by myself in Korea. I developed BTM based on my own experiences of failure and success in English acquisition; the testimonials of other people for successful English acquisition; my own study and research in linguistics with focus on language acquisition; failed experience of teaching FL in South Korea and USA; and experiments for successful and unsuccessful application of BTM at University of Colorado at Boulder and a private program as well.

The conclusion I obtained from all those experiences is that intensive Babble Training over real input is a must factor that had to be enforced to acquire language. My experiments clearly showed that any compromise to waive the intensive Babble Training for extended time has resulted in failure regardless.

I had very minimal level of English grammar and vocabularies from middle school in Korea. In high school, which offered only one class hour per week, I studied English grammar for about 1.5 years from the 2nd semester of the 1st year to the end of the 2nd year steadily daily basis. Then, I had to give up as I found zero progress made for my English speaking skill. I didn't study English in the 3rd year, the senior year in Korea.

After high school, I didn't go to college but got a job. I started studying English again. I started with Babble Training using textbooks for conversational dialogues with audio tapes. A year or later, I added the babble to learn reading. A year or later again, I also added the babble to learn writing with writing daily journal. Things worked very well to my surprise. I became quite confident with speaking, reading, and writing in English. I would say it took roughly about 3 years. When I came to the USA to study linguistics later after graduating from a college in Korea, I was lucky to get a freelancer job as a professional Korean-English interpreter for the US courts as well as for the Colorado state courts.

I introduced the study method which was surprisingly successful for me to a college student who later became my better half. She started with Babble Training just like I did. She later added the babble to learn listening. She didn't do much of Babble Training to learn reading and writing compared to what I did. Yet, she also very successfully became a convenient speaker of English.

I also know a few Korean American I met in the USA who were in their 40s and very fluent in speaking English. Believe or not, it's very rare to find pure Korean Americans who moved to the USA after their 30 plus years of age, who lived in the USA for over 10 or 20 years, and who are fluent in speaking English. I found that they had experiences of failing in English just like I did. I also found that what they did tenaciously to acquire fluent English skills in Korea for many years were what I now call Babble Training.

Before I came to the USA, I taught English for high school and college students in Korea for a few years following the traditional methods: Grammar, reading, TOEFL, TOEIC. I had no choice of developing my own method for them. None of them successfully acquired speaking skills of English. Even those students who got very high scores in TOEFL or TOEIC had no meaningful speaking skills of English.

I taught Korean at University of Colorado at Boulder. I designed BTM program to fit the class environment. The program was designed to help students to retain all the realistic expressions introduced during the class. For example, students are required to be able to play any given roles in the class any day for randomly selected piece of scenarios introduced during the semester.

For quizzes, students are required to write down the corresponding Korean expressions for randomly chosen English messages from the scenarios. For tests, students are required to record their own voice of saying the corresponding Korean expressions for 100 or 150 randomly chosen English messages.

This way, typically, students would learn and retain about 800-900 realistic expressions in a semester. They would become very talkative in Korean by the end of the semester. If the students would continue taking the class for at least 3 semesters, it would be very likely that the students would pick up about 3000 realistic expressions, and would build a strong foundation to acquire quite fluent level of speaking skills in Korean by continuing Babble Training by themselves to retain them for another year or so at least.

However, students would complain that the class is too much demanding compared to other language programs, and most of them would not come back for the next semester, which is very discouraging to me, the teacher. So, based on BTM's working hypotheses, I believe that the students must have completely failed unless they had continued Babble Training by themselves over the expressions they learned during the semester.

As the students complained and did not come back for the next semester, which lowered the comeback ratio of the students, which would make my teaching look not good, I developed and applied a program more like the traditional FLE method: Grammar, reading, and conversation for a couple years. Students liked it much better as the demand for the class is somewhat similar to other language programs.

Almost all students paid intensive attention on the grammar even though I emphasized the conversation skill to be more important. Their performance of conversation was very poor. They didn't retain the expressions they learned in class through out the semester as the program didn't require it. At the end of the semester, none of them were able to communicate with me for simple situation conversation using the expressions introduced to the class. No chance for them to pick up Korean at all. This result was not a surprise to me at all.

I taught English to many small groups of Korean Americans in metro Denver area, Colorado. It was a one-year program with one class a week for two hours. They were in their 40s to 50s, working full time jobs.

I designed the program to fit their situation as a group. I would give them weekly homework, and when they come to class, I would divide them into several groups of two people, and ask them to play the scenario between the two regardless of the characters.

This way, we don't need to worry about matching the number of characters. I would circle around the groups listening to their articulation, and help them with correct articulations. After playing the scenario by each group, I would use a projector to present the scenarios in Korean, and ask the students to say the corresponding message in English.

The students learned about 2,500 expressions. It was quite successful for some students who dedicated serious efforts and time to acquire all the expressions. They were grateful to me for being able to use the expressions they learned in their jobs and businesses.

There was one lady who learned how to apply BTM to acquire English. She could not come to my class due to her schedule conflict. She taught English to herself with BTM method using the material I designed. She was so happy to see how well BTM worked for her, and told me, "You are the 2nd most grateful person after God I have ever met."

4

Real Input vs. Optimal Input

Krashen's input theory presents optimal input as the best input for learners, and story listening and guided reading are the best method for learners to get the optimal input.

The optimal input is to provide students with language that is comprehensible, interesting, and abundant. It's idea is that students acquire language and literacy through such optimal input. It has four characteristics as follows:

1. Comprehensible: The input should be understandable, even if it contains some incomprehensible bits.
2. Compelling: The input should be interesting and engaging so that students temporarily forget it's in a foreign language
3. Quality: he input should be rich in language and include new words or structures that are slightly beyond the student's current level.
4. Quantity: The input should be abundant so that students have more opportunities to acquire language.

Meanwhile, BTM uses output oriented real input. That is, BTM uses real input or practical input designed for respectively required output. Depending on student's age, environment and required output, real input can be arranged accordingly.

Real input is the practical or realistic input that learners can acquire and actually use in his/her real life environment. Depending on intended outputs, real input can be specified as real input to learn talking, reading, listening, and writing respectively. Input which lacks the features like usability, context, interaction, and voice which are required to facilitate the acquisition of the intended output, is not qualified as an effective real input.

Instead of tackling indefinitely new and abundant input, BTM, for the purpose of effective and fluent acquisition, emphasizes repeated Babble Training over real inputs which people use daily basis in various situations of regular environments. BTM wants students to chew those real inputs as much as and as often as they can and store them in their Language Acquisition Device to be able to use them whenever needed and to maximize their linguistic intuition on the target language.

Detail method of effective Babble Training can be found in later chapters to follow.

I will not say it is absolutely impossible for students to acquire a language through story listening and guided reading of optimal input. Especially, I would agree that easy languages may be acquired to a degree by such intensive story listening and guided reading of optimal input.

Even though I heard testimonials from people who bragged about their children acquiring a language after reading over a thousand storybooks for the entire elementary school period, I am doubtful of their evaluation. For example, people who don't speak English would comment someone who can barely order hamburgers at a McDonald as a very good English speaker. If anyone became fluent in a foreign language, it means that the person must have a lot of Babble Training by oneself over the input.

Anyway, FLE is not to be for such handful of special students only.

BTM primarily aims for every student to be fluent in their daily environments in one to two years or so by acquiring a couple of thousand real input to learn talking. Which is really doable for most committed students. Then, BTM aims for acquisition of fluent reading, listening, and writing skills gradually just like all normal people do over time.

Short examples of real inputs to learn talking and reading will be introduced later in this book.

5

Geocentric Approach (Traditional Methods) and Heliocentric Approach (BTM)

The truth has never changed. It always has been the earth that rotates and moves around the sun giving us days, nights, and seasons. It took so long for man to recognize the heliocentrism as a truth of the universe. They were wrong for long time to believe in geocentrism.

The truth has never changed. It always has been through Babble Training that man acquired language. The linguists and teachers have been wrong for so long to believe in the traditional methods of teaching grammar, reading, listening, and conversation.

Most of the linguists and language teachers are so stubborn that they have insisted that man should learn language with grammar, reading, listening, or conversation, which can be categorized as the traditional methods. The linguists and teachers have dedicated themselves to develop advanced FLE programs within the frame of the geocentrism-like traditional methods.

That's how the linguists and language teachers have caused irreparable damages to hundreds of millions people worldwide. Because of such linguists and teachers, including myself as well, the students wasted time, money, and life over learning language in vain.

To make it easy to understand how fundamentally wrong the traditional methods have been from the very beginning, I claim that the traditional FLE methods are the FLE methods of geocentrism era, or the geocentric methods. Also, to make it easy to understand how fundamentally right Babble Training Method ("BTM") has been from the very beginning, I claim that BTM is the FLE method of heliocentrism era, or the heliocentric method.

Geocentrism seemed to have answers to all questions people had for long time like how days and nights change, and seasons change and etc, and then that was good enough for everybody for long time. Yet, some astronomers found that there were a couple of issues man could not get answers from geocentrism: the change of Venus' phases and sizes. Also, a mystery with Mar's movement could not be explained with geocentrism. Eventually, the mystery gave a birth to heliocentrism.

Just like that, the geocentric methods of the language education satisfied the linguists and teachers as it seemed to have answers to the questions on how to analyze sentence structures, how to read, and how to write in target language. They believed that geocentric methods would solve all problems in language education.

However, the geocentric methods have failed to resolve the mystery that none of the A+ students have become fluent in their target languages. So, the linguists and teachers have developed all kinds of methods with creative ideas to supplement the traditional methods to resolve the issue. Yet, they just kept failing over and over again.

Still, not many of those linguists and teachers see the heliocentric method of BTM effectively and surely resolve the unsolved mystery of language acquisition. BTM is the only method to acquire language and all realms of language like speaking, reading, writing, listening, and grammar at the same time. None of the traditional methods can do this.

Krashen's input theories can only fail simply because it still belongs to the geocentric approach of the traditional methods.

Now, in order to provide a clear answer for all the repeated failures of the traditional methods, and Krashen's input theories as well, I offer BTM's working hypotheses of acquisition and input-output, which will be introduced later.

Understanding the hypotheses, one will find out what have been missing in the Krashen's theories as well as in the traditional FLE methods.

I introduced BTM to be the only one way to acquire language, regardless of easy or difficult languages. For sure, we all acquire a language the same way through Babble Training over real input.

I don't mean to say that those inputs and those manners suggested by Krashen are absolutely ineffective. For example, I agree with Krashen that students would acquire language when comprehensible input is constantly offered in an immersion environment, where Babble Training would naturally take place to survive. It is because in an immersion environment, students are voluntarily or involuntarily enforced to perform very intensive Babble Training to survive. However, this type of method is very unrealistic for the absolute majority of learners.

Babble Training over due amount of real input and time[14] is the only universal way for all men to acquire language. No language is acquired without Babble Training. No input with Babble Training means no acquisition.

BTM is very easy, simple, and realistic. BTM can be applied to a class of many students. BTM teacher does not have to be fluent in the target language. BTM drives the LAD to work very effectively

---

[14] Due amount of real input and time varies depending on individual's linguistic resistance against TL and degree of mental immersion to learn TL. Concrete discussion will be introduced later.

just like in mother language acquisition. With BTM, students can do Babble Training over real input by or among themselves.

One can use audio device to do Babble Training. It does not necessarily require in person interactions. It does not require partners. One can do Babble Training without a teacher. It does not require going around the world to be immersed. One can babble alone at home, at work, or on the bus.

Learners and teachers can apply BTM's working hypotheses introduced above as a tool to find if any elected FLE program, textbook, or theory would work or not for acquisition.

It's neither reading nor listening to comprehensible input, but repeated Babble Training over real input that makes acquisition inevitable.

6

Can AI Solve the Problems with FLE? No and Yes.

As a part of research on effective foreign language education methods, I had once reviewed about 300 papers written by Korean researchers and scholars on various subjects related to effective methods of the English programs in Korea. Literally, all the ideas dealt with in the papers were of how to apply the contemporary technologies in the English programs. None of them acknowledged the failure of the traditional FLE methods. No wonder they focused on such subjects as how to help students understand the English grammar better and easier using the technologies; how to use online conversation partners; and how to apply graphic images to help with reading, and etc.

Now that we have AI, which we already have started to rely on more than human resources, a lot of ideas on how to utilize AI in FLE will appear soon. Then, almost all people will be misled to believe the AI based programs as if they are the best or standard ways of learning language. AI will be able to do a lot of things for teachers and students as well. AI can be a good conversation partner; it can provide very efficient reading materials; it can help students with learning grammar; it can help students with training to acquire listening skills; it can help students with writing skills; and it can do a lot of other things that the teachers and friends have done so far to help students

However, one should understand the nature of AI. AI can be self-learning and generative. So, AI will learn from the huge amount of FLE data and generate FLE programs based on the data. It can improve and produce much more productive and effective programs.

However, when there are no data that AI could learn from, AI cannot be generative. This means that what AI can learn and generate is bounded by the scopes of the data. It cannot generate a totally different scope of service that is not supported by the data provided. That is, AI would perform better than human only when there are equivalent codes or data provided to AI.

One should know that the reason for the traditional FLE methods to have failed so far was not because there were no good conversation partners; textbooks for listening skills; good teachers to teach how to read and write; or better grammar books. They have failed just because none of them are proper methods to teach or learn language.

Consequently, given the fact that the traditional FLE methods have failed for students to acquire oral proficiency, it is very obvious that all the programs which AI would generate based on the data from the traditional FLE methods would also fail for students to acquire oral proficiency as well. AI would not be able to generate the BTM training methods due to the fact that there are no data yet for the BTM training methods.

As BTM training is the only method to assure language acquisition, we can provide BTM training codes to AI. Then, in a near future, it will bring the best results for students to pick up the language of their choice.

CHAPTER 3

Examples of Real Input

Following examples of real input in this chapter are from *BTM Real English* series, which is designed for English programs based on real inputs useful for different levels of various situations in daily activities.

BTM Real English textbooks are composed of 4 books as follows:

1.   Book 1 for children
2.   Book 2 for juniors
3.   Book 3 for adults
4.   Book 4 for listening and phonetics

Audio files for all books are available at YouTube: #BtmRealEnglish

1

Real Input To Learn Talking 1: What Time Is Dad Getting Home Today?

2	Mom:	Tim!
3	Tim:	Yeah?
4	Mom:	Where are you?
5	Tim:	I'm in my room.
6	Mom:	Do you want something to eat?
7	Tim:	Sure.
8	Mom:	(comes in with a tray of food) Here, eat something. What are you up to?
9	Tim:	Just building things with my legos.
10	Mom:	That's impressive! Is that a ship?
11	Tim:	Yep, it's a ship.
12	Mom:	What's her name?
13	Tim:	Tim Ocean. I named her after me.
14	Mom:	I like that name.
15	Tim:	I'm making it for Dad's birthday. So, don't tell him, okay?

16	Mom:	I promise. I'm sure Dad will love it. How long do you think it will take?
17	Tim:	I'm not sure. Maybe two hours or so?
18	Mom:	Two hours? What time will that be?
19	Tim:	Well, what time is it now?
20	Mom:	It's half past three.
21	Tim:	Okay, I think I can finish it by five thirty. Mom?
22	Mom:	Hmm?
23	Tim:	What time is Dad getting home today?
24	Mom:	Around six, as usual.
25	Tim:	Perfect! I'll be done with this just before he gets home.
26	Mom:	What are you going to do after that?
27	Tim:	Can we catch a movie after dinner?
28	Mom:	Sure. What movie?
29	Tim:	Batman. There's a showing at seven thirty and another at nine thirty.
30	Mom:	Nine thirty is too late but the seven thirty showing will work. We'll eat at six thirty.
31	Tim:	Mom?
32	Mom:	Yes?
33	Tim:	What time are we getting up tomorrow to go to the airport?
34	Mom:	We leave at seven, so at six twenty at the latest.
35	Tim:	Why are we leaving so early?
36	Mom:	It takes an hour and a half to get to the airport.
37	Tim:	When's the flight?
38	Mom:	Nine forty five.

39	Tim:	How long does it take to go to Grandma's?
40	Mom:	A little over two hours.
41	Tim:	That's it?
42	Mom:	Well it takes another half hour from the airport to Grandma's house.
43	Tim:	What time will we get there then?
44	Mom:	Probably around a quarter till two. Chicago is an hour ahead of us.
45	Tim:	When are we getting back?
46	Mom:	We'll be back in Denver around quarter to five in the afternoon on Sunday.
47	Tim:	So, we'll be home around six thirty?
48	Mom:	Yeah, that sounds about right.

2

Real Input To Learn Talking 2: Can We Talk About Pets?

2	Mom:	Hey, sweetie! How was school today?
3	Tina:	It was okay.
4	Mom:	That doesn't sound too good. What happened?
5	Tina:	Nothing.
6	Mom:	You sure?
7	Tina:	Yeah I just didn't like the lunch.
8	Mom:	What was for lunch?
9	Tina:	Chicken.
10	Mom:	What was wrong with it?
11	Tina:	It was gross.
12	Mom:	That's it?
13	Tina:	Yeah.
14	Mom:	I see. Well, let's go home.
15	Tina:	Mom?
16	Mom:	Yes?
17	Tina:	Can we stop by the grocery store on our way home?

18	Mom:	Why? Do you want something to eat?
19	Tina:	Yeah, I want some ice cream.
20	Mom:	You do realize that you've been having ice cream everyday for the past week, right?
21	Tina:	Yeah. Is it bad to have it everyday?
22	Mom:	Of course. Eating anything with too much artificial flavoring and sugar everyday is bad.
23	Tina:	Oh okay...
24	Mom:	Do you have homework?
25	Tina:	Yeah, my teacher said to talk to our parents about animals.
26	Mom:	Animals?
27	Tina:	Yeah, animals you can have as pets!
28	Mom:	Hmm, interesting. Do you have any other homework?
29	Tina:	I do have some reading to do.
30	Mom:	Do the reading first, then we'll talk about pets after dinner.
31	Tina:	That's what I was going to do.
32	Mom:	Perfect!
33	Note:	(after dinner)
34	Tina:	Dad?
35	Dad:	Yes, princess?
36	Tina:	Can we talk about pets?
37	Dad:	Is this for homework?
38	Tina:	Yes.
39	Dad:	Okay, sure. Start by listing animals people can have as pets.
40	Tina:	Dogs!

41	Mom:	That's right! Many people have dogs because they're very smart and loyal to their owners.
42	Dad:	Exactly.
43	Tina:	Can we have a dog?
44	Mom:	We can discuss that later!
45	Dad:	Yes, we can discuss that later. What other animals can you think of?
46	Tina:	A cat?
47	Mom:	Yes, of course!
48	Dad:	Many people do indeed have cats as pets!
49	Tina:	I want a cat too!
50	Dad:	Tina, I don't think we can have a cat and a dog.
51	Tina:	It would be so much fun to have both though!
52	Mom:	I know, I know, but taking care of them would take so much time and effort.
53	Tina:	But all of my friends have a cat or a dog!
54	Dad:	I understand, but we can't afford to have a pet!
55	Mom:	Sorry, sweetie, maybe you can have both when you grow up!
56	Tina:	Okay.
57	Mom:	Good girl. Now what other animals can people have as pets?
58	Tina:	How about rabbits?
59	Dad:	Rabbits?
60	Tina:	Yeah! People have rabbits, don't they?
61	Mom:	They do!
62	Dad:	I don't think so…

63	Mom:	Of course people do, Honey.
64	Tina:	What about snakes?
65	Dad:	Oh yeah, I know a few people who absolutely love snakes.
66	Mom:	I don't like snakes...small snakes, big snakes, colorful snakes--I hate them all. They're gross!
67	Dad:	Yeah, I don't like snakes either.
68	Tina:	Dad, what other animals do people keep as pets?
69	Dad:	A cow!
70	Mom:	Hon, that's not exactly a pet.
71	Tina:	Oh, what about a horse?
72	Mom:	That's not a pet either! Those are animals raised on a farm.
73	Tina:	Oh, okay.
74	Tina:	What about roosters?
75	Dad:	Those are also raised outside on a farm! Well, in chicken coops.
76	Tina:	How about a tiger? Can you have a tiger for a pet?
77	Mom:	I don't think so.
78	Dad:	I've never heard of anyone raising a tiger.
79	Tina:	What about monkeys?
80	Mom:	Probably not. Those are animals at the zoo for people to see when they want!
81	Tina:	I saw all kinds of animals there last year!
82	Dad:	I bet you did! We can go to the zoo this weekend, if you would like to.
83	Tina:	Really?
84	Dad:	Of course.

85	Tina:	Thanks Dad.
86	Dad:	Anything for my girl.
87	Mom:	Is that it for your homework?
88	Tina:	I think so. Thanks for helping me!
89	Dad:	Sure. Any time.
90	Mom:	I'm glad I could be of help.

3

Real Input To Learn Talking 3: I Don't Want To Get Up

2	Note:	(Part 1: Mom wakes Tina up)
3	Mom:	Tina! Good morning!
4	Tina:	Good morning. I don't want to get up.
5	Mom:	Why not?
6	Tina:	I just don't feel like it.
7	Mom:	Did you not sleep well?
8	Tina:	I don't know. I had a dream though.
9	Mom:	Oh, sweetie, was it a nightmare?
10	Tina:	Nope.
11	Mom:	Oh, okay. What was it about?
12	Tina:	My friends were in it.
13	Mom:	Who?
14	Tina:	I didn't know them.
15	Mom:	Oh, really?
16	Tina:	Yeah. But they were nice.
17	Mom:	What did you guys do?
18	Tina:	I don't remember.
19	Mom:	It's okay, I never remember my dreams either.

20	Tina:	What time is it?
21	Mom:	It's a quarter till seven.
22	Tina:	Mom?
23	Mom:	Yes?
24	Tina:	How's the weather?
25	Mom:	It's sunny! I'll open the curtains.
26	Tina:	Is it Wednesday?
27	Mom:	It's Tuesday. You have swim lessons on Mondays and you had a lesson yesterday, remember?
28	Tina:	Oh, yeah. I remember.
29	Mom:	Good, good. Are you ready to get up now?
30	Tina:	Yeah. What's for breakfast?
31	Mom:	That's up to you! What do you want?
32	Tina:	Cereal in milk!
33	Mom:	Sounds good. Make your bed and get ready while I get that ready for you.
34	Tina:	Okay!
35	Mom:	Good girl. I love you, sweetie.
36	Tina:	What should I wear?
37	Mom:	Anything you want.
38	Tina:	Which pants, Mom?
39	Mom:	The yellow ones look good, sweetie.
40	Tina:	Okay.
41	Mom:	I'll be in the kitchen. Come down once you wash up and dress!
42	Tina:	Okay. Is Tim up yet?
43	Mom:	I think so. Dad's in his room now.
44	Note:	(Part 2: Dad in Tim's room)
45	Dad:	Good morning, Son! Time to get up. The sun has risen.

46	Tim:	Good morning, Dad!
47	Dad:	Did you sleep well?
48	Tim:	Not really.
49	Dad:	Why not?
50	Tim:	There were sirens going off all night.
51	Dad:	Oh, I didn't hear anything.
52	Tim:	Yeah, they woke me up a few times.
53	Dad:	Huh, I must've been in a deep sleep.
54	Tim:	Dad?
55	Dad:	Yeah?
56	Tim:	Can I get a phone?
57	Dad:	A phone?
58	Tim:	Yeah.
59	Dad:	I'll talk to Mom about it. In the meantime, get dressed and come down for breakfast.
60	Tim:	Thanks, Dad.
61	Dad:	I'm going to open the windows to freshen up the air.
62	Tim:	Do you know what's for breakfast?
63	Dad:	Nope, we'll see.
64	Tim:	I hope it isn't cereal in milk…
65	Dad:	Why?
66	Tim:	Because we have that every morning.
67	Dad:	It's still good though.
68	Tim:	I know, but I want something different.
69	Dad:	We can talk to Mom about it.
70	Tim:	Dad, can you give me a ride to school?
71	Dad:	What's wrong with the bus?
72	Tim:	I don't want to walk to the bus stop.
73	Dad:	I don't think that's a good reason to ask for a ride.

74	Tim:	Can I bike to the stop then?
75	Dad:	It's only 300 yards! Besides, you should get a little bit of exercise everyday anyway!
76	Tim:	Okay.
77	Dad:	Alright, get up and make your bed now.
78	Tim:	Okay.
79	Dad:	(as he is walking out of the room) And get ready for school after that!
80	Note:	(Part 3: Kids getting dressed)
81	Tim:	(in his room) Mom!
82	Mom:	Yes?
83	Tim:	Where are my socks?
84	Mom:	They should be in the small drawer.
85	Tim:	There aren't any in the small drawer!
86	Mom:	(to husband), Honey!
87	Dad:	What's up?
88	Mom:	Can you get Tim a pair of socks from the laundry room, please?
89	Dad:	Of course.
90	Mom:	Thank you!
91	Dad:	Sure thing.
92	Tina:	(in her room) Mom!
93	Mom:	What now?
94	Tina:	I can't find my hair band!
95	Mom:	Look around.
96	Tina:	Ok, I found it. Never mind, Mom.
97	Tim:	Where is my shirt?
98	Mom:	I'm busy making breakfast. Ask Dad.
99	Dad:	What are you looking for?
100	Tim:	My shirt!
101	Dad:	Which one?

102	Tim:	The one with cars on it.
103	Dad:	Oh I think I saw it in the dryer.
104	Tim:	Right, I'll go get it.
105	Mom:	Breakfast is ready!
106	Dad:	Let's go eat.
107	Tim:	Okay, I'll be there soon after I get my shirt!
108	Dad:	Okay. Hurry, please.
109	Note:	(Part 4: At the breakfast table)
110	Tim:	Mom!
111	Mom:	Yeah?
112	Tim:	Can I get some apple juice?
113	Mom:	You don't like milk?
114	Tim:	Not today.
115	Mom:	Okay, I will get you some apple juice. Here you go.
116	Tim:	Thanks, Mom.
117	Mom:	Any time.
118	Tina:	I like milk in the morning. It's refreshing.
119	Dad:	Good, I'm glad you like milk in the morning but you should have some fruit too, Tina. You too, Tim.
120	Tim:	I will.
121	Tina:	Mom!
122	Mom:	Yes, sweetie?
123	Tina:	What's for lunch?
124	Mom:	Just buy lunch at school today.
125	Tina:	Oh, okay.
126	Dad:	What time does school end today, kids?
127	Tina:	Dad, you always ask the same question!
128	Tim:	Honestly. It ends at two thirty everyday.

129	Dad:	(laughs) What are you guys doing after school today?
130	Tina:	You ask that every morning too.
131	Mom:	But you guys don't do the same thing after school everyday.
132	Dad:	Exactly.
133	Tina:	I'm going to hang out with some friends.
134	Tim:	Me too.
135	Dad:	What are you going to do with them?
136	Tina:	We don't know. Just go out.
137	Tim:	I think we're going to go biking for a while.
138	Dad:	Alright, sounds good! I'm glad you chose that over video games!
139	Tim:	Why don't you want us playing video games?
140	Mom:	It's a lot healthier to be playing outside!
141	Dad:	Most definitely.
142	Mom:	Alright kids, it's time to go catch your school bus!
143	Dad:	Go brush your teeth and get your backpacks.
144	Tina:	(leaving home for school) Bye, Mom! Bye, Dad!
145	Tim:	Bye!
146	Dad:	Have fun!
147	Mom:	Wait, wait! I'll walk you to the bus stop.
148	Tina:	Okay!
149	Tim:	Okay.
150	Dad:	Okay, well I need to get going.
151	Mom:	Alright, bye! See you tonight!

4

Real Input To Learn Talking 4: After School

2	Tim:	(Tim comes home) Mom, I'm home!
3	Mom:	Hi, sweetie! How was your day?
4	Tim:	It was good!
5	Mom:	That's good to hear.
6	Tim:	Can I get something to eat?
7	Mom:	Are you hungry?
8	Tim:	No. I just want something to eat.
9	Mom:	How was the lunch today?
10	Tim:	It was okay. Chicken nuggets and salad.
11	Mom:	That doesn't sound too bad. Well, I will go bake some potatoes right now.
12	Tim:	Can I have some ice cream instead?
13	Mom:	Sorry, sweetie. We ran out.
14	Tim:	Oh, can Dad get some on his way home?
15	Mom:	You can ask him.
16	Tim:	Okay. I'll call him. What time is it now?
17	Mom:	It's almost four. He should be in his office.
18	Note:	(Tim calls Dad)

19	Dad:	Hey, Tim!
20	Tim:	When are you getting home today?
21	Dad:	Around six, why?
22	Tim:	Could you stop by the grocery store and buy some ice cream on the way home?
23	Dad:	I don't see why not.
24	Tim:	Thanks, Dad!
25	Dad:	Sure, see you later.
26	Mom:	What did he say?
27	Tim:	He said he will buy some on the way home!
28	Mom:	Oh, how nice of him!
29	Tina:	(gets home) I'm home!
30	Mom:	How was school, sweetie?
31	Tina:	Not bad.
32	Mom:	Did something happen?
33	Tina:	No, not really.
34	Mom:	You look down.
35	Tina:	I'm just tired.
36	Mom:	Okay. Do you want some baked potatoes?
37	Tina:	Yes! I love baked potatoes!
38	Mom:	I know you do! They'll be ready in just a few minutes.
39	Tina:	Okay.
40	Tim:	Guess what?!
41	Tina:	What?
42	Tim:	I called Dad and he's buying ice cream on his way home today.
43	Tina:	Great! What kind?
44	Tim:	I don't know but probably cookies and cream as usual.
45	Tina:	That's my favorite!

46	Tim:	Mine too. Chocolate ice cream is good too.
47	Tim:	Mom!
48	Mom:	Yes, Honey?
49	Tim:	Can I go play video games?
50	Mom:	No, how about you go read instead?
51	Tim:	Can I play some video games afterwards?
52	Mom:	I don't think you'll have time to play video games after you finish reading. You have piano, remember?
53	Tina:	Tim, don't you remember what Dad said?
54	Tim:	What?
55	Tina:	He said it's not healthy to play video games all the time.
56	Tim:	I know.
57	Mom:	The potatoes are ready! Come eat!
58	Kids:	Coming!
59	Note:	(at the table)
60	Tina:	Could you pass the cheese, Mom?
61	Mom:	Sure.
62	Tim:	Tina, can you pass me the salt?
63	Tina:	Here you go.
64	Tim:	Thanks.
65	Mom:	Do you have homework today?
66	Tina:	Yes, but not much.
67	Tim:	Same here.
68	Mom:	Go out and play with some friends after you eat, okay?
69	Tim:	Mom, can I go to Kevin's?
70	Mom:	Of course. Remember to behave yourself, okay?
71	Tim:	Don't worry, Mom. I'm not a baby.

72	Mom:	Tina, what about you?
73	Tina:	I'm going to go biking.
74	Mom:	Be careful and make sure you have your helmet on.
75	Tina:	I will. What time should I be back by?
76	Mom:	Six. Also, make sure you close the door all the way when you go out.
77	Kids:	Okay.
78	Tim:	By the way, what's for dinner?
79	Mom:	Chicken soup.
80	Tim:	Delicious. I'm done with my potato. See you later!
81	Mom:	Okay.
82	Tina:	I'm ready too! Bye!
83	Mom:	Bye.
84	Note:	(after a while)
85	Dad:	Honey, I am home!
86	Mom:	Hey, Honey! You're early today!
87	Dad:	Yeah, my field meeting was cancelled.
88	Mom:	Oh good. How was work today?
89	Dad:	Great! Great!
90	Mom:	You always say 'Great!'
91	Dad:	Because I like it when it's great. How about you?
92	Mom:	I'm a bit tired. I had some issues at work.
93	Dad:	Relax, Honey. Don't let them bother you.
94	Mom:	Thanks, Honey. I like how you handle things like that.
95	Dad:	I'm flattered.
96	Tim:	I'm home, Mom!
97	Dad:	Hello!

98	Tim:	Hey, Dad! Did you get the ice cream?
99	Dad:	What do you think?
100	Tim:	You got it?
101	Dad:	Of course. Who do you think I am?
102	Tim:	You're my dad!
103	Dad:	That's right!
104	Tina:	I'm back, Mom! Hi, Dad!
105	Dad:	Hi, sweetie!
106	Tim:	I'm hungry!
107	Mom:	I know. Dinner will be ready soon.
108	Dad:	How'd you do in school, kids?
109	Tim:	I did alright.
110	Tina:	I did alright as well.
111	Mom:	Could you set the table, please?
112	Dad:	Of course!
113	Mom:	Thanks, Honey.
114	Dad:	Any time.
115	Mom:	Dinner's ready!
116	Kids:	Coming!
117	Dad:	Did you kids wash your hands?
118	Kids:	No. Not yet.
119	Dad:	Please go wash your hands.
120	Kids:	Okay.
121	Tim:	Chicken soup! My favorite.
122	Tina:	Could you please pass the salt and pepper?
123	Mom:	Of course. Here you go.
124	Tina:	Thanks, Mom.
125	Mom:	You're welcome.
126	Dad:	This is really good. You're a great cook.
127	Mom:	Thanks! Help yourself.
128	Tim:	I wish the soup wasn't so hot.

129	Dad:	Blow on it before putting it in your mouth. That should help.
130	Mom:	Also, eating fast is not a good habit.
131	Tim:	Okay. Is there enough for seconds?
132	Mom:	Of course.
133	Note:	(after dinner)
134	Tim:	Thanks for the dinner, Mom. It was really good.
135	Mom:	Of course sweetie, I'm glad to hear that.
136	Tina:	I enjoyed the dinner, too. Thanks, Mom.
137	Mom:	Thanks, sweetie.
138	Tim:	Can we have ice cream for dessert?
139	Mom:	Sure.
140	Tina:	Yes! I'll get it. Where is the ice cream, Mom?
141	Mom:	It's in the freezer.
142	Tim:	I'll get the scooper. Where's the scooper, Mom?
143	Mom:	It should be in the silverware drawer.
144	Tim:	Dad, how much do you want?
145	Dad:	Two scoops, please.
146	Tim:	How about you, Mom?
147	Mom:	Same here.
148	Tim:	Okay. What about you, Tina?
149	Tina:	I'll get mine myself.
150	Tim:	Okay. I will take five scoops.
151	Dad:	That's a little too much, Tim.
152	Tim:	Four scoops? (Dad nods)
153	Dad:	Kids, are you done with homework yet?
154	Tina:	Not yet, but I don't have much. It shouldn't take long.
155	Tim:	Me neither. I will do it soon.
156	Dad:	Sounds good.

157	Mom:	Take a shower before you start your homework, alright?
158	Kids:	Alright.
159	Dad:	Brush your teeth while you're at it!
160	Tim:	I will.
161	Tina:	Yes, Dad.
162	Mom:	Remember to put your dirty clothes in the laundry basket as well.
163	Tim:	I know.
164	Tina:	Yes, Mom.
165	Dad:	Do either one of you need help with homework?
166	Tim:	No, I don't think so. I just need to do some reading.
167	Tina:	I'm fine. I'll let you know if I need help, though.
168	Dad:	Good!
169	Tim:	I'm done eating. I'll shower first.
170	Dad:	Kids, could you please take your dishes to the sink?
171	Tina:	Okay.
172	Dad:	Thanks. That helps a lot.

5

Real Input To Learn Talking 5: Q&A On Personal Info

2	Guard:	Hi, how may I help you?
3	Hannah:	Hi, I came to apply for SSI.
4	Guard:	Okay, pick a number and have a seat over there, please.
5	Hannah:	Thank you.
6	Officer:	R231 window 5, R231 window 5, please....(no one shows up) Last call for R231, window 5, please.
7	Hannah:	Hi.
8	Officer:	Can I get your number, please?
9	Hannah:	Sure, here you go.
10	Officer:	Thank you. How may I help you?
11	Hannah:	I want to apply for SSI.
12	Officer:	Okay, sit please. What's your first name?
13	Hannah:	Hannah.
14	Officer:	How do you spell it?
15	Hannah:	H-A-N-N-A-H
16	Officer:	What's your middle name?

17	Hannah:	I don't have a middle name.
18	Officer:	I see.
19	Officer:	What's your last name or family name?
20	Hannah:	Park.
21	Officer:	Can you spell it also for me please?
22	Hannah:	Sure, P-A-R-K.
23	Officer:	Just double checking, your full legal name is Hannah Park?
24	Hannah:	Yes.
25	Officer:	What's your maiden name?
26	Hannah:	Maiden name? I don't understand.
27	Officer:	Have you gone by any other names?
28	Hannah:	I am sorry. Could you say it again please?
29	Officer:	Okay. Have you used any other names?
30	Hannah:	Yes, I used to go by Hannah Chang.
31	Officer:	Is Park your husband's last name?
32	Hannah:	Yes.
33	Officer:	Are you a U.S. citizen?
34	Hannah:	No.
35	Officer:	Are you a legal permanent resident?
36	Hannah:	Yes, I am.
37	Officer:	When did you become a permanent resident?
38	Hannah:	July 26, 1998.
39	Officer:	Can I see your ID please?
40	Hannah:	Sure, here it is.
41	Officer:	Did you bring your passport and permanent resident card with you as well?
42	Hannah:	Yes, here.
43	Officer:	Great. Thank you. Let me make copies of these. I will be right back.

44	Hannah:	Okay.
45	Officer:	What's your mother's first name?
46	Hannah:	Youngsook
47	Officer:	Is she a citizen of the United States?
48	Hannah:	No.
49	Officer:	What's your father's first name?
50	Hannah:	Taesun
51	Officer:	Is he a citizen of the United States?
52	Hannah:	No.
53	Officer:	What's your social security number?
54	Hannah:	My social security number is 999-99-9899.
55	Officer:	How old are you?
56	Hannah:	I am 66.
57	Officer:	What's your date of birth?
58	Hannah:	April 5th, nineteen forty seven.
59	Officer:	What country are you from?
60	Hannah:	Korea.
61	Officer:	What's the country of your nationality?
62	Hannah:	Korea.
63	Officer:	What's the country of your citizenship?
64	Hannah:	Korea.
65	Officer:	South Korea or North Korea?
66	Hannah:	South Korea.
67	Officer:	In which city were you born?
68	Hannah:	Excuse me?
69	Officer:	What is the name of the city or town you were born in?
70	Hannah:	Seoul.

6

Real Input To Learn Talking 6: Q&A On Employment Issues

2	Officer:	Do you work now?
3	Hannah:	Yes.
4	Officer:	Where have you worked for the past five years?
5	Hannah:	Right now, I work for a small dry cleaners.
6	Officer:	What is the name of the business?
7	Hannah:	Sky Dry Cleaners.
8	Officer:	What's the address of the business?
9	Hannah:	4320 Broadway Blvd., Aurora, CO. 80523.
10	Officer:	What county is that?
11	Hannah:	I believe it's Arapahoe county.
12	Officer:	Good. Who's the owner of the business?
13	Hannah:	Mr. James Martin.
14	Officer:	Good. Do you have the phone number of the business?
15	Hannah:	Yes, 303-997-2456.
16	Officer:	What do you do there?

17	Hannah:	I am a presser.
18	Officer:	How long have you worked there for?
19	Hannah:	About 3 years.
20	Officer:	When did you start working there?
21	Hannah:	July first, two thousand nine.
22	Officer:	How often do you get paid there?
23	Hannah:	I'm sorry, I don't understand what you are asking.
24	Officer:	No problem. Do you get paid weekly, every other week, or monthly?
25	Hannah:	I get paid every other week.
26	Officer:	How much do you earn an hour?
27	Hannah:	I receive $15.20 an hour.
28	Officer:	How many hours per week do you work there?
29	Hannah:	It depends. But around 30 hours per week.
30	Officer:	How much do you earn before taxes?
31	Hannah:	Typically, I earn about nine hundred and fifty
32	Officer:	So, what's your net income after taxes then?
33	Hannah:	About $900.
34	Officer:	Do you have any other income?
35	Hannah:	No.
36	Officer:	Where did you work before there?
37	Hannah:	I worked for a liquor store.
38	Officer:	Where is that store located?
39	Hannah:	It is in Thornton, Colorado.
40	Officer:	How many years did you work there?
41	Hannah:	7 years.

7

Real Input To Learn Talking 7: Q&A On Marital Status

2	Officer:	What's your current marital status?
3	Hannah:	Excuse me?
4	Officer:	Are you married?
5	Hannah:	Yes, I am married.
6	Officer:	When did you get married?
7	Hannah:	June twenty fifth, 2000.
8	Officer:	What's your husband's name?
9	Hannah:	Young Hoon Chang
10	Officer:	How do you spell it?
11	Hannah:	First name: y-o-u-n-g, middle name: h-o-o-n, and last name: c-h-a-n-g.
12	Officer:	Is he a US citizen?
13	Hannah:	Yes.
14	Officer:	Does he live with you?
15	Hannah:	Yes.
16	Officer:	How old is he?
17	Hannah:	He is 68 years old.
18	Officer:	What's his date of birth?

19	Hannah:	February thirteenth, nineteen forty five.
20	Officer:	What's his social security number?
21	Hannah:	I am sorry. I don't remember.
22	Officer:	I need to know his social security number.
23	Hannah:	Can I call and let you know later?
24	Officer:	Sure, I will give you my phone number. Here is my phone number.
25	Hannah:	Thank you very much.
26	Officer:	You are very welcome. How many times have you been married?
27	Hannah:	Twice.
28	Officer:	What's your ex-husband's name?
29	Hannah:	Young Bin Park.
30	Officer:	How do you spell it?
31	Hannah:	y-o-u-n-g b-i-n p-a-r-k
32	Officer:	How did the marriage end?
33	Hannah:	I'm sorry, I don't understand what you are asking.
34	Officer:	No problem. Did you get divorced?
35	Hannah:	No. He passed away.
36	Officer:	When did he pass?
37	Hannah:	September 7th, nineteen ninety eight.
38	Officer:	Thank you. Now, does your husband work?
39	Hannah:	Yes.
40	Officer:	Where does he work?
41	Hannah:	He works for 15th Ave. Liquor.
42	Officer:	What's that?
43	Hannah:	It's a liquor store.
44	Officer:	Where is it?
45	Hannah:	It's in Denver, Colorado.

46	Officer:	What's his hourly rate?
47	Hannah:	$12.50.
48	Officer:	How many hours does he work in a week?
49	Hannah:	Around 30 hours.
50	Officer:	How much does he make a month?
51	Hannah:	About $1,200 a month.

8

Real Input To Learn Talking 8: Q&A On Housing Issues

2	Officer:	Do you rent or own a house?
3	Hannah:	I rent.
4	Officer:	What's your current address?
5	Hannah:	4310 E. Yale Ave., Apt 345, Aurora, CO. 80412.
6	Officer:	Is this also your mailing address?
7	Hannah:	Yes.
8	Officer:	How long have you lived at your current address?
9	Hannah:	About two years.
10	Officer:	What are your addresses for the past five years?
11	Hannah:	Since May 2009, my address is 4310 E Yale Ave., Apt 345, Aurora, CO. 80412. From May 2007 till April 2009, my address was 1234 E. 17th Street, Denver CO 80220.
12	Officer:	What's your phone number?
13	Hannah:	Three oh three, nine nine nine, one four five six.

14	Officer:	Do you have an email address?
15	Hannah:	No, I don't have one.
16	Officer:	Who should we contact in order to reach you?
17	Hannah:	My son.
18	Officer:	What's his name?
19	Hannah:	In Sik Chang.
20	Officer:	His phone number?
21	Hannah:	Three oh three, five six nine, eighty seven thirty three.
22	Officer:	I need one more referral.
23	Hannah:	I have a nephew.
24	Officer:	Okay, please give me his name and phone number.
25	Hannah:	His name is Jack Hong, and his phone number is seven two oh six two five eighteen oh five.
26	Officer:	Thank you. Now, how much is the rent per month?
27	Hannah:	Seven hundred and fifty.
28	Officer:	Is that including utilities?
29	Hannah:	No.
30	Officer:	How much do you pay a month for utilities?
31	Hannah:	We pay a hundred fifty for electricity, eighty for gas, thirty five for water, and fifty for the phone.
32	Officer:	How much do you pay for food each month?
33	Hannah:	Well, it varies. But I think it's about three hundred and fifty dollars.

34	Officer:	How about medical expenses?
35	Hannah:	Not much, but about thirty dollars per month.
36	Officer:	Do you have insurance?
37	Hannah:	We pay four hundred and fifty every six months for auto insurance.
38	Officer:	Good. Health insurance?
39	Hannah:	No, we can not afford health insurance.

9

Real Input To Learn Talking 9: Q&A On Family Issues

2	Officer:	How many children do you have?
3	Hannah:	Three.
4	Officer:	What are their names?
5	Hannah:	Insik, Sukyoung, and Sungku.
6	Officer:	How old are they?
7	Hannah:	Twenty four, nineteen, and sixteen.
8	Officer:	Do they live with you?
9	Hannah:	No, Insik is in New York, but Sukyoung and Sungku live with us.
10	Officer:	Thank you. Do you know their birthdays and social security numbers?
11	Hannah:	Yes, I brought copies of them with me. Here you go.
12	Officer:	Excellent! Can I keep them, or do you need them back?
13	Hannah:	You can keep them.
14	Officer:	Great! Were they born here in the United States?

15	Hannah:	No, the first one was born in Korea, but the other two were born here in the USA.
16	Officer:	Who is their biological father?
17	Hannah:	My husband.
18	Officer:	What's his name?
19	Hannah:	Young Hoon Chang
20	Officer:	I see. What's the gross house-hold income?
21	Hannah:	I'm sorry, I don't understand.
22	Officer:	No problem. What's the monthly total income of your household?
23	Hannah:	Sorry, again. What do you mean by household?
24	Officer:	Household means like your family.
25	Hannah:	My husband, my sons, and myself?
26	Officer:	No, no, no. Your grown up sons don't count.
27	Hannah:	Oh, so just my husband and myself?
28	Officer:	Yes.
29	Hannah:	My husband makes twelve hundred and I make about eighteen hundred.
30	Officer:	So, the total is... Let me do the math here. Three thousand dollars?
31	Hannah:	Yes, that's right.
32	Officer:	Is that a gross or net?
33	Hannah:	Sorry, I don't know the difference between gross and net.
34	Officer:	It's okay. Gross means before tax, and net means after tax.
35	Hannah:	I'm afraid I still don't understand. Here are my tax returns for last year, though.
36	Officer:	Oh, great. Thank you. This is excellent. Do you need them back?
37	Hannah:	No, you can keep them.

10

Real Input To Learn Talking 10: Workshop For Marketing Strategy Development

2	Brad:	Good morning, everyone. Thank you for attending this workshop to develop marketing strategies for our products.
3	Brad:	As you know, our company sales have not picked up for the past two quarters this year.
4	Brad:	So, there was an idea that we should have a workshop on how to present our products to the consumers in the field, which I think is a great idea.
5	Brad:	Consequently, we made a post on this workshop on the company bulletin board asking you to come prepared for discussion and presentation, and for sharing your experiences.
6	Brad:	On the bulletin board, I announced that I would run this workshop in terms of a five step marketing strategy.

7	Brad:	Like (1) approaching customers, (2) introducing oneself and establishing rapport with customers, (3) presenting products, (4) opening a deal, and (5) closing the deal.
8	Brad:	Basically our customers are those who work in the purchase department. Especially those who are in charge of product research.
9	Brad:	When we approach customers, the best practice I believe is being patient, and steady. It takes time and it also takes courage to challenge.
10	Brad:	As our company and our products are rather new to the customers, we don't have high name value to rely on yet, and we need to build it up.
11	Brad:	As you all know, the best resource we have to compete against the competitors are the quality and price of our products.
12	Brad:	We have the best products and the unbeatable line of prices, which should be the best competition power ever.
13	Brad:	With that said, let's get started. Jenny will present a skit on a scenario of selling our products to a customer, Ryan.
14	Brad:	Let's watch the skit first, and have a discussion later to improve the scenario, if we can, in terms of the five step marketing strategy. (Jenny presents the skit with Tom, who plays Ryan)
15	Ryan:	Hello, STM, Ryan speaking.

16	Jenny:	Hi, Mr. Smith. This is Jenny, and I got your name and phone number from Sarah, your college classmate.
17	Ryan:	Did you say Sarah?
18	Jenny:	Yes, Sarah. She is with RMO, do you remember her?
19	Ryan:	Ah, Sarah. Yes, I do. In fact, she told me that you would call.
20	Jenny:	Do you have a minute? Sarah said you would love to hear about what I do. Oh, she also spoke very highly of you. If you are busy, I can call you later.
21	Ryan:	She is a nice friend. She always does that. But, I don't think I have time now. I need to get going for a meeting right now.
22	Jenny:	Sure, no problem. I will call you back later today. I would like to have a chance to talk with you about what I can do for you.
23	Ryan:	Okay. Why don't you give me a call later this afternoon?
24	Jenny:	Sure, I will. Thank you for your time. I will talk to you later. Bye.
25	Ryan:	Okay, talk to you later. Bye.
26	Ryan:	(Later in the afternoon, phone rings) Hello, STM, Ryan speaking.
27	Jenny:	Hi, Ryan, It's me, Jenny, again. Is this a good time to talk?
28	Ryan:	Yes, go ahead.
29	Jenny:	Thanks. How's your day going by so far?
30	Ryan:	So far so good.

31	Jenny:	That's good. I am just calling to see if I could get a chance to give you a brief presentation on the products I have, which I am sure you will be very interested in.
32	Jenny:	I am with 3CSI, which specializes in electric actuators. We have very attractive RP Series Electric Actuators for you.
33	Ryan:	Electric actuators?
34	Jenny:	Right. I am sure you are familiar with many kinds of electric actuators. However, our products have new features which are not available in other products.
35	Jenny:	You can apply our products to ball valves, butterfly valves, and dampers. They are all-purpose actuators.
36	Jenny:	I am very positive that our products are leading the edge with its technology.
37	Jenny:	On top of that, our prices are unbeatable for the features available.
38	Ryan:	That sounds very interesting.
39	Jenny:	Yes, with your permission, I will be very happy to make a presentation on our RP series electric actuators.
40	Jenny:	I know you are busy, and I didn't mean to talk too much over the phone. If you would like, I can come and present sample products for you to check out.
41	Ryan:	Sounds good. Why don't you send me some information on the products, and I will check it out before we get together.

42	Jenny:	Sure, I will send the information to you right away. Do you mind if I make a follow up call to you?
43	Ryan:	Of course not. Give me a couple of days to check it out though.
44	Jenny:	Sure, take your time. If you would have any questions in a meanwhile, please let me know anytime.
45	Ryan:	I will.
46	Jenny:	I thank you very much for your time today. It was very nice talking with you.
47	Ryan:	Likewise.
48	Note:	(A few days later Jenny makes a follow up call)
49	Ryan:	Hello, STM, Ryan speaking.
50	Jenny:	Good morning, Mr. Smith. This is Jenny.
51	Ryan:	Good morning, Jenny. You can just call me Ryan.
52	Jenny:	Thank you, I will. So, have you had a chance to review the information I sent you last time?
53	Ryan:	Yes, I actually forwarded that information to a couple of my colleagues, and they showed interest in your products.
54	Jenny:	Thank you, Ryan. That's great news. So, can I give you a presentation sometime soon?
55	Ryan:	Yes, I believe that's a good idea.
56	Jenny:	Great. When's the earliest convenient time for you, Ryan?
57	Ryan:	We normally have a new product meeting on Friday afternoons. So, how about this coming Friday afternoon?

58	Jenny:	Perfect. What time shall I be there?
59	Ryan:	The meeting starts at 2:30 and it lasts a couple of hours. You will have about half an hour to present your products to us.
60	Jenny:	Wonderful. I will be ready for that. Thank you very much for the opportunity. I am sure you will not be disappointed.
61	Ryan:	I hope not.
62	Jenny:	I will see you then, Ryan.
63	Ryan:	(at the new product meeting) Let me introduce Jenny. She's visiting us to make a presentation on her product. Go ahead, Jenny.
64	Jenny:	Thank you Ryan. Thank you everyone for letting me have this opportunity today. My name is Jenny Colts.
65	Jenny:	I work for 3CSI, a venture company specializing in electric actuators. I understand you had a chance to review our products. So, I will make a brief presentation, and answer your questions, if you have any.
66	Jenny:	I brought some brochures today for you to take a look at later. Let me show you our products with some PowerPoint slides.
67	Jenny:	As you can see, our products have about seven distinguished features. You can compare these features to the products by other companies.
68	Jenny:	We added the outside indicator to make it easy to check the valve tracks. This assures the valve operation to be checked by eyes.
69	Jenny:	The next key feature we added is the manual valve control to handle an emergency situation.

70	Jenny:	This manual valve allows you to rest assured that you can cope with any kind of emergency situation caused by power outage or the actuator being out of order for any reason.
71	Jenny:	Another feature I would like to emphasize is the Epoxy Polyester coating, which assures the durability of the product in a corrosive environment (Jenny continues the presentation covering other characteristics).
72	Jenny:	Last but not least, I would like to get your attention on the major specs of our products.
73	Jenny:	Our products have powerful output torques and quick operating time. And our products operate on various levels of input voltages.
74	Jenny:	With our products, you can rest assured that you will get the best quality products with maximum warranties on them. We are very confident and proud of our products.
75	Jenny:	Thank you very much again for giving me this opportunity. Now, I will be glad to answer your questions.
76	Ryan:	Thank you for the presentation, Jenny. It was good to know about your products. I want to know more about the unit price for your products.
77	Jenny:	Well, I forgot to tell you that price is one of the merits we offer. We believe that the price line of our products is unbeatable for their features.

78	Jenny:	Our regular retail price for the RP-002 series is $45 per unit; the RP-004 is $56 per unit, and the RP-006 series products start from $62 per unit.
79	Jenny:	As you can now tell, the prices are significantly lower than those of our competitors' products.
80	Jenny:	This is possible because we, as a venture company, do not have as much overhead expenses as our competitors have.
81	Ryan:	Do you offer a discount on a volume purchase?
82	Jenny:	For quantity purchase, yes, we surely do.
83	Ryan:	How much time do you need for delivery?
84	Jenny:	It depends on the quantity of the purchase. However, typically, we can deliver products within two weeks.
85	Jenny:	For a small order like less than 50 units, we can deliver within one week.
86	Ryan:	Thank you, Jenny. I guess we will let you go at this time. We will have a discussion on your products and let you know.
87	Jenny:	Thank you again.
88	Ryan:	(Jenny calls Ryan after a few days) Hello, STM, this is Ryan speaking.
89	Jenny:	Ryan, it's me, Jenny.
90	Ryan:	Hi, Jenny. I was about to call you regarding your presentation last week.
91	Jenny:	Thank you. How did they like my presentation?

92	Ryan:	We all liked it. We've decided to issue an initial purchase order for 100 units of the RP-002 series.
93	Jenny:	That's wonderful. Thank you, Ryan. Sure, I would love to get your PO. We will deliver the products as soon as we can but no later than two weeks from today.
94	Ryan:	Now, we need to talk about the price. How much discount can you offer us?
95	Jenny:	By policy, we offer 10% discount for the purchase of 90 to 100 units.
96	Ryan:	Come on, Jenny, come down a little bit more.
97	Jenny:	That's our policy. But, let me talk to my boss and get back to you. I will call you back right away.
98	Ryan:	(answers Jenny's phone call) This is Ryan.
99	Jenny:	Ryan. It's me, Jenny. My boss approved a 15% discount on your PO.
100	Ryan:	Thank you for the extra mile you went for us.
101	Jenny:	No problem. Please send me the PO, and I will have the products delivered.
102	Ryan:	Sure, I will. Talk to you again.
103	Jenny:	Thanks for your business. Bye.
104	Note:	(End of skit presentation)
105	Brad:	Wonderful. Thank you Jenny, and thank you Ryan. It was a great presentation.
106	Brad:	Now, let's start analyzing this skit into the five steps of marketing strategy. So, what about Jenny's first step of approaching the customer?

107	Tom:	Well, the skit doesn't show how Jenny got the contact info of the customer. So, it's a bit vague.
108	Jenny:	Let me clarify on that issue. I got the contact info from a lady in my book club. Her name is Sarah.
109	Brad:	Collecting and building up a contact list is a key practice for all of us. We all know that it makes our jobs much easier.
110	Tom:	Obviously, that's one good and easy way of approaching prospect customers. However, it's true that our contact list can't be endless.
111	Tom:	So, shall we talk about some other means of approaching the prospect customers?
112	Sue:	Has anyone tried cold calling?
113	Jenny:	I have, and I hate it. I've found it's not my type.
114	Sue:	However, there are some nice people who would allow you to talk.
115	Tom:	Yes, also it's more than a coincidence that you meet people who are looking for the very products that we have.
116	Note:	(Discussion continues to develop marketing strategies)

11

Real Input To Learn Reading and Listening 1 - And... I Am Off!¹⁵

2   One day after school, my mom asked me, "How would you like to backpack through Europe for two months?" I previously asked if I could spend part of the summer at my friend's house in France, but this was a far more exciting opportunity. When else would I be able to see Europe for free?

3   The nearer it got to my departure date, the more hectic life became. I was preoccupied with some last minute studying for final exams, but there seemed to be an inexplicable chaos building up all around in the background. With all that, I hardly had time to really consider what was involved in preparing to go on the trip until the last minute.

4   Always thinking ahead, my mom had arranged for me to volunteer with Habitat for Humanity in Poland my first week. I planned to pursue a degree in architecture

---

¹⁵ This article is from an unpublished book, *Seven Weeks Alone in Europe*, by Peter Kang LEE a.k.a. Jae Joon LEE.

and she felt this would be an excellent experience. All I really had to do was order my Eurail pass and a heavy-duty backpack (both due to arrive just before my departure date), and that just about sums up the preparation. When my backpack arrived, I filled it with toiletries, a few changes of clothing, electronics and chargers, and a "Let's Go Europe!" book. I had tried to construct an itinerary, but that did not happen. So I went without one.

5   Before I knew it, school was out and I was on a plane to Kraków, Poland. That was June 8th, 2012. I was due to return on the 29th of July. The thought of stepping off a plane onto a continent thousands of miles from home with not much of a plan scared me, but I tried not to show it. I told myself everything would be okay, because it was not okay for things to not be okay. Besides, I had everything I needed, clothes, shoes, water bottle, money, Eurail pass (to be delivered in Gliwice, Poland), and, at the end of it all, a plane ticket home. I even had an iPad, first aid kit, flashlight, and my summer reading books for school. And I realized, after giving it some thought, in reality it would have been nearly impossible to plan a two-month trip in advance. I was as ready as I was ever going to be.

6   The night before I left, I laid out my clothes for the next day, set up my backpack, loaded a gym sack (which would serve as my daypack for the next two months), and waited to fall asleep. I was so excited. I could not wait for the sun to rise.

7   I woke up in the morning with plenty of time to spare. I started my day by dropping off my beta fish at my friend's house. I'd just gotten it but obviously couldn't take it with me. I grabbed my packed gear, loaded it into our car, and we were off.

8   Everything was looking good until I got to the airport, where I encountered the first delay of the trip. Air Canada's whole computer system was down. We waited. And waited. And, waited some more. During that time, we met a family heading to Munich who, coincidentally, would be on all the same flights as I. My parents, worried that I would not be able to navigate all the airports alone, asked them if they would help me through my flight changes until we reached Munich. They kindly said they would. After this short interruption to the monotony of waiting, we realized my dad had to leave for work. So, I shook his hand goodbye, and my mom and I waited some more.

9   At last, after a two-hour delay, the computers came back up. They were able to assign seats and began boarding. I hugged my mom goodbye and followed my newfound German friends through to the gate. Although I was excited to finally be on my way, I felt a little uneasy, too. I was not sure I could pull this off. All the uneasiness faded, however, by the time I got to Montréal. I was hundreds of miles from home and there was no going back. Once in Munich, I thanked the Germans who had helped me through the past 10+ hours, and made my way to the gate for the flight to Kraków. A family of fellow Habitat volunteers was waiting to meet me. I was eager to get to know them better and looked forward to the project, but by the time I boarded that final flight, all I could think about was getting to Kraków and enjoying a nice hot shower.

12

Real Input To Learn Reading and Listening 2 - Kraków and Gliwice, Poland[16]

2   After many hours, we landed in Poland. I flew into Kraków, the former capital. I could not believe it. Of all the places in the world, I was in Kraków. It was just so surreal although I had known for months the city would be my first European destination. I had to pinch myself to confirm I wasn't dreaming. I started to reminisce about my arrival in Lima, Peru, two summers ago. I had felt the same sense of incredulity back then.

3   I followed along with the crowd from the plane to the airport entrance where I heard someone shout my name. It was my team leader, Tom. We had spoken on the phone before the trip but I didn't know what he looked like. For some reason, I just hadn't pictured him with a beard. But, there he was, bearded. Aside from his beard, however, he

---

[16]   This article is from an unpublished book, *Seven Weeks Alone in Europe*, by Peter Kang LEE a.k.a. Jae Joon LEE.

looked just as I had pictured him. He had short brown hair, thin metal-rimmed glasses, was slightly taller than myself, and of course, wearing our team shirt. I walked over and firmly shook his hand. The family of volunteers from the flight arrived and we all headed to a small café upstairs to wait for the rest of the team members to join us.

4   Over the next two hours, the others trickled into the café. Finally, everyone had arrived and we set off for our hotel by van. No one was very talkative on the ride, which suited me just fine. I hadn't been sleepy at the airport, but I could definitely feel my eyelids drooping once we got in the van. Not wanting to pass out on the ride, I distracted myself with thoughts of this incredible adventure I'd just begun. And, considerations of how far I was from the home I would not set foot in for the next seven weeks. After a bit of driving, our van arrived at our hotel. It was a three-star hotel, close to the town square. We walked into the air-conditioned building where the receptionist greeted us in English, which surprised me. We were efficiently checked in and given our room keys. I headed up to my room on the third floor with Kyle, a fellow Habitater just a year younger than myself, whom I had just met in the Munich Airport. Our room was a bit smaller and stuffier than the others, but that was the least of my concerns.

5   I opened up my backpack to find a bottle of mouthwash had leaked all over due to the pressure changes during the flights. It had soaked a few towels and shirts, and worse, had dyed my blue cardigan green... GREEN! I quickly took it down to reception to see if the hotel could wash out the stain. Unfortunately, I ended up paying big bucks for nothing; the damage was permanent. Despite my

disappointment, I had learned my first lesson of travel: Never bring along toiletries you can easily purchase at your destination.

6   The rest of the day passed without any additional life lessons. I busied myself socializing with my fellow volunteers and enjoying a bowl of white borscht, a popular Polish soup. Afterward, I took off to see some of the city before returning for a group meeting and dinner. I then headed up to my room to call my parents. I let them know I had arrived in Poland safely and told them my impressions and experiences so far. After hanging up, I washed up and got ready for bed, but I could not fall asleep right away. I lay awake thinking of the people I missed back home, even though I had only been away a little more than 24 hours. At some point all the faces started blurring together and I fell into a deep sleep.

7   The next morning, I woke up feeling more energized than ever, despite the fact that I'd only slept about three hours. I was now in a time zone seven hours ahead of home and by the time I awoke, it was already two in the afternoon back home. We had breakfast at the same place where we had dined the night before as it was located right next to the hotel and we didn't have much time. After breakfast, some of the group packed up their suitcases. Since I'd dealt with all that after the mouthwash fiasco, I headed out with a few new friends to do some sightseeing.

8   We first headed for the Barbacoa, an ancient defense tower located right outside the city walls. We did not really understand or know what we were looking at most of the time, but that was okay because we would return to Kraków in a week for a formal tour. We continued on and found ourselves by the Wawel Cathedral surrounded with a moat. We later found out the church housed the

crypts of many important figures in Polish history, including St. Stanislaus[1]. As we walked through Wawel, we suddenly realized it was almost past our call time and quickly headed back. When we arrived, we found the van waiting. No one else was ready to go yet but I retrieved my bags and headed for the lobby anyway. After idling around for a while, we piled into the van and were off to Gliwice, the Habitat for Humanity site where we would work over the next few days. As much as I wanted to stay awake to enjoy the scenery, I was fast asleep before I knew it.

9   I had been volunteering with Boulder County Habitat for Humanity for a little over a year, mainly due to my interest in becoming an architect. The opportunity to volunteer in Poland, thanks to my mom - as well as my many aunts, uncles and grandparents who helped me fund this experience - was the perfect chance to experience a different style of construction and to compare and contrast architecture styles of the world. When my mom had first approached me with the possibility of going on this trip, I had said I would love to because it sounded like a lot of fun, and it was.

10   But, the experience also taught me many valuable lessons. I learned a lot not just about construction, but about teamwork and collaboration as well. I learned that the goal is not to finish as quickly as possible and move on to the next project, but to give 100% and help each other out. Some of us were young; some were old. Everyone could not possibly have done the same work, but each contributed to the build equally. I came to realize that teamwork means every member putting in the same degree of effort. That it's important to recognize other member's strengths

and vulnerabilities so that as a group, there are no weak spots and the job is successfully completed.

11 All but the last two days in Gliwice were workdays. I was so jetlagged, I felt sleep deprived for most of the Habitat effort. I would go to sleep between 2 and 3:30 a.m. each night and although I didn't have to get up until 7:30, for some reason I kept waking at 5:30 a.m. So, I'd have to force myself to go back to sleep for two hours. Breakfast was the same every morning: bread, an assortment of cheese and meat, and a cup of coffee. I didn't mind, though.

12 During the school year, I usually woke up too late to eat breakfast, which was really disappointing as I liked having some food first thing to take me through the day. After breakfast, my daily routine was to grab my gym sack and join the rest of the group by the van for the half hour trip to the work site. Once there, we'd be given our instructions for the day and told the lunch menu. Once all questions were answered and lunch orders were placed, we would set off to work.

13 Not all days involved on-site work, however. On the second day, I was invited to go on a "field trip" with two of my team members. Since I was really curious about how house renovations in Poland compared with those I'd participated in back in the States, I jumped at the opportunity. Adam, the founder of Habitat for Humanity in Poland, drove us to Katowice, which is just a little under an hour away from our worksite. It looked like a fairly small, suburban town with roads lined with cobblestones.

14 Once there, we first visited a battered women's shelter to see if anything could be done about the deteriorated mouldings in the bathrooms and laundry rooms. The visit was short but I couldn't help but think about how

grateful I am for the life my parents have provided me. Doors lined the corridors leading to small rooms for the residents and their children. The rooms were only a little bigger than my bedroom, the size of a typical American living room. As we walked through and glanced into the rooms with open doors, I saw that instead of beds, there were only couches for people to sleep on. Although each room was different, each had to accommodate 1-3 people, and I could not help but feel a bit claustrophobic.

15   Unsure of how to behave, I stayed silent and followed our guide. We were led into a room where refreshments were provided and waited while Adam conversed in Polish with shelter personnel. They had quite a lot to review so our wait was long. I wanted to put this experience aside and not think of it again, but I couldn't. And perhaps that was a good thing, because although I could not do anything to help the people there, what I saw affected me in many ways. I was grateful for the world I live in, the people in my life, and the opportunity to witness the world through a different lens.

16   Next on our agenda were visits to two house renovations. Although these projects were not done by Habitat, I wanted to compare them to those I had worked on in the United States. For some reason, I expected the Gliwice renovations to be fairly spartan. I could not have been more wrong. The first renovation we visited was still in progress. It was a small project but the meticulous attention to detail really stood out. Although it was incomplete, I could see it was going to be very nice when finished. The second renovation had already been completed. In fact, the family (a mother of three, employed at a McDonald's) was holding an open house.

17   As soon as I entered, I was blown away. I was jealous, to say the least. As ridiculous and cliché as it was, I could not help but think of the saying: Don't judge a book by its cover. Not only did most buildings I'd seen look mediocre and rundown from outside, I had developed the mistaken impression that Poland didn't have the nicest standard of living. Seeing this very successful effort showed me that if we all contribute in even a small way, no matter the cause or location, we could significantly improve the lives of many people. This is just one more reason I love being a part of Habitat for Humanity.

18   Our work at the Gliwice schoolhouse was to mix cement and use it to stack pumice blocks against the walls of the building in order to improve insulation. We also transported heavy bricks (roughly 40 lbs.) up many flights of stairs via a daisy chain of volunteers. Handling the bricks roughed up my wrist to the point that I ended up with a decent scar on the left one, but I didn't mind. I looked at it as a kind of battle scar that later reminded me of this good experience.

19   During lunch one day, I went around the worksite taking photos. I happened to take one just a second before a future resident arrived. (Habitat policy is that residents contribute sweat equity to the building of the home.) The gentleman mistakenly thought I'd included him in the picture and promptly said, "No photos." I showed him the picture to prove he wasn't in it, but I could see from his expression he was still uneasy. However, he relaxed once we went back to work transporting the bricks, ending up right next to each other, and he realized we were on the same side, despite our different backgrounds.

20   The bricks were 25" x 7" x 3", and, given their weight, not easy to transport up the stairs. We made the best of

it, however, and it soon became a laugh-filled effort. It started with one of our older team members. He started to grunt obnoxiously every time he passed off a brick, I joined in and mimicked him. Soon, the Polish guy I'd met earlier joined in as well. Again and again, I reached over my right side to take bricks from the person below me and swung it across to transfer to my grunting friend on my left. The bricks hit the same part of my left wrist, just above my palm every time. The mark became red and then started bleeding. As painful as it sounds, I felt none of it. I guess I was having too much fun to care!

21   One day after work, we took a short – but very memorable -- trip to the radio tower in Gliwice. Maybe it seems crazy to get excited about a radio tower, but this tower just happens to be the tallest wooden lattice tower in the world today. It is the tower Hitler used to start World War II. He had attempted to form an alliance with Poland in order to attack Russia, but Poland refused to join him. Hitler then sent SS troops disguised as Polish soldiers to the tower in Gliwice. They sent out an anti-German announcement and an hour later, Hitler responded to his own message by declaring war against Poland. Although I've never been all that fascinated by history, I have to admit, I thought this story was pretty interesting. This was the real thing: A real place that had an impact on the whole world. This was History.

22   At the end of this tour, our team was shown through the Jewish quarter of Gliwice and taken for a dinner to close out our experience in the town. I may not remember what I ate, but I do remember the music, produced by a small band consisting of a pianist/vocalist, a trumpeter, and another vocalist. It was very distinctive. Upon leaving the restaurant, we headed out to look for an ice cream

vendor, but none was around. We slowly walked back to the hotel, where I headed to my room and promptly fell asleep after my exhausting and very full day.

23   The next morning, we jumped into the van one last time and headed to Kraków. The first day back, we mostly spent it with a guide who gave us a very thorough tour of the city. The weather was nice, the atmosphere lively, and the time flew by – just like the saying: Time flies when you're having fun. Everything about that day was perfect except when an ice cream vendor tried to rob me of 10 złoty (about $3.50). Here's the story: When our tour stopped for a 10-minute break, most of us scattered to find an ice cream stand so we could cool off a little. I paid with a bigger bill because I didn't have exact change. In return, I was handed a bunch of coins. Slightly annoyed, because I now had to count each bit of the unfamiliar currency, I started adding it up. I quickly realized I'd been shorted exactly 10 złoty. Just as I was thinking I had no options, the tour guide showed up. I told her what had happened and she accompanied me back to the stand.

24   Once there, we got in line. When it was our turn, the guide started questioning the cashier who quickly began yelling. The manager then appeared and asked what was going on. The guide explained and the cashier reluctantly handed me a 10zł bill. As we walked away, the guide explained that there were many small vendors who would rob tourists without a second thought. I wasn't particularly upset, after all thanks to the guide I had gotten my money back. I tried to understand that the cashier probably tried to steal from me because she was struggling and thought I was a rich tourist with money to spare.

25   The day ended on a much better note, however. The future residents of the project we had worked on set up a wonderful dinner for all the volunteers. The food was just phenomenal: steak, sausage, many different types of salad, an assortment of desserts, and Sprite. Sprite was sort of an inside joke on the job. My team leader dedicated it to me because Sprite was my drink of choice.

26   After dinner was over, we fooled around with a volleyball we'd found. It was funny or amazing, I'm not sure which, that even though we could not communicate, somehow we all knew how to play volleyball. There were language and cultural barriers, we'd all grown up thousands of miles apart, and yet, there we were, playing volleyball!

27   After that interlude, we were invited to look around one beneficiary's home. As I was leaving, I noticed a cage full of hamsters. I asked in English if I could hold one. The woman magically understood (my body language?) and allowed me to reach in and pick one up. After a few minutes of playing with the hamster, the woman suggested I take it with me. I was having so much fun, I accepted without a second thought. Just kidding! The first thing that crossed my mind was the idea of smuggling a hamster onto a plane and all the ways that could go wrong.

28   Working with my team in Poland was one of the greatest experiences I have ever had. The people, language, cities, culture, food, etc., helped open my eyes to how the world really is, as opposed to how I had imagined it from home. Volunteering with Habitat for Humanity in Poland, and honestly, in the U.S., too, has given me insight into the reality of the world outside the comfort zone where I live. I've come to realize there are many people with much

harder lives. It was quite overwhelming, not knowing how I could help all the people in need. I thought about this for quite a while, but it wasn't until much later that I came to understand, although I can't help everyone, through my small efforts, I contribute to a group which has a huge impact and dramatically improves the lives of many people: Habitat for Humanity.

CHAPTER 4

Language Relationships

Why are some languages easier to learn other languages?

Is there a particular language which is easier to learn for every body?

How can we figure out the relative degree of ease to be learned?

1

Easy Languages and Difficult Languages

Is there such a thing as the easiest language to learn? In order to answer the question, let me introduce some interesting stories.

One day when I was working as an editor-in-chief for the campus English paper of a college in Korea, two junior students visited me. They were very close friends to each other ever since high school. Soon after they entered the college, they made plans together for their future. One of the first plans was to take care of the mandatory military service first so that they could work straight on long term plans with no interruption.

Then, they made promises to each other that they would memorize every single words and idioms in Word Power[17] completely during the military services and before they get discharged from the army. Both of them were very proud that they kept their promises. They even asked me to test them on any word from Word Power. Also, they were very excited at the expectation that they would be

---

[17] This is a one-time famous dictionary type English vocabulary book of about 5,000 English words and idioms. During the decade of 1970's, it was considered as a must-study vocabulary book among the college students in Korea.

very good at English. Their plan was to pick up English so that they could go abroad to study.

They particularly asked me to teach them English grammar. They were so sure that they needed the English grammar to be very good at English. They strongly believed that once they get familiar with the English grammar, they should be able to speak English very well with the help of Word Power.

However, even though they memorized all the words and idioms in Word Power, their pronunciation was very poor. Even though they asked me to teach them the English grammar, I explained to them what I thought about the problems of studying grammar first. In a way, I forced them to follow my way of teaching. They reluctantly agreed with me to start with Babble Training. They struggled a lot because of the difficult pronunciations of English words, and more because of their doubts and hesitations to completely focus on Babble Training to talk. They would habitually turn their attention to the grammar, and spend extra hours every day to study the English grammar on their own wills.

For six months, they studied very hard to find out and conquer the secrets of English. They even would speak Korean to each other in the English word order so that they could be familiar with the English structure of speaking.

However, their English was so poor that they had no confidence to say anything in English. As a result, after six months, they told me that they would give up English because they did not get what they expected from the six months of English studying. It was very frustrating for them to fail to pick up English in six months after memorizing all the vocabularies in Word Power during the close-to 3 year military service. Instead, the two friends told me that they would start studying Japanese. They were told by some people that they could pick up Japanese in six months quite fluently.

Again, about six months after, they came and said to me that it was their very smart choice to give up English and choose Japanese.

They were very happy with what they had achieved during the six months of Japanese study. They told me that they studied Japanese very hard the same way they did for English.

Yet, in six months, they found that they could think and speak quite a lot in Japanese, and became very confident that they could do much better Japanese quite soon. It was much easier for them to find the secrets of Japanese. After graduation from the college, the two people left for Japan to continue studying. I will use a term of "Japanese Case" to refer to this story.

There is another interesting story. I met a business man, Mr. C, in Colorado. After graduating from a college in Korea, he went to Japan and stayed there for about 4 years. For the first year or so, he went to an institute to learn Japanese. After, one year of studying Japanese, he was able to communicate in Japanese very well so that some Japanese people would consider him as a native speaker of the Japanese language. Then, he went to England where he attended an English school to learn English. He stayed there for about 2 years, and went back to Korea. Soon after, he came to the USA.

When I asked him what language other than Korean he feels most comfortable to speak, he answered, "Japanese". He did not study Japanese in Korea at all, but he stayed in Japan for about 4 years right after the college. On the other hand, he has been staying in the USA doing businesses for a little bit over 9 years. Previously, he stayed in England for about 2 years. He received English education for about 10 years in Korea from a middle school to a college. He also tried to learn Chinese one time. Further, due to his business, he speaks Spanish enough to deal with the customers. He was not successful, he said, in picking up Chinese as he did not study for long time enough.

Among the four languages other than Korean such as Japanese, Chinese, English, and Spanish, Mr. C identified that Japanese was most comfortable to learn, and that Chinese was the next even though he does not speak it. According to him, English is the most difficult language for him to learn even after residing in the USA close to a decade. Spanish, which he started to learn at last among those four languages, was even easier than English for him to pick up. I will use the term of "C case" to refer to this story.

Based on the above two cases, I see that there is a significant relationship between the acquisition and the language similarities. That is, languages which share more similarities or common features with the learner's first language are easier to learn and maintain. Korean and Japanese are well known to share significant amount of common features or similarities between the two: word order, sound system, and quite a number of linguistic resources with minor sound differences. On the other hand, Chinese and Korean share significant amount of the linguistic resources.

Majority of the Korean noun forms are borrowed from the Chinese language, many of whose sounds can be easily related to each other. For reference purpose, I will use the term of **neighbor languages** for languages which share quite a lot of linguistic similarities and common features among themselves by being neighbors linguistically, not necessarily geographically, to each other like Japanese, Korean, and Chinese.

In this sense, it can be understood that, to the English speaking learners, learning one of the Indo-European languages such as Italian, German, French, and others would be much easier than learning languages which are not related to English. For reference purpose, I will use the term of **family languages** for the languages in such a relationship to each other. Family languages by nature share many same or similar features in many aspects such as writing system, sound system, grammar system, and linguistic resources. However, the relativity among the original family languages has been weakened as they have gotten divided further into different groups of families along with the time.

Hence, some languages do not seem to share any common features with each other. For example, Russian is categorized as one of the Indo-European languages like English, but Russian uses its own writing system, and does not share many features with other Indo-European languages. This is the same case to Hindi also.

Therefore, to identify the relativity among the languages of a family, it would be necessary to use such term as **cousin languages** for languages with many common features shared and **second cousin languages** with not many common features to be shared.

On the other hand, for English speaking person to learn Korean is very difficult, and vice versa as the two languages share very few significant linguistic features to each other. It goes the same for English and Japanese, I believe.

It seems even more difficult for Korean-speaking learners to acquire English than vice versa as the Korean sound features, which have no accents, intonations, and variations between the sounds and characters, are simpler compared to the English sound features. Arabic seems to be quite difficult for the speakers of English, Korean, Japanese, and Chinese as it has a totally different writing system with quite confusing vowel systems as well as totally different sound features. For reference purpose, I will use the term of **strange languages** for the languages in such a relationship to each other.

Now back to the question of whether there is such a thing as the easiest language to learn. My answer to the question is that no language is simple and easy enough to be picked up in one morning. All languages require a lot of efforts of Babble Training to be acquired. Second, compared to the neighbor languages and strange languages, family languages are relatively easier to learn from the beginning as they share a lot of common features to each other. Consequently, strange languages would require most amount of times and serious efforts to be acquired.

2

Linguistic Distance

People say that some languages are easy to learn in the beginning, but very difficult after the beginning level. Also, some other people say the opposite about some other languages. Are these realistic comments? Why would it be so? Also, why family languages or cousin languages in general would be easier to learn than strange languages? How can one explain the degree of being easy to learn particular languages which are not related to one's language. I believe that the answers to the questions lie in the similarities of linguistic features shared among the languages.

I already introduced such terms as family languages, cousin languages, second cousin languages, neighbor languages, and strange languages to refer to the relationships of TL to one's native language. However, to answer to the questions in more visible ways, the relationships among the languages need to be described in digitalized formats.

For the purpose of digitalizing the similarities or dissimilarities between languages, I would like to introduce the concept of linguistic distance. Linguistic distance means the degree of difficulties for learners to carry out to acquire TL. The distance or the degree of difficulty is measured by 'distance scores' based on the comparisons of the respective groups of systematic features of two languages. The systematic features are grouped into three categories: phonetic features, syntactic features, and lexical features. By nature, the phonetic features are related to the physical capacity; syntactic factors to the linguistic intuition; and the lexical features to the linguistic resources.

Let's look at how the linguistic distance table is produced. First, the linguistic distance for the phonetic features is measured by comparing such features as the vowels, consonants, suprasegmentals, letter-sound disparities, and principle of syllabification of both languages. Except for the suprasegmentals, which is given a base point of 10, whatever phonetic features of TL, which do not exist in the learner's MT, is measured by 1 point each.

For example, based on my research, English has at least 11 vowel sounds which Korean does not have. Therefore, the distance from Korean to English for the vowel features is 11. For the same token, the distance for the consonant features is 15, and that for the letter-sound disparity, which means the letters representing more than one sound, is 13. Based on this method, the total linguistic distance score for the phonetic features from Korean to English is 49.

However, the total score for the phonetic features from English to Korean is not the same as the scores for the other direction. This is because the phonetic features of one language can be much more complicated or simpler than that of the other language. Based on the table below, the total score for the phonetic features from English to Korean is 19. Compared to the total score from Korean to English, which is 49, this score is significantly lower, which means that the English phonetic features are much more complicated than the Korean phonetic features.

Second, the linguistic distance scores for the syntactic features and the lexical features are measured based on a base score system. The scores for each feature are decided by deducting the prorated scores from the base scores according to the statistical ratio of the given features of one's MT occurring in TL. For example, if the statistical ratio for a particular feature group of MT is about 30%

of all occurrences of such groups in TL, the distance score for given feature will be a number which is equivalent to the 70% of the base score point for given feature. As for the base scores for respective features of each group, I put prorated scores based on the degree of the weights which each feature appear to carry. Frankly, this is a quite subjective matter rather than being objective.

However, as long as one maintains a consistent and reasonable principle in judging the base scores for all the features, it should not cause a significant difference in evaluating the linguistic distance between any two given languages. Eventually, it would require a lot of discussions and works to be done by and among the linguists of the world languages to form a standard set of criteria to measure and compare objectively the distances of multiple languages in all directions. However, at this point, I will not worry about that far in the future yet. I also tried to reflect all of the language specific significant groups of features which are to be learned for effective communications.

Korean and English do not really share many common features in terms of the two groups, the syntactic and the lexical features. So, I gave the base scores for respective features except for the phrase structure, for which I put 3 against English based on the fact that, in Korean, an adjective phrase always precedes a noun phrase, and the fact that, in English, an adjective phrase can come either before or after a noun phrase depending on the types of adjectives. That is, I calculated the degree of difficulties for the unshared English phrase structure to be worth of 3 points. This type of phrase structure applies the same way to the adverb phrases which, in Korean, comes always before a verb phrase, but, in English, comes both before and after a verb phrase.

Feature Types[1]		Linguistic Distance Scores	
		Korean to English	English to Korean
Phonetic Features	Vowels	11	8
	Consonants	15	4
	Letter-Sound disparity	13	7
	Syllabification	0	0
	Suprasegmentals (10)	10	n/a
Subtotal for Phonetic Features		**49**	**19**
Syntactic Features	Phrase structures (5)	3	0
	Sentence structures (10)	10	10
	Interrogative (5)	5	5
	Prepositions (5)	5	n/a
	Postpositions (5)	n/a	5
	Voice (5)	5	5
	Affix Types (5)	0	3
Subtotal for Syntactic Features		**28**	**28**

	Alphabets (10)	10	10
	None Alphabetic (20)	n/a	n/a
	2nd set of alphabets (5)	1	n/a
	Use of 3rd alphabets (5)	n/a	n/a
	Use of a 3rd non-al-phabets (5)	n/a	1
Lexical Features	Case system (5)	5	5
	Gender system (5)	n/a	n/a
	Classifier system (5)	1	4
	Number system (5)	5	5
	2nd number system (5)	n/a	5
	Vocabularies (50)	50	48
	Honorific system (5)	n/a	5
	Modality system (5)	n/a	5
Subtotal for Lexical Features		72	88
Total Linguistic Distance Score		149	135

Now, based on the above table, let's look at the difficulties for Korean people to learn English first. The linguistic distance score from Korean to English is 149, which should be considered to be quite high compared to most of cousin languages, which should not exceed 50 at most. Among the total score of 149, the total distance for the phonetic features is 49, which is a little bit less than the 30% of the total distance. This explains why it is so hard for the Korean-speaking people to acquire English sounds. After over 10 years of English education from school, most of the Korean students still cannot articulate most of the English sounds accurately. This tells why most of them do not overcome the huddles of the English sounds.

On the other hand, many bilingual Korean people who acquired English as a second language told me that English is very convenient and easy to use. They even admit that Korean is quite complicated and not convenient because of so much personal-relationship oriented regulations on the usage of the Korean language. This tells how well they assimilate themselves with the syntactic features and lexical features after acquiring the phonetic features, speaking features.

Now, let's look at the degree of the difficulties for English people to learn Korean. The total distance score for the phonetic features is 19; the score for the syntactic features is 28; and the score for the lexical features is 88. The phonetic feature distance score tells that the difficulty for English-speaking people is about half of it for the Korean-speaking people. This seems to be very accurate based on my teaching experience even though the English people learning Korean for the first time would feel that it is still very difficult to learn the sounds. Except for some unsteady students, most of my students would pick up the sounds of the Korean language in one to two semesters quite fluently: they could read sentences, listen and comprehend native speaker's sounds, and, also, produce quite accurate Korean sounds when they speak or read without much accent from English. They don't have problems with reading any written Korean words with accurate sounds.

However, for the Korean-speaking students to be able to read, listen and produce English sounds quite well, I believe it takes at least 6 to 8 or more semesters. Yet, the students still cannot figure out all the sound qualities by looking at the written English words, and the proper stresses on words. Based on this comparison, two semesters can be said to be quite short time for the students to be able to learn all of the Korean sounds.

However, the English speaking bilingual people who learned Korean as a second language complain about the difficulties of the never-appear-to-be-possible-to-conquer honorific systems as well as the un-known number of modality markers, which shows the speaker's various attitudes about the people involved, and about the information being conveyed. After all, the usage of lexical items properly in Korean is very difficult for foreigners to overcome in a high level of Korean.

According to the above linguistic distance table between English and Korean, which is in a developing stage, the linguistic distance from Korean to English is 149. On the other hand the distance for the opposite direction is 135. Apparently, the distance score from English to Korean turned out to be less than the score for the other way. So, the Korean-speaking people would have more difficulties to acquire English than the English speaking people would to acquire Korean.

While it is true that no language is easy to learn, it is also true that some languages can be easier to learn than other languages. Ideas of how much TL is apart from MT can be displayed by the linguistic distance table. So, with the information on the linguistic distance to TL, one can get an idea of which part of TL is to be most difficult to learn for learners.

Consequently, the cousin family languages should have very low scores as they share a lot of features in common. The neighbor languages should gain quite higher scores compared to the scores of the family languages. Accordingly, the strange languages should gain quite high scores to each other like the scores for the pair languages of Korean and English. Using the table, one can see that the difficulty of learning TL is proportional to the distance score.

Based on the concept of the linguistic distance as shown in the table above, I would say that any language with the total linguistic distance of around 50 from MT are relatively quite easier to be acquired. For, such languages, students would not need to acquire a new set of the acquisition factors[18] of TL. On the other hand, any languages with the total linguistic distance of over 100 would require a new set of the acquisition factors to be acquired.

To find out concrete ideas in terms of the relationships between the learning process and the linguistic distance, and also to be able to utilize the distance score information for better fitness, the measurement of linguistic distance introduced here needs to be developed more thoroughly. To produce accurate and reliable linguistic distance maps between particular languages, it would require the cooperation of many linguists of the languages. With more systematic approach to the linguistic distance between MT and TL, it would help FL teachers to understand the dynamic relationship between the two languages and designing the classes.

---

[18]   The definition of this term is introduced in a later article.

3

Linguistic Distance and FLE Methods

It has been taken as granted that related or family languages which have very low linguistic distance score can relatively be learned easily and fast. This means that students who learn family languages with very low scores of linguistic distance in general can achieve much higher level of proficiency for the same period of time. However, students who learn strange languages with very high distance scores in general do not achieve the same proficiency level in acquisition for the same period time.

Then, should different FLE methods be applied for teaching different groups of languages depending on the linguistic distance relationship to TL? For example, if MT and TL belong to a same family language group, and the linguistic scores are very low like less than 50, what would be the best method to teach? Since the two languages are so similar, would it be the best way to introduce and focus on the grammar from the beginning so that the students can easily understand the differences between the two languages?

On the other hand, if MT and TL are totally strange languages to each other, what would be the method to teach? Since the two languages so drastically different in every linguistic aspect, should we start with teaching the dramatic differences one by one? Or, should we just start with teaching Babble Training to talk?

The answer to the questions is again to watch the natural way of acquiring the family languages, and the neighbor or strange languages by children, for example. One thing to be sure is that no matter how much strong linguistic intuition toward a family or a neighbor language one would have, the language specific phenomena belong to the realm of linguistic skills to be acquired rather than that of linguistic knowledge to be understood. One can understand the method of developing such linguistic skills clearly by watching the process of natural language acquisition.

By watching the natural way of language acquisition, we can be sure at least one thing that it leads learners to the development of the fundamental linguistic skills, the capability of speaking. The natural way of language acquisition starts with building the fundamental linguistic skills first. In this sense, it drastically contrasts to the various types of the traditional methods which have focused on teaching grammar based linguistic knowledge, non fundamental linguistic skills such as reading and writing, or superficial listening and speaking skills at most.

The reason I use the expression of 'teaching superficial listening and speaking skills' is that language cannot be acquired through unconditional exclusive activities of listening, and, also, through some occasions of inconsistent face to face conversational practices. One may not be sure whether that would be the most effective way for adult students to learn a second language. However, as the FLE based on various methods has not been successful, we could assume that a method which utilizes the natural language acquisition method may be the best way through which people acquire second language.

Accordingly, the answer to the questions is that, regardless of the linguistic distances between MT and TL, basically the most effective teaching methods should be the same. For this, I insist that regardless of the language relationships between MT and TL, we should start with teaching the level 1 babble, Babble Training to talk, and continue to the next levels of Babble Training to meet and improve the proficiency level of the students.

Of course, depending on the linguistic distance to TL, students could make very fast or slow progresses toward higher levels of the babble process. The lower the distance score to TL, the faster will be the progress to the higher levels of the babble process. The higher the distance score, the slower will be the progress to the higher levels of the babble process.

Above questions on the differences and methods for teaching family languages, neighbor languages, or strange languages can be likened to the questions on the differences and methods for teaching similar or strange musical instruments to students. No matter how the musical instruments are similar or strange to one's own instrument, the teaching process basically cannot be different from the prototypical teaching methods. That is, the teachers should require the students to practice a lot every time. The difference would simply be that students would pick it up much quickly or slowly depending on the similarity or differences of the new instrument.

Also, as the lower distance score means that students already have higher linguistic intuition, physical capacity, and linguistic resources toward TL, it would take less intensive trainings, less amount of time, and less quantity of efforts for students to acquire TL. For many of the IE family languages, it is true that a lot of the acquisition factors are still shared by the speakers of each language. Accordingly, students who learn such TL would acquire TL with relatively less intensive babble process to learn talking, reading, listening, and writing.

This is the main reason, I believe, that the traditional grammar translation method has been the strongest trend of FLE. That is, before the 20th century, FLE was in general mostly focused on teaching quite strong family languages which were being used in the neighbor countries. As the linguistic distance is so close between MT and TL, the grammar translation method was still quite effective method in that it helped the students acquire such communicative skills as reading and writing by simply being able to distinguish the grammatical differences between the two languages.

On the other hand, students who learn a strange TL with really high linguistic distance scores would need to overcome a lot of difficulties of going through very intensive Babble Training process with quite large amount of expressions to build the linguistic intuition, physical capacity, and the linguistic resources strong enough to acquire TL. Especially, students who challenge to learn a strange language whose linguistic distance score for the phonetic features is very high would have a lot of difficulties from the very beginning level. In fact, many students would end up not overcoming the level 1 Babble Training because of not being able to afford the amount of efforts and time required.

As a conclusion, all languages require the linguistic intuition, physical capacity, and linguistic resources to be acquired. It is just like all sports activities require athletic senses, physical capacity, and all sorts of skills available. Therefore, just as the sports activities would require the same routine intensive practices to learn, languages require the same routine intensive and focused Babble Training process to be obtained, no matter how similar they are to one's MT. After all, the linguistic distance to TL should not change the methods of FLE; instead, the distance would influence over the speed of the progress being made.

CHAPTER 5

Evaluation Methods

Can we teach independently from the general trends of evaluation criteria?

No matter what we teach, students will lean toward the trends of the evaluation criteria.

1

Transitions of Foreign Language Evaluation Methods

As far as FLE is concerned, it is quite obvious that the most intensive and worldwide prevailing FLE program is TESL. Countless number of English education related textbooks, audios, videos, and reference materials fill the walls of every bookstore in the non-English speaking countries. Just looking at the English language market in South Korea is beyond the astonishing level. Every month, new English education reference materials are introduced to the market.

In the USA, I don't see FLE programs of any particular language being so intensive as in Korea. Not so much enthusiasm and fanatic social atmosphere to learn a FL I see in the USA either. I understand that other Asian countries like Japan and China are not much different from Korea with respect to the issue of FLE. I assume that it would be quite same to most of the other non-English speaking countries also. As I am much more familiar with FLE programs in Korea and in the USA, I will discuss FLE situation with comparisons between the USA and Korea.

Compared with the serious concerns of every body for FLE in Korea, the people in USA relatively look quite generous and relaxed about what they get out of FLE. The outcome of one's FLE in the

USA does not make so critical influence on one's promotion or progress continuously through out one's whole life as in Korea. In general, the students in Korea try to get more than 100% out of what was taught as an input for FLE because, otherwise, they would fall behind in the critical competition. Accordingly, the students in Korea, most likely in other countries also, almost have no choice but blindly studying very hard whatever being taught in the English class.

Now, I want to discuss how the worldwide TESL has evolved. The trends of worldwide TESL have been led by the trends of the English evaluation methods which have gone through dramatic changes over the last 20 years. Some people may argue that it could be the other way also. However, I believe that historically the trends of the English evaluations have had more controls on the trends of TESL compared to the control by the TESL on the trends of the English evaluation.

Prior to the 1970's, the students in Korea were evaluated based on heavily grammar-oriented tests. So, whoever was very good at English grammar could make the life much easier and successful in school and work as well. Again, I assume that most of the non-English speaking countries have shared the same pattern of the trends as in Korea. Then, up to the 1980's, they were evaluated by the grammar and reading oriented tests.

Accordingly, people studied very hard to be able to read and understand quite lengthy English paragraphs, compared to very short example sentences used to explain the grammars before 1980's, by analyzing each of the sentences based on the grammar knowledge. Since the 1980's, the TESL of the world countries has been led by the ETS as TOEFL and TOEIC by ETS were considered as a worldwide standard English test program. The English teachers and students adjusted their orbits of English education following the trends of the ETS evaluation since then.

So, as the ETS tested the students based on the grammar, reading and listening skills through TOEIC and TOEFL, the TESL added the listening skill on its focus in addition to existing grammar and reading skill oriented education. Then, as the ETS added writing test to its evaluation in 1990's, every body got much busier to prepare for the writing test on top of the tests for the grammar, reading, and listening comprehension of English.

However, with the beginning of the 21st century, the ETS realized the serious problems of its own programs. The problem was that very few of those who have very high scores in TOEFL or TOEIC could speak English well. Most of them, especially those from the countries of non-European language countries, have turned out not even to be able to make a simple communication well enough in English.

As a result, the ETS has developed the iBT TOEFL including the test of the speaking skill. Also, the ETS decided that the grammar evaluation should be done in the writing and speaking rather than in a separate grammar section. These new changes to TOEFL only seemed to make the students feel more confused and harder to tackle English. Even though the ETS dropped the grammar section from iBT TOEFL, nobody seems to consider it as meaning 'no separate grammar study is necessary'. Even the ETS clarified that grammar skill would be tested in the writing and speaking skills, because of which people still strongly believe that separate focused English grammar study is very necessary.

By adding those test areas in such a sequence, the ETS, with the authority naturally bestowed upon it through its highly renowned reputation as the world's best professional English test program agency, seems to have silently ratified the traditional sequence of TESL focusing on the grammar and reading first.

In other words, with the sequence for traditional methods of evaluation, the teachers were led to teach the grammar first, and then reading second. Based on the sequence of the additional subjects having been added to the test programs of the ETS such as TOEFL, the teachers were further led to teach writing, listening comprehension, and speaking skills in the same sequence as they were added to TOEFL respectively.

As a result, the speaking skill training is still considered as the last course of the school English education program, and the program would not have enough time to reach to the level of speaking skill training for many reasons. The program would spend most of its time on grammar and reading comprehension. Then, the program would cover very marginal trainings for writing and listening skills.

Therefore, to me at least, it is very natural and not so much surprising to find that the people with near 10 years of English education cannot speak English at all. As we have not taught it, students simply cannot do it. It is a very logical consequence. We taught them English grammar, reading, writing and listening. Therefore, the students are well equipped with the skills of grammar, reading, writing, and listening skills to the proportional degree they have been educated. In this sense, the English education worldwide has been very successful. We can't complain about it because they learned what we taught very well.

However, somehow, we are very upset with the very logical consequence that the students cannot speak English so well. This tells that we have been teaching English with the greatest unbelievable misunderstanding that student would be able to speak English after learning the English grammar, reading, writing and listening. Everybody mistakenly believed that teaching grammar, reading, writing, and listening should precede teaching speaking.

At a glance, it sounds so plausible, but it is a great misunderstanding. They completely did not know that once the speaking skill is acquired through thorough Babble Training, not through superficial speaking training, all the other matters such as grammar, reading, writing, and listening will be resolved at once. Even at present, the reality is that most of the FLE educators have so strong belief in such an unbelievable misunderstanding, and raise their voices arguing for the traditional methods.

The reason I introduced how the worldwide TESL has evolved is because it has very significant influence not only on FLE of the USA but also on that of all the countries in the world.

The USA seems to be quite unique in that there is no particular language that every body is committed to learn for many years, and that, compared to many other countries, quite a number of languages are offered even from the elementary schools to the students with a quite equal weight. Also, it is also very unique and fortunate for the students in the USA that almost all of the variety languages are taught by the native speakers everywhere nationwide. Few countries in the world have such a luxury of a variety of human resources.

However, problems still exist. That is, many of the native speaker teachers of such variety languages are the ones who received FLE in their countries before they came to the USA. This means that they underwent the traditional TESL courses in their countries. The TESL programs in abroad are mostly influenced by the teachers who were strongly influenced by the traditional sequence of TESL based on the new developments of the ETS evaluation criteria.

Consequently, most of FLE teachers in the USA as well as in other countries have seen and experienced school environment FLE only: TESL in their countries. Therefore, even though one may strongly deny it, they were naturally led to believe that the traditional methods of TESL are the most systematic and well designed methods for FLE.

As a result, I believe many FL teachers in the USA are equally, if not more, biased on the language teaching sequences of grammar, reading, writing, listening, and speaking respectively, or somewhat to similar to this sequence, just like the English teachers in Korea and many other countries also. One may say, "So what? What is wrong with such a sequence?" However, there is one big thing wrong with the sequence, which I am very concerned about.

The biggest problem is that the traditional TESL based on such sequences prior to the iBT TOFEL generation has been proven for long time and by millions of people to have failed to produce solid English speakers. With its very short history, the iBT TOFEL is yet to be waited and seen. However, I don't see how the students would reach to the level of the iBT TOFEL by following the traditional study tracks. It would take forever even before they are ready for the iBT TOFEL.

As the traditional TESL has not been successful to produce fluent English speakers, most of the native speaker FLE teachers in the USA, who were raised and educated in the school TESL environment in their countries, didn't really pick up English from the schools. They were mostly able to read and write English well.

Then, at some special environments after regular school curriculum, or after their arrival to the USA, they picked up the English language through a lot of intensive babble activities. Solely based on and limited to their own experiences, many of them believe that it is not possible for one to pick up TL fluently without being raised and educated in the society of TL.

Now, one could see where my concerns come from with respect to FL teachers who would stick to and insist on the traditional tracks as they do not know any other tracks around to teach FL.

I understand that many language teachers realize that there are problems with the traditional FLE, and work hard to come up with better ideas by reviewing the language classes they have taught, reading language pedagogy books and attending conferences on FLE. Yet, without realizing the true sources of the problems for the traditional FLE methods, the teachers would not be able to overcome the influences coming from one's own experiences with the traditional TESL methods in making decisions to build FLE programs.

What should we do to find the real issues with the traditional FLE? We should think carefully about how all human beings have acquired the language.

2

Proficiency-oriented Evaluation Method

Since it was hatched in the late 1970s and the early 1980s, the concept of proficiency movement has formed major discussions and gatherings of many FLE professions and FL teachers in the USA. It has been quite influential on FL teaching in that it provided the motivation for many FL teachers to review the various types of FL teaching methods they have adopted.

How much it has been successfully implemented by the teachers is yet to be seen. It also has brought up a lot of concerns and objections. Many of the concerns and objections are related to the unclear definition for some of the terminologies such as proficiency, proficiency teaching, proficiency testing, function, proficiency-based instructions, and etc. Also, the unreasonable emphasis on grammatical accuracy and corrections from the earlier stage invited critics.

Through exchanges of criticism and responses, the positions of those who support the proficiency movement have been clarified quite a lot. Also, the misunderstanding or misinterpretation on the significance of the proficiency guidelines and the oral proficiency interview (OPI) by the American Council on the Teaching of Foreign Languages (ACTFL) became clearer. The supporters of the proficiency-oriented curricula claim that the OPI is less important as an evaluation instrument than as an agent for change. This statement clearly helps us how we should look at the proficiency-oriented guidelines and the OPI. That is, the OPI itself has much room to be improved, but it clearly points a new direction for FL teaching.

The proficiency movement has two parts in it: the proficiency-oriented instruction and the OPI. At the center of the movement is the OPI, which grades student's oral proficiency in four levels: Novice, Intermediate, Advanced, and Superior, all of which, except for the superior level, have three sub levels of low, mid, and high respectively. To help FL teachers plan and design syllabi in accordance with the criteria of the OPI, the proficiency-oriented instructions have been suggested through the following five working hypotheses:

1. Opportunities should be provided for students to practice using language in a range of context likely to be encountered in the target culture.

2. Opportunities should be provided for students to practice carrying out a range of functions likely to be necessary in dealing with others in the target culture.

3. There should be concern for the development of linguistic accuracy from the beginning of instruction in a proficiency-oriented approach.

4. Proficiency-oriented approaches should respond to the affective needs of students as well as to their cognitive needs. Students should feel motivated to learn and be given opportunities to express their own meanings in a non-threatening environment.

5. Cultural understanding should be promoted in various ways so that students are prepared to live more harmoniously in the target-language community.

Even though proficiency-oriented instructions are not claimed to be FL teaching method, the hypotheses clearly show teachers how FL classes should be oriented. Also, supporters of the proficiency movement emphasize the balance of the four language skills as well as the culture of TL. The issues which are introduced by the hypotheses are truly good points to talk about, but they cover so limited areas only in FL teaching. They do not indicate how to start FLE, and how to put the students up in the high level of acquisition. They sound flashy, but they do not really carry the weight.

The hypotheses tell the farmers only about how to raise chicks. The hypotheses simply assume that the chicks will hatch and reproduce by themselves. There is no consideration reflected on the hypotheses about the most important works of how to hatch the chicken from eggs. If one would design the curriculum according to the hypotheses, one would have hard time to start the very beginning level classes. Also, even if one would manage to start the very beginning level classes, the students would not be able to improve to higher levels of acquisition than the intermediate level according to the OPI guidelines.

The hypotheses also seem to impose quite a burden on the international FL teachers around the world except for those in the USA, most of whom are not native speakers of the subject language, and do not know the cultural context of TL very well. For most of other countries than the USA, the FL class environments are way different from those of the USA.

Some of the major reasons for the non-native TL speaking teachers to insist on focusing on intensive grammar based teaching is, I believe, they do not speak TL fluently; they do not understand how a language is acquired very well; and they do not know much about TL other than the grammar and how to read TL based on the grammar.

Before they became FL teachers, most of them were naturally led by the traditional FLE situation they went through while in school to believe that grammar is a must-to-do basic before anything else. Therefore, they don't doubt that they are teaching right things by teaching grammars most of the time every day and every year.

Even though the proficiency-oriented instruction guidelines clearly stimulate FL teachers to seek new directions, I believe that the hypotheses are not clear and strong enough to change the mainstream direction of FL teaching methods. The hypotheses do not warn the serious problems of being addicted to the grammar-oriented teaching methods. Such teaching methods so far only have produced countless number of expert grammarians of TL in different levels such as novice, intermediate, and advanced.

We know that grammarians do not have to be able to speak TL fluently as long as they can analyze the grammar of TL based on collected texts and write papers on them. Also, some of us know how, unless they acquired TL previously, most of the grammarians speak TL, like a retired 286 processor computer with a very poor speaker attached frequently failing with assembling the data. As a matter of fact, instead of warning such problems, the hypotheses give excuses for the grammar-oriented teachers to stick to their traditional methods.

Also, most of the hypotheses do not apply to those who could not afford the school with FL teachers, and, therefore, would like to teach FL to themselves. For those adult people in the world who challenge to teach FL to themselves, the hypotheses are only discouraging. Do we need separate sets of working hypotheses of the proficiency-oriented instructions for different FL class environments and for different group of students?

On the other hand, I understand the confusion with the concept of proficiency. It could mean all different things and different levels of performance. It needs to be clear and specific for one agreed understanding by every body. Yet, the hypotheses in a sense make the concept unclear. It is just like the traditionally confusing concept of English to many people in those countries where English education is so crucial and mandatory.

For example, when people say, "Eric is very good at English" it means many different things. He could receive such a compliment by one of the followings: He always gets high score from the school English tests; he is very good at English grammar; he is very good at English reading; he writes English with no grammatical errors; he received a very high score in TOEIC or TOEFL; he teaches English to students at a school or private institute; he won a prize at an English speech contest; or he speaks, reads, and writes English very well.

Even though I take the concept of proficiency as mainly referring to the oral proficiency based on the hypotheses and the guidelines, I still cannot get rid of such a belief that the hypotheses, which lay the foundation for the proficiency based instructions, seem to be of too rough ideas to be a trust winning hypotheses. It is because I believe they failed to address the very key ideas of what it takes for students to achieve successful proficiency.

In other words, the hypotheses do not show any consideration on such factual factors as oral proficiency cannot be achieved without first acquiring TL; the teaching methods for acquisition may not necessarily be the same as them for developing the proficiency; and it requires tremendous efforts of repetitions and experiences to develop the proficiency.

Offering opportunities to express their own meanings in a non-threatening environment could be fun and motivating. However, for beginning students, it is not feasible for them to do so from the beginning. It also is only a minor part of the whole class operation. We, FL teachers, know that it takes much more than simply offering such opportunities. The hypotheses failed to link the proficiency of TL to the acquisition of TL. In other words, they clearly overlooked the fact that the successful proficiency of TL cannot be achieved without successful acquisition of TL.

Consequently, the hypotheses surely let the FL teachers overlook the acquisition process of TL, and focus on the proficiency of TL. In other words, what the OPI focus on does not seem to be the acquisition of TL. As proficiency of TL cannot be achieved without acquiring TL first, it contradicts by itself.

Even with such issues I pointed above, I welcome the concept of proficiency-oriented instructions, and especially the OPI as an agent for change. At least it is good to see a great turning point in FLE methods. Thanks to the OPI, many FL teachers already have reviewed and would continue reviewing and updating the methods of their teaching, evaluation, curriculum, course design, class environment, and student-teacher relations to comply with the criteria of the OPI.

Unfortunately, not many of us, FL teachers, could teach our own languages independent of the evaluation trends. Not many of us have independent goals apart from meeting the requirements of the prevailing evaluation method. Almost all of us would follow the contemporary trends of evaluation methods as almost all of our predecessors have done. That is why it is so important to have a new method of evaluation for good or bad. Otherwise, many of us, FL teachers, would not be motivated much for change for better or worse. For this reason, I really want to see the OPI develop as the method to evaluate the students' acquisition level of TL.

As the proficiency-oriented instructions and the OPI guidelines claim not to be the proficiency-oriented method but to be an agent for change, we are back to our own tradition, continuing what we have been doing traditionally. We now have learned one more concept on how to teach FL, which is called proficiency-oriented instructions, in addition to a dozen of the existing traditional FLE methods. Yet, we don't know what to continue and what to trash away from the dozen of the traditional methods for the proficiency-oriented instructions. We don't know how much of what respectively needs to be taught to meet the criteria of the OPI. The job to develop teaching methods for our students to acquire TL is back to us.

3

Questions for Ourselves, FL Teachers

Who are we? We are FL teachers. What is our duty? Our duty is to teach our languages to the students. These may be the common answers we may easily share in response to many possible questions for us, FL teachers.

To somewhat more sophisticated questions like what methods should we use to teach FL; what should be the bases of planning for the curriculum; and what should be the ultimate goal of our teaching, one would need to play with the questions for a while to induce the answers one might want to get. To the detail questions with 'how' and 'why', we would have no way to expect one prevailing answer over others.

At least for FL teachers in the USA, with the concept of the proficiency-oriented instructions dominating the discussions on FL teaching methods, it is true that it provided opportunities with the teachers to consider the methods we have used so far. Even though many of us are still quite confusing and not clear what and how to do, it is true that most of us feel it necessary to review the methods we have used for many years.

Why do we pay so much attention to the teaching methods? Why now? Why not before? Would it have been the same way without the powerful driving force of the OPI by ACTFLE? No, I don't think so. Without the OPI, the concept of the proficiency-oriented instructions would have not received so much attention from FL teachers just as most of FL teaching methods introduced have not so far.

However, it could have been in the record of history like the many FL teaching methods. So, from the concept of proficiency-oriented instructions, what have we found to be added on top of what we already have been doing? Or, what have we found to be discontinued from the methods we have been using so far? Not many of us have found the answers to the questions yet, I believe. Rather, many of us got confused and are getting back to what we have been doing.

Very similar movements have started since the last several years around the world in the countries where English is considered as one of most important subjects in the school. The urgency for change in English education in those countries was accepted as reality as ETS started the iBT TOEFL since several years ago, which added the evaluation of the English speaking skills, and dropped the grammar section. The English education related school and government authorities have put spurs in search for teaching methods for the students to gain high scores in the iBT TOEFL or next generation TOEFL.

So far, they started teaching very intensive grammar to lay strong foundation for reading comprehension, and, then, they added teaching the listening skills toward the end of their multi year English education system. Yet, they now find not enough time to add the teaching of English speaking on top of the existing curriculum. They don't think they can stop teaching grammar, nor reading, nor listening. Therefore, I would not be surprised to see that, without choice, they would choose to increase the English education classes and hours to teach the speaking skills.

Why these changes should happen every once in a while? Can we not make a clear and ever consistent goal of our teaching? Or, are we naturally supposed to change the goals of our teaching each time whenever new types of evaluation method are introduced? Let's say that we spend years of time to develop a successful teaching method based on the criteria of the OPI, or based on the criteria of the iBT TOEFL. Can we be sure that this is the last time for change? What if the ACTFEL come up with something like OPIW by adding the writing proficiency evaluation to the OPI with a vague set of working hypotheses? What if the ETS comes up with EOPI for the English oral proficiency interview? Then, are we again going to fly back and forth to attend the seminars and conferences on how to change our teaching methods? Where are we driving our students to? Is the destination of our teaching to the skills for successful evaluation, or to the complete acquisition of TL?

We should establish one all time goal of teaching our languages, shouldn't we? The ultimate and all time goal of our teaching should be to help the students acquire TL and develop the advanced level oral proficiency of it, shouldn't it be? We should keep developing our teaching methods to achieve the consistent goal, shouldn't we? Once the students acquire TL and develop such high level oral proficiency, they should be able to deal with whatever types of TL evaluations, shouldn't they? So, if we really teach our students for acquisition and oral proficiency, we do not need to be led by the types of evaluations, don't we?

We, as FL teachers, are responsible to develop teaching methods which most fit to our students at given situation toward the efforts of acquiring TL. FL teaching methods should not be driven by the methods of evaluation because the methods of evaluation, none of them being perfect, are to change ever. It should not matter whether ACTFEL or ETS would evaluate intensively on the grammar, reading, writing, or oral proficiency to us because our priority job is to assist our students to acquire our languages. Then, we are sure that, once they acquire TL and pick up the oral proficiency in some years, they will handle such types of evaluation successfully.

We FL teachers over the world should get together to discuss the best FL teaching methods and to gather ideas of effective FL class management. We should not gather to find out the secret skills for our students to gain high scores in particular types of evaluations. We should not compromise our all time goal with any skills for scoring high scores because the best way to prepare our students for evaluations is always to help them pick up the oral proficiency of TL first as much as they can.

Now is the time to seriously ask ourselves of who we are, what is our job, what the all time goal should be for our teaching. Now is the time to really set ourselves apart from the concerns of the various types of the evaluation criteria and methods; to gather our pure thoughts and reviews on the teaching methods we have chosen; and to overcome the typical prejudices we have built against or in favor of particular methods. Now is the time we need to be independent and establish very firm foundation to the benefit of the students.

CHAPTER 6

BTM Theories

The terms 'babbling', 'babble', or 'the babble' used in this book are originated from the verbal acts of babies during the process of acquiring mother tongue.

I use the term 'babble', 'the babble' or 'babbling' to mean the learner's repeated acts of mimicking, copying, talking to oneself, memorizing, using, and practicing over Real Input with a purpose of acquiring language, especially oral proficiency. However, in a broad sense, I also use the term to mean the learner's repeated practice acts of listening, reading and writing after Real Input with a purpose of acquiring respective skills.

Acquisition is achieved most effectively through intensive Babble Training; and oral proficiency is developed most effectively through intensive performance training. Therefore, to ask for beginning learners to perform TL would not be an effective teaching technique.

1

What is BTM?

Looking into the traditional FLE methods such as Grammar Translation Method, and Reading Method, which in sequence seem to have been applied most generally to the current FLE, the main idea of those methods seems to be that the acquisition of the system of rules of TL will make it easier for the students to learn TL or expedite the process of TL acquisition. Or, the main idea of the traditional methods could be to offer the skills for the students to be able to read and understand TL.

If the first idea is the real intentions of the methods, FLE based on these methods have clearly failed. Not only that, it clearly produced more handicapped students in learning TL than any other methods. However, if the second idea is the real intentions of the methods, one could say that FLE based on these methods has been successful. However, if this has been the true intention of the traditional FLE, we now should consider upgrading the main idea more realistically to meet the expectation of the modern society for FLE.

The ideas for the follow up methods to the traditional FLE methods such as Direct Method, Technical Approaches, and Content Based Method seem to be that immersing the students directly into TL and forcing them to speak in TL would lead the students to acquire the oral language of TL. Yet, based on my teaching experience and observation, the students who are not familiar with the spoken forms of TL could not really participate in such an abrupt in-class immersion. Especially, it seems not so much realistic for the students who are heavily educated under the traditional FLE methods to adjust themselves into the sudden in-class immersion. They have been trained to break down the sentences of TL and assemble the components into their language system before they understand TL sentences, and vice versa before they produce TL expressions which they want to say.

This kind of strong habits would not be silent when the students try to immerse into TL. Instead, the habits would interfere very strongly with the speech process when the students try to react to a situation where they are requested to show response in TL, which results in significant delay of the responses and interruptions of the linguistic performances. This is the horrible side effects coming from the traditional FLE methods.

BTM, which I propose in this book as an oral proficiency-oriented FLE method, is based on the working hypotheses on language acquisition and inputs & outputs, and on the very obvious fact that all human beings have successfully acquired their languages through the babble process. It is also based on my own experiences of acquiring English as TL, and teaching English and Korean as TL to students.

I say this way because the only thing the babies do, that seems uniquely to be related to their language acquisition, is, I believe, the babble over the inputs from the babble leaders. The people who failed to acquire the verbal forms of their languages are the ones who were not able to perform the babbling for whatever reasons. The people who did the sign Babble Training acquired the sign language.

I really don't see any better proven ways to acquire language than the babbling. As a matter of fact, based on the fact that very young children with less fully operative brains acquire their languages in 36 to 40 months with the easy and relaxed babbling, Babble Training seems to be the easiest, simplest and most effective way to acquire a language. At least, we know for sure that at the end of Babble Training is the acquisition of language.

I believe that Babble Training is a unique universal feature that all human beings have performed to acquire given natural languages. Also, the language education method adopted by the parents to their children is a unique universal feature that has been always successful for the learners to acquire given languages except for such extraordinary situations as physically unable children.

The language education by the parents can be categorized into three main levels: speaking, reading, and writing. No systematic grammar teaching is introduced at all by the parents to the young children. Also, the language education by the parents is purely oral proficiency-oriented. Such language education process by the parents is the role model of BTM.

The term babble in nature refers to the repeated vocal acts of mimicking target expressions and attempting to produce own expressions by young children, which I see as a preparation or practice process of acquiring the linguistic intuition, the physical capacity, and linguistic resources, which are very crucial factors in language acquisition.

Based on such nature of the babble, I define the babble in general as the primary training process to acquire the acquisition factors of TL. In a narrow sense, I also use the term, babble, to mean repeated efforts to acquire individual expressions of TL. Therefore, depending on the objects of Babble Training, I use such terms as babble to talk, babble to read, babble to listen, babble to write, and babble to free talk.

Based on such unique universal feature of Babble Training as the training process of language acquisition, the main idea of BTM is to apply the whole process of natural language teaching process to FLE in the most effective manners.

For this effective BTM, I propose the following five areas of Babble Training for FLE: Babble Training to talk, Babble Training to read, Babble Training to listen, Babble Training to write, and Babble Training for free speech activities. According to BTM, these five areas of babbles are deployed into the following levels.

Types	Babble Levels	Babble Subjects Being Added
Babble Training for acquisition	Level 1	Talking
Babble Training for oral proficiency	Level 2	Add reading
	Level 3	Add listening
	Level 4	Add writing
	Level 5	Add free talking
Option	Level 6	Add TL grammar

BTM starts with the level one, teaching the students to do Babble Training in TL. This level 1 is designed for the students to acquire enough language skills to participate freely in communicating with people in TL utilizing the expressions and vocabularies learned during the babble process. The goal of level 1 is to acquire TL to the level of MT acquisition by 36-40 months old kids, when many kids start reading.

From level 2, it is a process of building up the oral proficiency by developing and expanding the language skills, which is acquired through level 1, into higher quality.

As level one successfully settles and continues, Babble Training to read in TL is added for level 2. Babble Training to read is very important in preparation for the next levels of Babble Training as students are expected to collect a lot of linguistic resources as well as the intuitive understanding power of the TL sentence structures through the reading process. Without the strong vocabulary power and the intuitive understanding power of the TL sentence structures, the following levels of Babble Training for listening comprehension of normal speed TL and for free talking in TL would be extremely difficult for students.

For level 3, the babble for listening comprehension of TL is added to level 2. So far, students are familiar with the conversation type expressions, which are different from the general expressions used in the media. To understand the general media languages effectively, intensive training for listening skills is necessary.

Then, for level 4, which is adding Babble Training to write in TL, is introduced to the students. Babble Training to write in TL is to help students to acquire the linguistic logic of TL, and to train them to practice for expressing one's ideas in creative and productive manner.

Finally, upon successful settlement with level 4, the babble for free talking in TL is added for level 5 Babble Training. As Babble Training for free talking is the actual stage to improve one's oral proficiency, it is very important to have a lot of free talking experiences on various topics.

The last but an optional level in BTM of FLE is level 6, Review of TL system, which is the grammar class of TL. Unlike the areas of babbling, grammar is not an object of babbling. It is rather a study subject, and not so much crucial as the various babble subjects in language acquisition and performance.

However, it does not mean that all of these six levels should be completed for the students to be able to use the language. I suggest that these levels should be completed to achieve high level of oral proficiency. Students can still get to speak TL quite well to deal with most of the personal life activities in TL by continuously focusing on level one of Babble Training about 500 daily activity related independent expressions[19] collected from various real personal life situations. That is, with successful level one education for TL, one still can acquire the skills to communicate in TL utilizing the expressions one acquired during the process of level one. The illiterate people, who can speak but cannot read one's mother tongue, show that language can be acquired by people without having to be able to read and write it.

The goals and detail teaching ideas of each level will be introduced in later chapters. The following sequence diagram shows how each of the six levels should be processed with minimal amount of real inputs required to acquire language to a base level. For higher level acquisition, higher amount of real inputs is required.

More detail and concrete ideas for effective Babble Training can be found in the last chapter of this book, Chapter 14. Even though the last chapter is for self Babble Training, it is also designed for teachers to build an effective BTM programs.

---

[19] I define the term 'independent expressions' here as those expressions which are not part of a pattern to each other. For example, such expressions as 'How are you?', 'How is he?', 'How is she?', and 'How is your sister?' are considered as belonging to one pattern, and, therefore, they are all together counted as one independent expression.

The BTM Diagram[20]

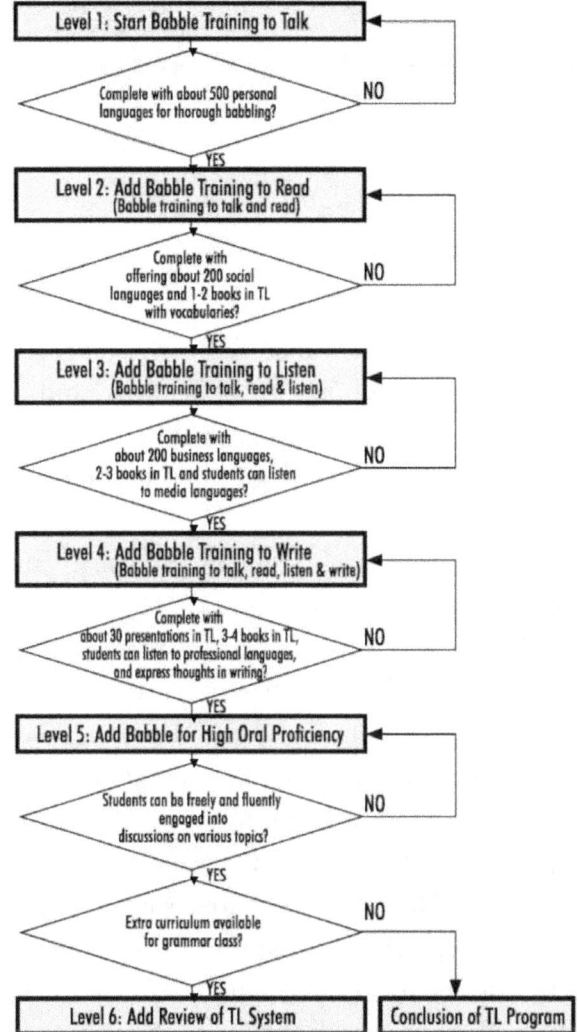

The Babble Training Method Diagram

Level 1: Start Babble Training to Talk

Complete with about 500 personal languages for thorough babbling? — NO

YES

Level 2: Add Babble Training to Read
(Babble training to talk and read)

Complete with offering about 200 social languages and 1-2 books in TL with vocabularies? — NO

YES

Level 3: Add Babble Training to Listen
(Babble training to talk, read & listen)

Complete with about 200 business languages, 2-3 books in TL and students can listen to media languages? — NO

YES

Level 4: Add Babble Training to Write
(Babble training to talk, read, listen & write)

Complete with about 30 presentations in TL, 3-4 books in TL, students can listen to professional languages, and express thoughts in writing? — NO

YES

Level 5: Add Babble for High Oral Proficiency

Students can be freely and fluently engaged into discussions on various topics? — NO

YES

Extra curriculum available for grammar class? — NO

YES

Level 6: Add Review of TL System

Conclusion of TL Program

* The fulfillment of these conditions for each level requires discretional judgment of teachers as the conditions may not be satisfied by every student in the class.

---

[20] The fulfillment of these conditions for each level requires discretional judgment of teachers as the conditions may not be satisfied by every student in the class.

2

What is Language Acquisition?

Before I go further, I would like to clarify the definition of language acquisition that I want to talk about. Otherwise, people will rely on their own convenient meanings of the concept, and cannot avoid huge conflicts of understanding. In a general linguistics sense, one may apply the concept of acquiring linguistic competence of a language as language acquisition.

Here, according to the definition of a dictionary, the term competence refers to speakers' knowledge of their language, the system of rules which they have mastered so that they are able to produce and understand an indefinite number of sentences, and to recognize grammatical mistakes and ambiguities. It is seen as in opposition to the notion of performance, the specific utterances of speech.

To acquire such kind of linguistic competence, especially for a foreign language, one does not have to be able to command the oral language very well. Of course, for native speakers, they obtain the knowledge of the language by acquiring first and performing the language. That is, speaking the language. They don't have to make any particular efforts to obtain the knowledge about their language as they obtain it somehow by just acquiring and speaking it.

However, for those people who learn a language as FL, they don't have to focus on acquiring the oral language to obtain the linguistic competence or the knowledge of TL to be able to produce and understand an indefinite number of sentences, and to recognize grammatical mistakes and ambiguities.

In fact, many FL students do succeed in obtaining the knowledge by studying only the system of rules of TL. In other words, there are two different ways of obtaining the linguistic competence: with the acquisition of the speaking skills and without having to acquire the speaking skills.

As a result, the concept of obtaining linguistic competence as a definition of language acquisition realistically brings about quite a contradiction. It is a huge contradiction to consider who knows the grammar of TL very well, but cannot speak TL so well, which is not an unusual situation in this world at all.

The concept of obtaining linguistic competence without having to acquire the speaking skills is not the concept that I use in this book to refer to language acquisition. Nor the concept of having to obtain linguistic competence with the speaking skills is what I acknowledge as language acquisition either.

Also, the general concept of acquiring a language is quite vague, and it does not seem to appreciate the individual performance levels. So, if someone says to have acquired a language, the person is likely to be considered as a master of the language. Based on this kind of concept, no one will acquire a language.

The concept that I use for language acquisition for FLE purposes is the acquisition of the basic levels of linguistic intuition, physical capacity, and linguistic resources for the meaningful performance of the incoming and outgoing flows of the oral language.

The linguistic resources here in this book means, in a narrow sense, the vocabulary, but, in a comprehensive sense, it means the words, phrases, idiomatic expressions, and the realistic expressions.

Meanwhile, the basic levels of linguistic intuition, physical capacity, and linguistic resources refer, for example, to the acquisition level of the typical 36-40 month old children. The typical 36-40 month old children seem to have acquired the basic levels of linguistic intuition, physical capacity, and linguistic resources enough to perform the incoming and outgoing flows of the oral language.

In other words, they seem to understand the oral language aimed to them, and deliver their meanings in oral language without particular difficulties. In their oral language activities, they seemed to be restricted only by their limit of linguistic resources. The oral proficiency level of these children can be the barometer to judge the degree of one's language acquisition.

The traditional FLE methods have focused on promoting the students to learn the linguistic competence rather than on the acquisition of the linguistic intuition, physical capacity, and linguistic resources. Also, many people strongly believe that obtaining such linguistic competence should happen first in order for one to acquire TL. This is based on their belief that teaching students to obtain the knowledge of the systematic rules of TL would naturally lead to the acquisition of TL.

It would lead to obtaining of the linguistic competence, but not to the acquisition of the basic levels of the linguistic intuition, physical capacity, and linguistic resources for the meaningful performance of the incoming and outgoing flows of the oral language. Further, they seem not to recognize the serious problems caused by the traditional FLE methods for the students who later try to acquire the oral language skills in TL. I will handle this issue later.

As I have noted repeatedly, I believe it has been proven by the history of FLE that the traditional FLE methods with the main focus on teaching the students to learn the linguistic competence without having to acquire the speaking skills have failed to produce solid bilingual speakers.

I believe that the traditional FLE methods in Korea have produced many students with the linguistic competence in TL. For example, through very intensive English education in Korea, hundreds of thousands of students obtain near-native-speaker level knowledge of the English language by the time of graduating their high schools. Most of them can read and understand English very well.

By the time of graduating colleges, numerous students can listen and understand English very well on top of the high level of knowledge of English as well as very good skills in reading and writing English. Yet, no students have picked up the oral English from the public school's English programs to the degree of solid bilingual speaker.

One may say that the traditional FLE methods in Korea have been successful as the students have obtained English competence in the grammar, reading, writing and listening skills. However, I cannot agree with such an argument because I strongly believe that language acquisition should be accompanied with the acquisition of the fluent oral skills in the language.

In conclusion, for the purpose of improving the traditional FLE methods, the concept of language acquisition should be understood in terms of acquiring the basic levels of linguistic intuition, physical capacity and linguistic resources for meaningful performance of the incoming and outgoing flows of the oral language. Yet, such language acquisition would not be achieved without the sufficient amount of accumulated linguistic resources individually acquired to the fluent level.

3

Language Acquisition vs. Oral Proficiency

All FLE programs pledge to bring foreign languages to the acquisition by the students. All FL teachers internally as well as externally proclaim to develop syllabi and curricula for students to speak TL fluently. Yet, what most of the schools have offered, and what most of the FL teachers have done actually in the class so far have not made such pledges and proclaims realistic. I have identified many reasons for such failure in earlier articles. If I add one more reason for that, it would be because of the misleading and misunderstanding of the concept of language acquisition.

As I pointed out in the previous article, the traditional concept of language acquisition has failed to identify the definition properly in relation to one's real language skills.[21] Also, the general concept of language acquisition is such vague that it does not define individual language skill levels properly either. They either misidentify or do not clearly indicate what are required to acquire a language. Therefore, it causes confusions and misleading for FL teachers in

---

[21] I use real language skills as a reference to the realistic language skills for students to effectively communicate in his/her real environment.

adjusting and rearranging the teaching methods to help students to acquire TL.

Therefore, for the purpose of FLE, I defined the language acquisition in the previous article as the acquisition of the basic levels of linguistic intuition, physical capacity, and linguistic resources for the meaningful performance of the incoming and outgoing flows of the oral language. The key ideas in this definition are those of the 'acquisition of the basic intuitive physical capacity', 'meaningful process', and 'the oral language'.

The word 'intuitive' is used here as opposed to the concept of 'knowledge based'; the term 'meaningful' is used as opposed to the idea of 'unacceptable', but not necessarily of 'ungrammatical'; and the phrase 'physical capacity' is used as opposed to the meaning of 'mental skills'. Then, the key expression of 'oral language' is used as opposed to the concept of 'written language'.

Also, the idea of 'linguistic resources' means the accumulated sets of various expressions which can be used with high proficiency anytime. These key ideas clearly indicate what needs to be done for students to acquire a language. We can find such kind of basic intuitive physical capacity on oral languages from the children of about 36-40 months old who are raised in natural MT environment. Such kind of basic intuitive physical capacity can be achieved by intensive Babble Training as can be seen in children. In other words, it does not require any particular knowledge or reading/writing skills of TL to acquire the TL.

Then, let me introduce the concept of the oral proficiency. It seems that no particular definition was given to the concept of oral proficiency. Therefore, I would define the oral proficiency as one's capacity to make fluent performance of the incoming and outgoing flows of the oral language. To develop such oral proficiency, one should acquire the advanced levels of linguistic intuition, physical capacity, and linguistic resources.

The concepts of language acquisition and that of developing oral proficiency are almost identical except for a couple of words: 'the advanced levels' vs. 'the basic levels'. Based on the two concepts, it is clearly shown that there is a sequential relationship between the two. That is, language acquisition should take place first before the development of oral proficiency.

However, it does not necessarily mean that one can achieve the oral proficiency by simply continuing the same methods to acquire TL. The basic level skills can be acquired most effectively by imitating after the role model, which is what Babble Training is for, but the advanced level skills require creative efforts of one's own, which is what the performance training is for.

The reason I introduced these two separate but closely related-to-each-other terms is because I believe that achieving language acquisition and developing oral proficiency are two closely related but different concepts. Accordingly, the methods of teaching FL for achieving TL acquisition and for achieving oral proficiency should be developed appropriately.

In order words, intensive FL teaching with foci on achieving TL acquisition through out the program would not be efficient for students to achieve oral proficiency. On the other hand, intensive FL teaching with foci on achieving oral proficiency from the beginning would not be efficient either for students to achieve TL acquisition.

Based on the two concepts, now it becomes clear that FL teaching should start with the focus on achieving language acquisition, and that, after success with the acquisition, FL teaching should focus on developing oral proficiency step by step.

As a conclusion, the relationship between acquisition and oral proficiency development of FL is of one-way conditional relationship: acquisition serves as the foundation for oral proficiency to be built on. Accordingly, the FL education methods should reflect such relationship properly.

In other words, the training to develop oral proficiency should follow after the successful acquisition of TL by the students. I believe that the most effective way for students to acquire TL is through intensive Babble Training trainings; and that the most effective way to develop oral proficiency is through intensive performance trainings. Without strong foundation of Babble Training, no efforts of performance activities on the surface can be meaningful.

Consequently, teaching for acquisition should be completed first before teaching for oral proficiency starts. As no building can go up without the foundation being successfully completed, no oral proficiency can be accumulated without the acquisition of TL. A child should not be trained for running before walking.

4

Mystery of Language Acquisition

Many linguists and psycholinguists have performed researches on language acquisitions. They have waged many battles over the mystery of how a language is acquired. Many theories have been introduced on this mystery. The theories of nativism, empiricism, reinforcement, imitation, and the role of input have been the main stream studies to explain the mystery phenomena of an infant's acquiring a language. Yet, none of these seem to clearly show the detail process of how the language is acquired.

It is obvious that no human being is born with a language. However, I believe that the mystery of language acquisition can be understood in terms of the inborn human capacity of collecting data, developing intuition based on the recognized information from the data, and performing expected acts creatively. Without this assumption, nothing that we as human beings do seems to be explained. This way, I believe that human beings are born with the capacity to acquire language.

Yet, the actual process of acquiring language cannot happen without inputs of actual and correct linguistic data even though, sometimes, incorrect data can temporarily be approved without reinforcements. Also, it cannot happen without the process of building intuition to perform expected acts. The process of building intuition is made by repeated practices or faked performances based on the linguistic data collected. Through such repeated faked performances on the data, various types of linguistic information of the data are parsed into the intuition building system.

The Genie case explains the importance of the linguistic data and the intuition building process. Genie, whose real name is not revealed to the public and who was mostly locked in her bedroom without being exposed to typical human interactions until she was found by an authority at the age of 13, did not receive sufficient and proper linguistic inputs, and, accordingly, did not have the process to build the linguistic intuition.

As a result, she didn't acquire a language. Even though some researchers attempted to teach her language for a year or so, she was not successful. Many reasons could be speculated for her not being successful to acquire a language, but I believe that she fundamentally did not have sufficient amount of languages spoken to her as input so that she could process them to build linguistic intuition. I could use the piano analogy again to make it easier to understand the process. We surely know that all human beings are born with the capacity to acquire the piano skill. Yet, without being taught how to play a real piano, and without repeated practices of playing the piano, no one can acquire the piano skills.

With respect to the acquisition of native language, every single child shows the exactly same routine of language acquisition. Even though the progresses made by ages show a range of minor differences by individuals, the fundamental processes of the language acquisition by each child are identical. The teaching methods of native languages to the children are also universal worldwide. No parents or teachers in the world start teaching for the skills of grammars, reading, writing, listening, and speaking right away. No parents would give lectures on science subject to the babies. No parents would expose the babies heavily to TVs or movies expecting them to pick up the language. Parents and relatives would simply try to talk to the babies about very realistic and concrete situation, which lead the babies to babble over the expressions.

The only thing babies seem to do until they acquire the mother language is repeated Babble Training or imitations over the expressions which were told to them and they could follow to a degree. Even Babble Training of the babies does not seem to be so much focused or concentrated intentionally. No babies look to suffer from heavy stressful pressures to perform the babbling. Everything looks very relaxed and natural in the acquisition of the language by the babies.

Compared to the amount and intensity of the linguistic expressions from the parents and relatives to the babies, the amount of Babble Training by the babies does not seem to be so much or intensive. It seems that their languages just grow bigger with Babble Training as simply and naturally as their bodies grow bigger with time.

It is quite obvious that children acquire the linguistic intuition, physical capacity, and quite an amount of linguistic resources quite thoroughly through the babble so that they reach to the point where they could command the oral language very fluently to handle their daily matters. They reach to the point through Babble Training where it is only a matter of being able to recognize the letters and meaning of new words for them to read and understand written texts. Again, they reach the point where they could write down the language once they recognize the letters and the corresponding sounds.

For the babies to acquire such linguistic intuition, physical capacity, and linguistic resources to command the oral language quite semi-instinctively and fluently, and to reach to the points where they would get ready to deal with the written language, it only takes about as little as 30 to as much as 48 months at most of quite relaxed and loose Babble Training from the birth. Yet, the actual time for the babies to be able to perform the babble is about 20 months or so.

However, looking into the amount of the expressions which the children babble over for about their first 30 months or so, it is amazing to see the children produce expressions which don't seem to have been introduced to them before. This can be explained only with the assumption that human beings are equipped from the birth with the capacity to perform expected acts creatively based on one's intuition.

To sum up so far, based on the assumption of the inborn human capacity of collecting data, developing intuition based on the recognized information from the data, and performing expected acts creatively, two factors are crucial to acquire language: the input of data; and, the process of building intuition. With the kind of realistic and concrete data that our parents presented on us as inputs, and with the kind of babblings over such kind of linguistic data, we acquired our languages with ease the way as we did in the past. Had the inputs on us been the other way, the way we performed our language first time would have been different also.

As FL teachers, we know many bilingual speakers acquire FL like the same way as the children acquired their mother tongues. We also know that most of our students, after all such cooperative efforts between us and our students, have failed to be solid bilingual speakers through our teachings based on the traditional FLE methods. We have failed to turn our students into solid speakers of our languages, which even infants with very limited learning capacities can fully acquire in 36 to 40 months, after so much focused intensive multi year curriculums.

Looking back into FLE history, we have to confess that the inputs which we have presented to our students have been very unrealistic, non-actual, non-concrete, and many of them are even non-linguistic at all. Also, the ways we have taught our students for the process of building linguistic intuition have been also very unrealistic, non-actual, non-concrete, and many of them are even non-linguistic at all.

We now need to consider very seriously about what linguistic data we will present for our students to learn, and what process we will ask our students to build the linguistic intuition. For effective FLE, we need both correct linguistic data and correct processes. We as FL teachers are liable for these two. If we don't offer correct linguistic data and correct process of acquisition, we are also liable to the students for their time if we would offer incorrect directions for them to acquire our languages.

5

Working Hypothesis on Language Acquisition

What are needed for students to acquire a foreign language?

Would the thorough knowledge of a language make one be fluent speaker of the language? No, it would not. To equip students with a thorough knowledge on a language system, it requires at least a few years of intensive language classes on the system. This is true at least based on most of the contemporary FLE programs on many different languages. However, we know the answer from the history and the results of the Grammar Translation Method FLE. Few people can speak a language fluently out of such knowledge no matter how thorough it may be.

Would one be able to speak a language fluently if one knows the grammar very well, and could read a foreign language? No, one would not. We know this answer from our own experiences, or from the people we know who are excellent in the grammar and reading of a foreign language.

Would one could be fluent speaker of a foreign language, if one could read the foreign language loud with very good pronunciation on top of the grammar knowledge and the reading comprehension skills? No, it would not work. We know it from the real life world we live in.

Then, would the excellent skills of writing in TL make one be fluent speaker of TL? No, it certainly would not.

Could one be fluent speaker of a foreign language if one is equipped with tens of thousand vocabularies of the foreign language? No, surely it would not.

Could one speak a foreign language fluently if one could listen and understand the foreign language very well? No, it would not work either. We know this from the testimonials of so many people who achieved very high level of listening skills of a particular foreign language.

What if a person knows the grammar very well, have tens of thousands of vocabularies, and could read loud, write, and listen and comprehend TL very well? Could this person speak TL fluently? Unfortunately, based on many testimonials of those who achieved very high scores in TOEFL or TOEIC and the observations on numerous people who have such strong various skills, the answer is a clear negation.

Can one be a fluent speaker by taking conversation classes for a year or so where teachers apply Direct Method? Not really. I know many people who went to a Direct Method teaching private English conversation schools for a year or so, but not successful in picking up the language other than very basic communicative skills, which disappear from their memories pretty soon after they quit the school.

Can people acquire a foreign language by being immersed into the language community for a year or so? No. Almost all of the people who came to the USA from Korea to learn English, and whom I met in this country, went back to Korea with not much English language after few years of stay in the USA.

Then, why a language is not conquered after so much dedication of every body's efforts, time, and money? What causes the failure? What makes a success in acquiring and developing the oral proficiency of TL?

To answer the questions, I hypothesize that language acquisition requires babbling[22] over due amount of real input[23] and time[24] to acquire the following three acquisition factors simultaneously: (1) Linguistic intuition, (2) Physical capacity, (3) Linguistic resources.

The three acquisition factors should be concurrently acquired first for one to be able to acquire and command TL fluently. For a person to be a fluent speaker of a language, these acquisition factors of the language should be acquired concurrently. Without one of these three factors, one would not be a fluent speaker of TL.

Accordingly, the relationship among those three factors is rather of multiplication than of addition. Mathematically, it can be put as 'Acquisition(%) = Linguistic intuition (%) x Physical Capacity (%) x Linguistic Resources (%)'. One may speak TL only to the degree of one's acquisition of these three factors.

This is the very crucial concept that we should keep in our minds when teaching our languages to the students. Again, without very harmonious and natural operation of these acquisition factors of TL, one cannot be a fluent bilingual speaker. One can acquire a

---

[22] I use the term 'Babble' or 'Babbling' to mean the learner's repeated acts of mimicking, copying, imitating, or practicing linguistic input with a purpose of acquiring language, especially speaking skills. However, in a broad sense, I also use the term to mean the learner's repeated practice acts of listening, reading and writing after linguistic input with a purpose of acquiring respective skills.

[23] This is a term I use as a reference to the realistic input that learners can acquire and actually use in his/her real life environment. Depending on intended outputs, real input can be specified as real input for talking, reading, listening, and writing respectively. Input which lacks the features required to acquire the intended output is not qualified as an effective real input.

[24] Due amount of real input and time varies depending on individual's linguistic resistance against TL and degree of mental immersion to learn TL. Concrete discussion will be introduced later.

language only so well as the degree of one's acquisition level of these acquisition factors.

I use the term of linguistic intuition in reference to one's intuitive linguistic skills to recognize the sounds, structures of words and sentences, interpretation of meanings, and usage of linguistic resources such as sets of expressions, morphemes, words, idioms, and other useful expressions of TL. It is also one's capacity of intelligence to naturally and instantaneously process the linguistic information coming in and going out.

Such linguistic intuition is, I believe, most effectively developed or acquired through repeated experiences of performing over numerous real input. Intuition is a dynamic stream of semi-instinctive recognition for such process, not a package of static knowledge stored in the brain to be manually retrieved as a reference to coordinate the language pieces. In order to be able to process the incoming and outgoing linguistic information or resources such naturally and instantaneously, one should acquire the intuition on the sound phenomena, word/sentence structures, and the usage of the language.

Any knowledge of system based artificial or manual skills to process the linguistic information are yet to be considered as linguistic intuition based performance. One may acquire this linguistic intuition of TL by being exposed to TL environment through either reading a lot in TL, or listening to TL media for long time. One also may pick up some of the physical capacity as well as the linguistic resources passively as byproducts during the process. Yet, such linguistic intuition of FL with such passive physical capacity and linguistic resources would not make a solid bilingual speaker.

I use the term of physical capacity in reference to the physical capacity of the speech organs to perform speech activities in a fluent manner. The skill to operate the speech organs semi-instinctively in harmony with the linguistic intuition does not come from the great knowledge of how to articulate each of the individual phonemes correctly. It cannot be acquired simply through imaginations based on the information of particular sounds one would get by listening to the sound a lot. Rather, it requires tremendous repeated exercises of the physical speech organ. With knowledge of the phonetics and phonology of TL, one may carry out each sound phonetically correctly for the purpose of demonstration.

However, such knowledge and demonstrative skills alone would not make one speak the language instantaneously from the intuition. Also, one may be able to build such physical capacity by simply focusing on reading media texts loud repeatedly after the sounds of a model without the efforts of developing linguistic intuition based on the recognized information from the texts. That is, one may obtain such physical capacity through intensive training without the process of building the linguistic intuition.

I use the term of linguistic resources in reference to such linguistic elements as various sets of ready-to-use independent expressions, words, idioms, and other useful expressions, which are required for people, in their real life environment, to convey desired messages in both verbal and written forms of a language. Linguistic knowledge of TL such as grammar, phonetics, morphology, syntax, and semantics, is not necessarily part of such resources. Such resources are very important for the students to be able to communicate in TL for survival until they acquire and develop oral proficiency of TL.

Such linguistic resources are also very important in that they serve as the data on which students rely on to collect linguistic information and to develop the linguistic intuition as well as the physical capacity based on the information. If the linguistic resources collected by students or offered by TL teachers would offer only grammatical information, or only meaning interpretation information, the students could do only so much.

Also, if we, as FL teachers, would require the students only to focus on listening comprehension, the students would be limited to building linguistic intuition based on the information obtained from the sounds. Accordingly, the linguistic resources offered to students should include complete sets of information for students to build the intuition and the physical capacity.

Based on the hypotheses, one would be defined as having acquired TL by earning, to the equivalent or higher level of a typical 36-40 month old native speaker, the three acquisition factors concurrently, the comprehensive linguistic intuition, the physical capacity, and the linguistic resources of TL.

Once language acquisition is achieved, the teaching methods and efforts should be adjusted to focus on building up high level oral proficiency by strengthening the comprehensive linguistic intuitions, physical capacity, and especially the linguistic resources of TL.

6

Working Hypotheses on Input and Output

For the sake of my arguments here, I define the concept of 'input' as the individual materials in a narrow meaning, and the categories of the materials in a comprehensive meaning which are introduced to students for FLE purposes. Commonly known input categories which have been used in the public FLE programs are the grammar, reading comprehension, listening comprehension, writing, vocabulary building, and direct speaking of TL. Also, I define 'output' as what students actually acquire as a result of the transition process on the inputs.

Then, what is the significance of talking about the input? How important is it to apply proper types of inputs for different levels of language acquisition processes? To find out answers to such questions, one should think about many important factors required concurrently for achieving successful FLE such as the time spent by the students, the efforts invested by the students, the motivation of the students (so far, the "student factors"), and the program itself (the "program factor"). These are all interdependent from each other so that any one of them failing could result in a total failure. This shows how hard it is to carry out a successful FLE program.

Among the factors, the program factor is the only factor over which students don't have much control, while students have pretty much of the control over the student factors. Accordingly, for the students who can control and afford all the student factors very well, the program factor is the only factor which, as they don't have control over, they would need to rely on for successful learning of TL.

However, as far as I know, through out most of the public FLE programs, very few people have successfully achieved fluent oral proficiency of TL, which is why I believe that the public FLE programs through out the world have failed.

The fact that the FLE programs in public schools have failed to produce fluent speakers from millions of students around the world, of whom at least hundreds of thousands of hard-working students have fully dedicated their time and efforts to the program with a must-do-for-survival motivation through out the programs, tells us that the programs must have something to do with the failing legacy of the FLE programs.

Then, what are wrong with the programs? To figure out an answer to this, let's look at the elements of the program factor. Some of the most common elements of the program factor are the duration, frequency of class meetings, teachers, and the inputs. Among these four elements of the program factor, the duration, frequency of class meetings, and the teachers do not seem to be at least the major trigger for the legacy of failure because the results in terms of oral proficiency have been pretty much the same among the programs which have implemented varieties of such elements.

Consequently, it leads to the conclusion that the input element has been the major trigger of the failure of the FLE programs. So far, various types of inputs have been implemented as the demands for proficiency types have changed over time, and yet the results have not been successful in terms of oral proficiency.

Why is it so? To answer to this question, I propose the working hypotheses on input & output that, in the learning stage of a language, there are certain relationships between the input and the output as follows:

1. There is no mutation between input and output.
2. No input produces no output.
3. There is individual linguistic resistance to be overcome for meaningful transition from input to output.
4. The input the most real, simple, and well understood to the students produces the most effective output.
5. The proficiency level of the outputs depends on the quality, quantity, and the reality of the inputs retained in the student's linguistic resource pool.
6. The input is most effectively retained in the linguistic resource pool by being repeatedly performed on regular basis with the constant and strong level of mental immersion.
7. There is a certain sequence and combination of input categories which is most effective to acquire and develop oral proficiency as an output.

These working hypotheses explain the various phenomena of outputs in FLE. Also, they present ideas of what to offer as an input depending on expected outputs. They also offer clear insights into what have been mistaken by many of the students and teachers regarding what and how to teach or learn.

The 1st hypothesis tells us that the nature of the output cannot be different from that of the input. One should not expect different types of outputs from those of the inputs. For example, if an FLE program heavily focuses on offering Grammar-Translation based classes, students as the output would perform translating TL expressions and pointing out grammatical issues of TL.

Also, if an FLE program would offer Grammar-Translation based classes, and, in sequence, vocabulary oriented classes, the outputs would be the performance of grammar-based translation and of retaining the vocabularies. Countless number of students have shown that they could not demonstrate meaningful oral proficiency by combining the grammar and the vocabularies they acquired. Accordingly, the input should be carefully decided depending on the expected outputs.

The 2nd hypothesis clearly tells us one of the biggest reasons of why students from the traditional public FLE programs have failed to acquire oral proficiency of TL. There have been no proper inputs offered for oral proficiency in most of the traditional public FLE programs. Accordingly, no outputs of oral proficiency have been produced.

This hypothesis also stipulates that input includes intensive and repeated Babble Training for extended time period. Through the intensive Babble Training repeated over time, one can get all those required linguistic intuition, physical capacity, and vocal features of the individual input like pronunciation, intonation, stress or accent, and etc.

Therefore, lack of intensive Babble Training will produce unsuccessful output leading to failure of acquisition.

The 3rd hypothesis shows the relative productivity relationships between input and output depending on one's linguistic resistance. The linguistic resistance is the degree of one's physical and cognitive unfitness to process the input, which deters the production of output. The linguistic resistance is mainly caused by the linguistic distance from one's MT to TL, and by one's age. One's age shows the degree of the firmness of the physical and cognitive adhesiveness to the linguistic features of one's MT.

In addition, the linguistic resistance can be increased by any kinds of individual unfitness to process the input. The linguistic resistance explains why different languages are less or more challenging for students with different MT backgrounds to acquire them compared to other languages. It also explains why children in general can acquire a foreign language relatively faster than adults. Input is to suffer loss during the transitional process to output because of the linguistic resistance.

Accordingly, the higher the score of the linguistic distance is, and the older the student's age is, the more linguistic compensation is required for input to be produced as meaningful output. One of the most common ways to compensate input is repeated trainings of reintroducing the input to the students, for which I use the term 'Babble Training' in this book.

The 4th hypothesis tells us how to decide the priorities of the inputs. This also tells us that FLE programs should be student's necessity oriented. It also points out that inputs should be real and simple as much as possible as well. So, once a decision is made on the category of the inputs based on the 1st hypothesis to meet the specified goals of a program, the class materials can be produced based on the consideration of the students' needs.

The 5th hypothesis indicates how intensive an FLE program should be. Here, I use the term proficiency, and define it as the actual linguistic skills to command appropriate resources from the resource pool to perform linguistic activities.

Here, the quality refers to the actual fluency or the physical capacity of commanding the individual resources. Quantity refers to the amount of inputs retained; and the reality refers to the usefulness of the inputs retained to the individual learner.

Depending on the linguistic activities, the proficiency can be divided into grammar proficiency, reading proficiency, listening proficiency, oral proficiency, and etc.

The 6th hypothesis gives us ideas of how to deliver the inputs to the resource pool. It also tells that simply introducing inputs and going forward would not leave much inputs retained in the pool. In other words, FLE programs should be designed in such a way where students are required to carry out repeated performances regularly over the inputs introduced.

Another important element pointed out in this hypothesis is the mental immersion. This mental immersion is directly related to the motivation or commitment to learn TL. Constant and strong mental immersion or motivation is what grabs and holds tight the inputs in the resource pool. It helps students to stay away from being disturbed by many other things going around.

To acquire and build proficiency, one should first of all retain the inputs in the resource pool, which is the memory area of the brain. Without retaining the inputs in the pool, no proficiency can be built successfully. Then, to improve the levels of proficiency, the quality and quantity of the inputs retained in the resource pool need to be improved as much as possible. Also, the reality of the inputs stored in the resource pool plays very significant roles as impractical resources would not provide many opportunities for the students to experience the actual usage of them.

The quality of retained inputs here refers to the acquisition level of all linguistic skills required to obtain the inputs without loss. For the inputs of colloquial expressions, as an example, one should at least acquire the listening and speaking skills for respective expressions.

Therefore, any retained inputs that cannot be spoken well would not be considered as a full acquisition of the required skills. It should be instead considered as partial acquisition. Retaining inputs with partial acquisition would lower the proficiency level. For the inputs of grammar, on the other hand, the full acquisition would only require to retain thorough understanding of the grammar. This way, the grammar proficiency level can be built very high.

The 7th hypothesis denotes that the categories of the input should be sequenced and combined in such a way to be most effective for students to acquire and develop oral proficiency of TL. Based on what we have seen on the consequences of the traditional FLE methods, one can suppose the sequence and combination of the input categories which have been deployed by the traditional

FLE programs have not been effective. Traditionally, the categories of the inputs for most of the FLE programs have been more likely similar to the following sequence:

Step 1: Grammar
Step 2: Reading added to step 1
Step 3: Writing added to step 2
Step 4: Listening added to step 3

However, most of the traditional public FLE programs have not had enough time to go beyond the step 2 as it took so many years to do only steps 1 and 2. Consequently, most of the programs did not offer the inputs for writing and listening much less for oral proficiency.

Some other programs have offered very minimal inputs for oral proficiency from the outset of the program. However, as the weight for oral proficiency was so minimal, while the weight for other types of inputs such as grammar and reading were heavily prevailing, no sufficient amount of the student factors was invested for oral proficiency, leaving minimal amount of fully acquired colloquial expressions retained.

Consequently, with an empty resource pool for colloquial expressions, no outputs of colloquial performance can be expected from the students.

From informal observations on many people who have acquired the oral proficiency of foreign languages, and also from the observations on the process of natural language acquisition, I have found grounds to build a certain sequence of combining the input categories to produce outputs for oral proficiency very effectively, which is the foundation of Babble Training Method (BTM).

The following figure represents the key concepts of the hypotheses on the input and output relationships. The linguistic resource pool represents the storage space in the brain where the inputs are to be retained and processed for the learner to build the intuition and the linguistic resources required to acquire and develop the proficiency of TL.

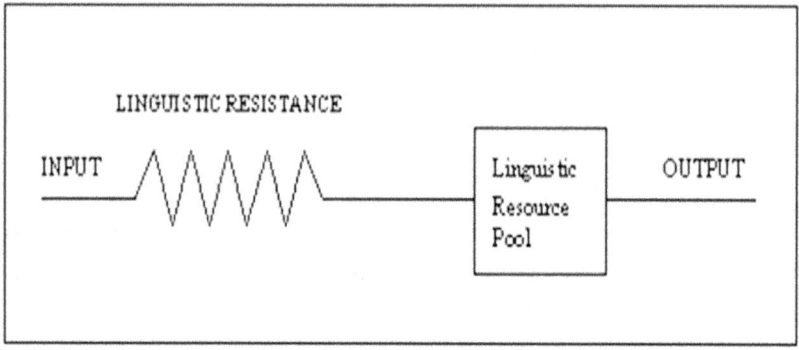

7

An Idea to Evaluate Oral Proficiency - LCST

Earlier, I quoted the general language skill level acquired by 36-40 month old children as the criteria to judge the acquisition of TL. Whoever has acquired TL to such language skill level of 36-40 month old child can be considered as to have successfully acquired TL. With that much acquisition of TL, any students would not suffer from not being able to make communications on daily life activities. Even though a student has acquired such a level of TL skills on the daily life activities, he or she would still need to develop the oral proficiency of TL to perform fluent communications in TL on somewhat more sophisticated subject matters like the social and business life activities.

In other words, even though the acquisition of the language skills of TL and the development of the oral proficiency of TL are mutually related to each other in a sequential relationship, they belong to different process of TL acquisition and should be clearly distinguished without confusion.

Then, how can we verify whether students have acquired TL or not? How can we compare the amount of linguistic resources acquired by 36-40 month old kids with that acquired by the students? If the kids can understand about 1,700 vocabularies and command about 300 expressions, how can we find whether our students have reached to the same level of TL acquisition?

Even though we may be able to find a lot of concrete data from various books and papers on the language skill level of the 36-40 month old kids, it would not be easy to use such data to judge the students' acquisition level of TL. If so, what would be the method for us, FL educators, to rely on to relatively easily find whether the students have acquired TL or not?

To develop a method to measure students' acquisition of TL, we need to stay aside for a moment from the idea of relying on the number of vocabularies and expressions acquired by the kids, and to pay more careful attention to the linguistic phenomena which are shown by the kids of 36-40 months old.

One of the phenomena which are shown by the kids who have acquired language is the act of copying languages. That is, they would mimic or quote languages spoken by others as part of instant communication. Such language copying can be frequently found during the playful exchanges of languages with kids. Or, kids sometimes copy the languages between their dads and moms.

This type of copying is different from babbling. Kids would copy languages sometimes to enjoy showing their language skills. When copying languages, kids mostly copy languages in contextually correct manner. Kids sometimes would copy a whole expression as is, and, some other times, parts of expressions to fit into contextually correct manner.

The act of copying languages normally cannot be done without the supports of the three acquisition factors. If the linguistic intuition acquired is not strong enough, it would be very difficult for one to copy or restructure, without having to memorize, the expressions said by others instantaneously to fit into given context.

Even if one might have acquired the linguistic intuition, it would still be quite difficult for him or her to articulate the expressions so fluently if the physical capacity to articulate TL had not been acquired. Yet, it can be possible that students can copy languages in poor manner, depending on the difficulty levels, without having to acquire very strong physical capacity.

However, it would simply show the levels of the speaker's immature acquisition status of the required physical capacity. Further, kids seem not to copy languages which they don't understand. When one would copy languages without understanding the meaning, the copied languages can easily be found to be out of the context.

Consequently, based on the observations on how kids copy languages, and based on the logical relations between the acts of copying languages and the acquisition status of the three acquisition factors, we can utilize the skills of language copying as a way to measure the students' acquisition levels of TL.

Then, how can we test students for language copying skills? First of all, the language copying skill test ("LCST") would better be utilized as a part of the various regular evaluation methods in the general curriculum. The concrete methods to utilize the language copying skills may vary depending on various unique situations given.

However, in general situations, students can be tested in the following manner:

1. Present some daily life related TL expressions in regular speed to the students via audio equipments or in person through one to one interaction. The forms of TL expression should be such that the student would need to modify parts of the expressions to come up with contextually correct forms. For example, yesterday the *teacher didn't teach* because the *teacher* could not come to school for cold.
2. Request the student to explain the meaning in the source language.

3. Request the student to restate the TL expressions for his own meaning: Request the student to modify or manipulate parts of the expressions to make his or her own story.
4. Depending on the student's age, school level, and the difficulties of TL expressions, the number and forms of TL expressions to be copied by the student may vary.

The idea of asking the student to explain the meaning first is to interrupt the possible unconscious process of memorizing the expressions, and, therefore, to check the work of linguistic intuition on TL. Also, it is obvious that we can verify, by asking the student to explain the meaning, whether the student has acquired the necessary level of the linguistic resources of TL.

If the student has not acquired strong level of the linguistic intuition of TL, it would be very unlikely that the student could come up with contextually correct forms of TL. If the student's physical capacity is not strong enough, we would be able to find that the student would show poor articulation in copying TL expressions. Also, if the student has not acquired sufficient linguistic resources of TL, the student will show the problem in explaining the meanings.

8

An Idea to Evaluate Oral Proficiency - OMT

Another idea for evaluating students' TL acquisition or oral proficiency level is the oral matching test ("OMT") method on a number of colloquial expressions both in and out of context.

This idea also can be used as for evaluating students' performance as part of the regular evaluation tools during the semester. Even though this idea can be useful to all levels of students, from the beginning level to the advanced levels, it is especially effective to the beginning and intermediate level of students who are still in need of accumulating a lot of useful and real TL expressions to build an underlying linguistic capacity to deal with TL very smoothly. Also, the OMT can be utilized as a good tool to screen applicants based on their oral proficiency of TL.

Basically, the idea of OMT here is to present a number of expressions in source language and have the students perform the matching expressions in TL. As a way of general comprehensive evaluation for students' acquisition or oral proficiency level of TL, an evaluator can produce a written list of whatever number of colloquial expressions, for example 100 assorted expressions among the various levels of expressions such as beginning 1, beginning 2, intermediate

1, intermediate 2, advanced 1, and advanced 2 levels according to the expected levels of acquisition or oral proficiency. Then, students should be asked to say the matching expressions in TL.

Also, OMT can be utilized as a method of regular evaluation of students' TL performance. Through BTM, students typically are introduced to and asked to acquire various colloquial expressions through different sets of useful and real dialogues.

This way, students can pick up the sets of expressions as a whole quite effectively. However, it does not necessarily mean that they can detach and utilize each individual expression in a real life situation independently from the sample contexts where the expressions are introduced.

To evaluate how well a student has acquired, and can detach and utilize the individual expressions, regular based OMTs through out the semester can help a lot. For this, FL teacher can produce a list of a number of assorted expressions, in source language, from all the expressions introduced to the class to the point of test, and have students speak the matching expressions in TL.

This way, students are expected to maintain all the expressions introduced from the class fluently through out the semester or school year. Students who acquired the individual expressions better will perform better in OMT.

The underlying idea of the OMT is a working hypothesis that it indicates the acquisition or oral proficiency levels of TL by each student: More number of expressions will be matched fluently by students with higher level of the TL acquisition or oral proficiency. Also, the lower level of the TL acquisition or oral proficiency a student has, the lower level of expressions will be matched, and the fluency is expected to be poorer.

Unlike LCST and other types of oral performance evaluations, OMT has its merits in that it is relatively simple and convenient to be done for multiple students at a time. In other words, it can be done without in-person interviews with the students if necessary.

Also, it can be done without providing oral expressions to the students. Evaluators can simply produce and provide the OMT list to the students, and students can record their answers to be evaluated later by the evaluator. For the sake of convenience for grading afterwards, students should be asked to record their voice for respective questions (or at least the respective question ID numbers) and answers together.

For general comprehensive evaluation purposes, depending on the levels of students, such criteria as meaningful completion, appropriate vocabularies, articulation, vocabulary conjugations, manner of presentation, and time restriction should be considered with prorated performance scores assigned depending on the practicality based weights of respective criteria.

For time restriction of a general OMT with all levels of assorted expressions, an average of 10 to 12 seconds per question seems to be reasonable. For example, if the total number of OMT expressions are 100, 17 to 20 minutes would be reasonable. In case a student would skip or could not finish any number of expressions due to time restriction, those expressions would be counted for zero points in all categories of the criteria. For example, one can assign various fixed points per expression as follows:

10 points on MC (Meaningful Completion)
7 points on AV (Appropriate Vocabularies)
6 points on FA (Fluent Articulation)
4 points on VC (Vocabulary Conjugation)
3 points on MP (Manner of Presentation)
30 total points per expression

For convenience sake, each of the criteria above can be evaluated based on a 10 point system which can later be converted into the respective points. Also, prorated unit scores can be assigned for different levels of difficulties of each expression. For example, one can assign various fixed points for each level expression as follows:

4   points per B1 (Beginning 1) with under 5 words
6   points per B2 (Beginning 2) with 5 to 8 words
8   points per I1 (Intermediate 1) with 9 to 12 words
10 points per I2 (Intermediate 2) with 13 to 16 words
12 points per A1 (Advanced 1) with 17 to 20 words
14 points per A2 (Advanced 2) with 21 to 24 words
Total score: 54 points (for 6 expressions, one from each level)

The following OMT score table shows the ideas of prorated scores for respective criteria and the difficulties of each expression:

Levels of Expressions (Unit Scores)	Performance Scores					Total Score (30)	Net Unit Score
	MC (10)	AV (7)	FA (6)	VC (4)	MP (3)		
Beginning 1 (4)							
Beginning 2 (6)							
Intermediate 1 (8)							
Intermediate 2 (10)							
Advanced 1 (12)							
Advanced 2 (14)							

OMT Score Table

In the OMT score table above, the numbers in parentheses show the maximum points of respective categories. According to the score table above, the maximum total performance score per each expression is 30 points. That is, a student can earn 30 points by performing an expression with no unacceptable mistake. Then, the total score of each expression gets converted into a net unit score.

For example, if a student receives 30 points total on an Advanced 1 level expression, the students would get 12 net unit points. However, if the student would earn 15 points total instead on the same expression, he/she would get 6 net unit points, which is obviously a failing score. Then, let's say we have 60 questions total, 10 questions from each level. Then, the total maximum possible net unit score is 540.

Now let's see how we can utilize the OMT table above to judge a student's oral proficiency of TL. The simplest way to utilize the table is to use the total of the net unit scores for all levels. Based on the total score, it would be easy to screen the students from the highest score to the lowest score.

However, it does not show an analysis of each student's language skills on TL. Therefore, to analyze a students' performance on each level, one can look at the sum of the net unit scores of each level, and apply 'high', 'mid', and 'low' grading, based on the percentage achieved, for over 90%, 80%, and 70% respectively. Here, 'high' means very fluent oral proficiency, 'mid' means mediocre fluency, and 'low' means poor but able fluency of TL.

As an example, let's assume that Student A received the following scores shown in the table from an OMT with assorted expressions of all levels:

Levels (Total Points)	Performance Scores					Total Score (30)	Level Score Total	Percen- tage (%)
	MC (10)	AV (7)	FA (6)	VC (4)	MP (3)			
B 1 (40)	9.0	7.0	5.4	3.6	2.7	27.7	36.9	92.3%
B 2 (60)	9.0	6.3	5.4	3.6	2.7	27	54	90%
I 1 (80)	8.0	5.6	4.8	3.2	2.4	24	64	80%
I 2 (100)	6.3	4.9	4.2	2.8	2.1	21	70	70%
A 1 (120)	3.0	2.1	1.8	1.2	0.9	9	36	30%
A 2 (140)	0	0	0	0	0	0	0	0%

OMT Summary Table (Total Number of Expressions: 60)

According to the OMT Summary Table above, Student A's oral proficiencies on given TL by each level are: Beginning 1 (high), Beginning 2 (high, Intermediate 1 (mid), and Intermediate 2 (low) respectively. The student has not gained any oral proficiency of the advanced level yet.

9

FL to Adults vs. MT to Children

It is a simple and unquestionable fact that children acquire their mother tongues regardless of the language types in about 30 to 40 months from birth. About 36-40 months after birth, children seem to be very active and creative in communicating with other people. They would surprise the parents with new expressions which parents would not expect the baby to be able to say.

By 36-40 months from birth, the children seem to have acquired the language to a level where they have quite strong linguistic intuition enough to produce various types of expressions with regular pattern forms. They semi-instinctively create regular forms for those expressions which have irregular forms. For example, some children would say "car goed by" instead of "a car went by". Also, they seem to have acquired the physical capacity to carry out the communication with no problem. The operation of their speech organs seem to be quite native like except for some particularly difficult words for them to articulate.

By 36-40 months after birth, I believe that children's linguistic intuition and physical capacity are quite fully developed that their language skills are only limited to their linguistic resources. Speaking of the linguistic resources, they probably have around 300-400 vocabularies which they use in their actual speech activities. Even if they would have 500-600 vocabularies, it is not really a lot. With such intuition, physical capacity, and with the vocabularies, they become very fluent in commanding the language.

Considering that babies really don't start active Babble Training until 10-15 months due to their immature physical conditions, it comes down to less than 30 months for babies to acquire the language to so much fluent level. Then, how much actually would it take for the babies to acquire the language like that? Let's look at the milieus for the babies to pick up the language in detail.

Categories	Description
General span of time to acquisition	About 36-40 months after birth; considering the fact that they don't start babbling until 10-12 months after birth, it actually takes about less than 30 months.
Actual daily hours of babbling	To adults' stand point, children do not do the babble intensively. They do it intermittently. They do it more as they grow but not so much during earlier months. Over all, in average, they may not spend more than 3 hours total a day for active babbling.
Activities	Mostly listening to input sources and babbling. Not much two way verbal interactions with the care provider until quite late. No reading, no grammar, no writing, and no media listening. Most of a day is spent on sleeping in early stage.

Input sources	Care providers: mostly parents and baby sitters. No medias like TV, audio equipments, or movies are really used for language acquisition purposes.
Physical conditions	Very limited compared to adults. Their brain is yet to be fully developed, and their physical movements are not fully operative. The sense of understanding and judgment is yet to be developed.
Linguistic intuition	Born with the capacity of collecting data, developing intuition based on the recognized information from the data, and performing expected acts creatively. Zero linguistic intuition to begin with; and later acquires the intuition strong enough to be productive and creative with the regular pattern language after 36-40 month of birth.
Physical capacity	Zero to begin with; quite limited through out most of Babble Training stage.
Linguistic resources	Zero to begin with; and, by 36-40 months after birth, about 300-400 daily life need based and kinship related terms.

Then, can adults[25] acquire FL in about 30 months by doing Babble Training to the same level as the 36-40 month old kids acquire the mother tongue? Sure, they can. Actually, they can do a lot better than what 36-40 month old kids can do. Depending on individual efforts and time spent on the babble, I see it very possible that adults can acquire FL in 30 months through intensive Babble Training to the level of elementary school students.

Compared to the language acquisition milieus of the kids for the mother tongue, those of the adults for FL do not seem to be so much unfavorable especially with the help of the technologies. Rather, it seems to be much more favorable to adults learning FL than to the kids learning MT. Most of all, adults have fully developed brain and speech organs. They can understand, learn, and proceed the babble process a lot more and faster as well as more effective than the young children can do. Adults can actively focus and exert hard efforts to achieve goals while young children seem to be less active to carry out Babble Training to the adult's stand point. On top of that, adults can utilize the letters to help with memory, and to represent the sounds.

Not only that, but adults also can utilize the technologies to be tireless input sources at any time and anywhere one wishes to have it. They can carry the input sources with them always, and do babble after the sources as much as they can physically afford.

The most unfavorable factor for adults to learn FL may be the fact that they have acquired a native language for so many years. In other words, their linguistic operations have been totally preoccupied with the linguistic features of their languages so that the features would interfere with the process of acquiring another language.

---

[25] I use the term 'adult' here to mean relatively young adults of school ages like from middle schools to college, or graduate schools.

One of the most typical problems the adults suffer from when learning and speaking FL is the difficulties with pronouncing FL. That is, the strong linguistic features of one's mother tongue would show up as an accent when speaking TL. Strong accents are particularly vivid with the adults who did not do Babble Training a lot. As one starts learning FL older, the accent tends to get stronger. The stronger one's accent is the more difficult it is to learn and speak FL.

Therefore, they need to overcome the subconscious interference of such features with one's performance of FL, which, if one would try intentionally by applying the knowledge of systematic process, is not easy to do. To overcome such barriers coming from one's native language, especially the accents, one should focus on simple and physical Babble Training much more rather than on the rules and the system of TL.

10

How Languages Are Lost

Some years ago, I read an article about an old Korean person about 60 years of age who was found to have lost the Korean language completely after 15 years of life in a foreign country prison. It is said that the person spoke Korean fluently just like other native Korean speakers of his age before he was imprisoned. I was very surprised to find the fact that a native language for over 40 years of time could be lost just like that.

I also have a friend who told me in a recent meeting that her brother seems to have lost the Korean language almost completely in 13 years of life in the USA. Her brother came to the USA when he was 13 years old. According to her, he really forced himself to lose Korean by not using Korean to learn English more effectively. He went to schools where nobody spoke Korean. He made friends with only English speaking people. He works at an English only speaking company.

On the other hand, I know several people around me who once seemed to have lost Korean quite completely and regained it in a very surprising short time period. They picked up Korean as a mother tongue from home and used it until around the graduate time of elementary schools or so, and then lost it for over 10 years by not using the language before they regained it. They said to me that it took about one to two years for them to regain the language to very fluent level by getting along with Korean people due to marriage life or work. Their Korean sounds so fluent with no accent that it is not easy to imagine that they once lost the language for such a long time. It is just like a little bit rusted machine working fine after a while of being oiled and adjusted.

Based on my observation of these people around me, I came to believe that people lose the linguistic resources first and the linguistic intuition and physical capacity remain for long time. In other words, people lose the vocabularies and the expressions of a language rather quickly compared to the intuition and the physical capacity. I don't know how long the intuition and physical capacity remains, but it seems that they could at least remain over 10 years in such a status as to be reactivated quite easily by being recharged with the linguistic resources.

Accordingly, when one is said to have lost one's own mother tongue which one had fully acquired and used at least for 10 years prior to losing it, chances are, in most cases, that one has lost the vocabularies and the sets of expressions from one's memory; and that the linguistic intuitions and the physical capacities are still quite available.

Among the acquisition factors for one to be fluent speaker of a language, the linguistic intuition, and the physical capacity share a common feature, which is that they both are of instinct. While, the linguistic resources, the remaining factor, is different from the other three in that it is of memory. This shows that the semi-instinct lasts much longer than the memory or knowledge.

Anyway, all the examples by the people around me show that language without maintenance is to be lost. Especially, the memory or knowledge factor of a language gets lost much more quickly than the other two factors.

Then, how the students lose the languages we taught them so quickly and completely? Then, how they don't seem to regain the language so easily?

I know many people who learned foreign language for many years and have lost the language completely. One of my social friend said to me that he learned French for 7 years in the USA. He said he started studying French at school when he was 7th grade, and continued to the 2nd year in a college. The first five years of the classes were mostly of the Grammar Translation Method, and the 2 years in the college was of going to a lab to listen to French and do the pattern based drills, which is the method of Technological Approaches. He said that ever since the college he does not really remember anything about the language, and yet could read it, but could not understand it.

He is not the only one who has lost completely what he learned from school language classes. As a matter of fact, most of the students who learned FL from us, FL teachers, for many years have the same issue. It is not surprising result at all. What makes me sad is the trend that every body accepts it as natural and granted. Surprisingly enough, nobody has raised complaints about such results of FL teachers' job performance.

Now, let's admit that whatever we teach for memory would disappear rather quickly. Based on my experience as FL student, most of them disappeared upon the finish of the quizzes. I would have to prepare again from the scratch for monthly, midterm, and final exams respectively.

So far, we have not taught enough for the students to acquire the linguistic intuition, physical capacity, and the linguistic resources on our languages. Rather, we have used all different methods to cram the information on the rules and systems of our languages into the brains of our students, which do not take long time to be lost.

From the beginning, students have not been trained to acquire any semi-instinctive factors like linguistic intuition or physical capacity. So, it is very natural that students have learned nothing to remain for long time.

CHAPTER 7

BTM – Only FLE Method
To Succeed

Who do not babble will not acquire it.

1

Direct Method vs. BTM

Among FLE methods introduced so far, the direct method is unique from other methods in that it focuses on direct verbal interactions between the teacher and students in FL by conducting all instruction in TL with no recourse to translation. Other than reading and writing are taught from the beginning, this method seems to have been an FLE process most similar to the natural process of language acquisition. Based on what the concept of the method implies, one would think that it should work and it would work. In a sense that the direct method puts the weight on oral language education, it apparently seems to have quite similarities with BTM, which puts focus on the training process to acquire language skills. So, it would be helpful to clearly understand the differences of the two.

One of the best examples of applying the direct method in contemporary FLE education, I believe, is the ESL programs in many English speaking countries. In the USA, most of the state level universities run ESL programs; and many high schools and middle schools also have ESL programs for foreign students. Very few places offer ESL programs for elementary school students. The ESL programs offer English only speaking classes for grammar, reading, writing, speaking and listening. The college ESL programs also offer English grammar classes with quite weights on it. Most of the ESL programs offer 4-5 hours of English education a day for five days a week.

It is not easy to tell how much the ESL programs with direct method are successful due to various circumstances and results. For example, based on my observations on students around me from foreign countries, foreign students in elementary schools with no ESL programs seem to pick up English at least as well as, if not better, the foreign students in middle schools or high schools with ESL programs. While, the students in the college ESL programs, who seem to study a lot more at school and do a lot more homework at home compared to the non-college ESL students, obviously do not seem to pick up the oral English as good as the younger students in the schools with or without an ESL program. It seems to be a paradox.

There is a theory called puberty theory which claims that foreign language education after the puberty age would not lead the student to a native level speaker. So, some people would try to explain the above paradox case with the theory. Here, I would try to explain it in a different aspect: In the aspect of the babble.

My key to the paradox is the amount of the babble: based on the same condition, whoever does more Babble Training picks up better speaking skills. In the same token, whoever does more training to read picks up better reading skills; and whoever does more training to write picks up better writing skills. Further, whoever does the training to listen only would pick up the listening comprehension skills only. Regardless of the types of FLE methods being applied, no speaking skills will be picked up without sufficient amount of voluntary Babble Training by the student.

Looking into the daily lives of the foreign students, generally the students in elementary school with no ESL program seem to be most active in getting along with others. As students go higher in the school, both of the students, foreign and resident, seem to be more focused on their personal lives as the schools require more homework, and they get more busy with their own personal life styles. Also, older students seem to be more sensitive and not to like getting along with foreign students who do not speak the language. Therefore, foreign students in elementary schools confront situations where they would have to say something so much more frequently every day than the students in, for example, a college ESL program, where every body, except the teacher, in the class are non-English speakers.

Accordingly, the students in elementary school get to babble the same expressions, which they collected by observing the peers acting in various situations, many times a day repeatedly. In the beginning, they are not really talking by doing so. Rather, I would say, they are simply Babble Training what they know and observe the responses from the peers to adjust their Babble Training performance.

Meanwhile, the students in a college ESL program do not confront such situations so frequently every day as every body except the teacher are not English speakers. So, they don't get opportunities to speak English so often at school. Chances are that they would have people in the program who are from the same country as they are and speak the same language, which would not be helpful a lot for them to pick up the English language. There are other elements that I think cause many problems with the students in the college ESL programs trying to pick up oral languages. Based on these issues, it is no wonder that, as a result, one to two years of college ESL programs, where Direct Method is applied, are not so much productive as one had expected before leaving one's country to learn English.

Then, should we apply the direct method to beginning FL classes? I don't think it is a good idea because it would not be effective enough for students to acquire the acquisition factors: Linguistic intuition, physical capacity, and linguistic resources. Direct method is not the most effective method especially for the students who have not acquired the acquisition factors yet.

First of all, it would not be so much practical to give instructions in FL only to the adult students who are not ready yet to process TL. Giving instructions in TL only to the beginners would be just like putting the beginners of soccer directly into the games from the very beginning to teach them the soccer, asking them to figure out on their own how to play in the game. It would make the class so much more difficult and dry that students would lose interests in FL quickly.

Secondly, as it requires FL teacher and the students to get together, the students cannot study FL without FL teacher. This raises a most serious issue regarding the feasibility of the direct method for the public as well as private FLE. To secure FL teachers who could lead FL classes in TL only is very unrealistic not only for most of the schools in the world but also for the individuals who wish to teach FL to themselves.

Thirdly, the in-class direct method cannot offer the students to practice speaking the language enough. Simply leading the directions in FL only would not be sufficient enough for the students to acquire the physical capacity required to perform the communication in FL. Intermittent simple verbal interaction opportunities to a students would not develop the physical capacity to carry out fluent communication in FL. Also, such intermittent interaction with the teacher would not be enough for students to acquire the linguistic intuitions of TL.

Forth, even if Direct Method offers the opportunities for students to access TL in a live mode, one thing that should not be ignored is what is being taught through Direct Method. If the Direct Method classes would offer grammar based teaching just as most of the current Direct Method based ESL classes in many English speaking countries do, it cannot be considered as being effective so much because it would not produce fluent speakers of TL as it has been proven by millions of people in the world. The same goes for any reading based classes offered through the method. In other words, no matter how good the method may be, it could not be an effective method without focusing on the training to talk from the beginning.

Then, is the direct method useless? No, it is not. It has its own valuable worth. However, what I am trying to say is that applying the direct method to the beginners of FL is just like teaching how to sprint to the crawling baby students who yet don't know how to walk by demonstrating sprints to them.

Over all, the direct method is in the same category of being not effective to the beginners of FL as the other FLE methods. The biggest one common reason of all FLE methods for having failed to produce fluent speakers of FL is the fact that they all do not focus on the training process to acquire the acquisition factors for language acquisition. This is where a clear difference between the direct method and BTM stands out. In other words, the direct method puts emphasis on providing FL classes in TL only environment. On the other hand, BTM puts its emphasis on providing the students with strong and sufficient training process to acquire language skills first, and then to achieve high level oral proficiency.

With respect to the variety of FLE methods, someone has said that no one FLE method can be perfect; and effective FLE program depends on successful coordination of the various FLE methods. However, I would like to revise that statement as follows: No one FLE method may be perfect, but no combination of FLE methods without a method emphasizing Babble Training to talk, preferably in the very beginning stage, can be successful.

There is only one proven way through which all human beings of the world history acquired the language. That is the babble. No normal human beings have failed to acquire the language by simple babbling. I strongly believe that developing and applying an effective Babble Training method will bring effective FLE program.

2

Sentence Memorization vs. BTM

Many people argue that sentence memorization ("SM") is very helpful in learning FL. Yet, no concrete means of the SM method have been introduced or known to people. One can only guess the means of the method simply based on its self explanatory concept. No systematic teaching on sentence memorizing seems to have been carried yet as far as I know. Therefore, it is very difficult to find people who have actually consistently carried out the method.

Many FL teachers I know have expressed negative comments on the SM method. Even though, I do not support the SM method per se either with clear reasons, I still see many merits of SM method over the traditional FLE methods because I see the method can be quite useful depending on how one carries out the method.

Then, what is the difference between BTM and the SM method. For the sake of a clear comparison, let me review the concept of the babble. I earlier defined the concept of babble as the training process to acquire language skills. Among the language skills are speaking, listening, reading, and writing.

To acquire such language skills with proficiency requires the three acquisition factors of the linguistic intuition, the physical capacity, and the linguistic resources. As a most effective education method for students to acquire such acquisition factors, I have developed a systematic Babble Training procedure which includes serial trainings for reading, listening, writing, and free talking.

Meanwhile, no particular definition of the concept of sentence memorization is known. Accordingly, for the comparison purposes, we will take the common sense definition implied by the terms of sentence memorization: memorizing TL sentences. SM presumes that memorizing TL sentences will allow students to speak TL.

First of all, based on the respective concepts shown above, one can easily find the outstanding difference between the two methods in that the SM, unlike BTM, only focuses on memorizing TL sentences which are selected by no systematic principle, and does not contain concrete process for the acquisition of such skills as speaking, reading, listening, writing, and the development of oral proficiency skills.

Ultimately, the main focus of the SM is for students to acquire the basic level speaking skills of TL instead of acquiring all of the language skills. In other words, the SM is considered to be no more than a fragmental method to learn limited language skills of TL, which happens to be the basic level of speaking. Especially, just like all of the other FLE methods specialized on particular areas of the language skills, the SM method does not contain the systematic teaching process and methods on such various areas of language skills as the basic level speaking, listening, reading, writing, and advanced level of oral proficiency.

As a result, the SM method does not present a solution for the dilemma of the traditional and contemporary FLE situation in disorder. In other words, the SM does not have an answer to the questions of what, when, how, and how much to teach first and to follow up among the areas of grammar, speaking, reading, listening, writing, and advanced levels.

Meanwhile, BTM focuses not only on teaching for students to acquire all of the language skills in a very systematic manner but also to develop oral proficiency. Therefore, the SM cannot be matched to BTM in terms of the ultimate language skill areas and levels pursued by each method. Even though the SM cannot be matched to BTM, the fact that the SM basically focuses on acquiring the speaking skill of TL by students, it is worthy to compare the SM with Babble Training of BTM.

Over all, the difference between the SM method and Babble Training can be summarized in short as the difference between memorization and acquisition respectively. The one simply refers to saving something into the memory, and the other refers to obtaining, developing or acquiring a skill. In other words, the purpose of SM is of saving learned sentences of TL into the brain to utilize them later again as necessary.

Meanwhile, the purpose of Babble Training is, on top of acquiring the fluent speaking skill of TL, to establish strong foundation to develop high level of oral proficiency by acquiring the three acquisition factors. In this sense, the SM can be considered as a partial process of gathering linguistic resources, one of the three acquisition factors. That is, the SM in a sense can be regarded as a part of Babble Training to talk.

To find out the relationships between the memorization and Babble Training in terms of language acquisition, one needs to look into the characteristics for each of the three acquisition factors. One can easily find that, by nature, the linguistic intuition and the physical capacity are clearly of semi-instinctive skills.

On the other hand, the linguistic resources such as variety of expressions, idioms, and vocabularies are clearly of knowledge accumulation, which can be characterized as of memorization. In this sense, one can define the relationships between SM and Babble Training as the one being part of the other.

However, for meaningful acquisition of a language, as the acquisition factors cannot be acquired independently of each other, but, therefore, should be considered as one inseparable process, it is really difficult to say that simple memorization is a solid part of Babble

Training process to talk. Especially, as the simply eye reading based memorization without due process to the level of acquisition could result in wrong linguistic intuition and wrong physical capacity on TL, the eye-reading based SM by itself really should not be considered as a legitimate part of the language acquisition process.

On the other hand, the difference and relationships between the two concepts can be easily likened to the metaphor of a baseball pitcher: Memorizing versus acquiring the pitching skills. For the purpose of memorizing the skills, one can study the pitching skills written on a piece of paper like a cooking recipe and memorize them without actually being out to the field, or with little bit of trials out in the field. However, for the purpose of acquiring the pitching skills, one has to spend many months, if not years, out in the field practicing the skills.

The difference of SM and Babble Training also can be compared to the metaphor of playing the piano. One who has acquired all the skills of playing piano music can play various types of piano music very naturally. However, one who completely memorized the piano music still cannot play the music as it is supposed to sound like.

Even though the two methods are clearly different from their concepts as shown above, people may still be confused and consider them to be kind of the same thing. Let's look into the detail aspects of Babble Training and the sentence memorization to see where the differences are coming from.

One thing that is partially common between the two is that students need to store various sets of expressions in one's own linguistic resources database. However, the process of storing the expressions is quite different between the two.

One of the most obvious ways to distinguish the two from each other is in the ways people actually perform each of the methods. That is, one is possible, and the other is not possible to do without having to mobilize the speech organs. One can memorize sentences directly by simply eye reading or by listening to them. However, one cannot do Babble Training without mobilizing the speech organs. Memorizing sentences is basically static information storage process. However, Babble Training is in nature a very dynamic physical training process.

Another way to distinguish the two from each other is in the final destination of the expressions being stored. The final destination for memorized sentences to be stored is in a very deep and remote place of the brain[26]; while, that for the babbled expressions to be stored is on the tip of the tongue[27] which is trained to be synchronized with the brain. During Babble Training, it is very important for students not only to maintain the linguistic resources very well but also to be able to produce those expressions very fluently from the beginning.

One more way to clearly distinguish the two from each other is in the source types of the linguistic resources. The source for the students to do Babble Training over is the native or very fluent speaker's actual demonstrations of the oral language: either by listening directly to the native or very fluent speakers, or to the audio materials produced by native or very fluent speakers of TL. However, the sources for sentence memorization are various including mostly written texts and sometimes the actual sounds. Therefore, the input sources of the SM method generally do not include the accurate information for oral performance.

Further distinction between the two can be done in the sense of the things that are actually stored in the database. Depending on the

---

[26] This is a metaphoric expression to reflect the time taking process for one to retrieve memorized sentences to use in a real situation. It does not necessarily mean a physically deep and remote place.

[27] This is a metaphoric expression. It refers to the instant availability of the stored expressions on the tip of the tongue. It is obvious that nothing can literally be stored on the tip of the tongue. However, as a way of emphasizing the naturally synchronized interactions between the brain and the tongue which takes place through intensive training of Babble Training to talk, I am using a metaphoric expression here.

source types of the sentences, for the SM method, most-likely incorrect understanding/performance of the sounds, and the information on how to figure out the meaning, component, and the usage of the texts are stored. However, for Babble Training to talk, the physical capacity to carry out actual linguistic performance of given expressions are stored in addition to all of the information on the sound, meaning, component, and the usage of the texts.

Many FL teachers doubt the effectiveness of memorizing sentences as a way of studying FL. Many other people also believe that memorizing FL sentences would not help a lot for one to acquire FL. This is because language is not simply to be memorized but to be acquired. Therefore, for those who simply memorized sentences from textbooks with no practices for proper performance, the memorized sentences would not be much effective for one to communicate in TL.

However, during the process of memorizing the sentences, it is generally true that one gets to practice them to a degree, but typically not enough to acquire them. For this, depending on the amount of practice, SM method can be much more effective in terms of communicative skills when compared to the traditional grammar translation method. However, SM could bring about a bad habit of building strong accents by the repeated memorizing process of expressions with the sounds created by one's own imagination of the sounds.

Even though there are many issues with the SM method as shown above, the following case introductions will show that the SM method could still be a better method than those traditional methods in terms of being able to be communicative in TL. At least, even with quite clumsy manner and with one's own strong accents which require quite an attention from the listener, one can communicate in TL by utilizing those expressions memorized through SM to a level of managing one's daily matters.

3

The Relationship of the Babble with Memorization, Recitation, and Acquisition

In order to make a clear presentation on the relationship of the babble with memorization, recitation, and acquisition, it is necessary first to clarify the relationship among memorization, recitation, and acquisition. In FLE environment, the term of memorization has been used quite often. However, such terms as recitation and acquisition do not appear to have been quoted so commonly as memorization has been. In a sense, the term of memorization sometimes seems to have been used in a generic sense to include even the concepts of recitation and acquisition. It is just like that the term of water sometimes is used in a generic sense to include all kinds of water like warm water or distilled water.

However, for the purpose of distinguishing the physically changing status of the water precisely, and of understanding the relationship of the role of the media which causes such physical changes, it is very necessary to use specialized terms in accordance with the status of water. Likewise, for the purpose of understanding the changing status of students' language skills during the learning process of

TL, we should use specific terms rather than a vague and confusing generic term to denote different levels of the language skills being acquired by students. Therefore, for the purpose said above, I will use such three terms as memorization, recitation, and acquisition.

Then, first of all, what is the fundamental concept of memorization? As far as language learning is concerned, one can simply define memorization as storing the linguistic information of given TL expression into the brain. So, memorization is more related to inputting information, and, strictly speaking, outputting such information via specific performance does not belong to the realm of memorization.

Therefore, the most important issue in the level of memorization is to collect and store all of the linguistic information presented in most possibly accurate manner. This is because the quality of memorization will completely decide the quality of the next level. For example, if a student does not collect all the accurate linguistic information of "I won't play" when it was presented to him/her, and memorizes it with such sound as much more close to "I want pray", it would definitely bring about wrong outputs.

Another thing to note is that the amount of the medium, whatever it is, which is required to bring about memorization would not be sufficient to carry out the memorized linguistic information into concrete and correct linguistic acts. To output the linguistic information into such linguistic acts would require extra amount of such medium.

The next level to memorization is recitation. The fundamental concept of recitation in language learning can be defined as reciting the comprehensive linguistic information which is stored in the brain with concrete linguistic acts. Among such concrete linguistic acts, the act of producing articulations as accurately as possible to the level of the source is one of the most important issues in recitation. Here, it is assumed that the source is produced by a native speaker or a native speaker level teacher. Thus, any recitation based on such memorization of wrongful information cannot be an effective recitation.

As seen above, one can find it easily that memorization and recitation are in a sequence relationship. That is, memorization should precede recitation. Also, the quality of recitation cannot be better than that of memorization. Therefore, one should understand that, in achieving successful recitation, the quality of information stored in the brain plays so significant role, which means that sincere effort to collect and store accurate linguistic information during the process of memorization is crucial.

Then, what is the fundamental concept of acquisition in language learning? Acquisition can be metaphorically defined as a complete possession of given TL expression as a linguistic instrument. To possess an expression as linguistic instrument means that the expression has been processed into one's lingua pool of TL, and is ready to be utilized fluently and naturally anytime anywhere upon necessity. The lingua pool of TL is an imaginary place where all the linguistic phenomena of the acquired expressions are extracted and analyzed to produce linguistic intuition of TL. The pool is also where all personalized expressions are produced through one's linguistic intuition as well as physical capacity of TL. Here, the linguistic instrument of course means a tool for active interaction for communication, especially verbal communication which requires a lot more of instantaneous linguistic intuition, physical capacity, and linguistic resources of TL.

Based on the above concept of acquisition, one can infer the differences between recitation and acquisition: Recitation is of performing merely memorized expressions, while acquisition, in narrow sense, is of performing fully personalized expressions; and the result of recitation is more of temporary function of reproduction, while the result of acquisition is an all time available language skill. Also, acquisition is different from recitation in that the acquired or personalized expressions can be naturally transformed or utilized into different forms.

As shown above, the terms of memorization, recitation, and acquisition are not independent from each other, rather they are related to each other in a certain chain of feeding sequence. That is, memorization produces inputs to recitation, which again produces inputs to acquisition. In other words, they denote different levels of given expressions being acquired in TL learning process. Consequently, high quality of memorization is very essential to achieve successful recitation, which would eventually be crucial in deciding the quality of acquisition. So, none of the three concepts can be taken lightly in TL learning.

Then, what is the medium that moves the TL skills of students to the gradually higher levels in the order of memorization, recitation, and acquisition? That is, what leads the TL skills of students to memorization, to recitation, and to acquisition levels respectively? It is the babble. Students memorize, recite, and acquire given TL expressions through babbling. No memorization, recitation, and acquisition will be successful without babbling, active or inactive. Also, the quality of memorization, recitation, and acquisition purely depends on the quality of babbling, which includes the quantity of Babble Training also.

If an expression is memorized with, let's say, very inactive babbling, the quality of the memorized expression can be good only so much that, depending on the quality, the memory may not last long enough for recitation; then the recitation of the expression can be good also only to that degree; and, even if the expression would be acquired, it would eventually cause so much side effects in communication. Therefore, the high quality performance of Babble Training is so important from the beginning.

The relationship of the babble with memorization, recitation, and acquisition can be compared, for easy understanding, to that of heat energy with cold water, warm water, and distilled water.

254 | CHEOL BEOM LEE

That is, the heat energy is the only medium which causes the physical changes of water. The heat energy would change ice to cold water, to warm water, and to distilled water. Certain amount of heat energy is required to change ice into cold water; certain more energy to change the cold water into warm water; and certain additional energy to change the warm water into distilled water. After all, as the heat energy is required to cause the changes in the physical status of water, the babble energy is required to cause the changes in one's language skills of TL.

Just like insufficient heat energy would not melt ice into cold water, insufficient babble energy would not bring about memorization. Just as the heat energy which was sufficient only to melt ice into cold water would not warm the water, the babble energy which was sufficient only to bring about memorization of an expression would not help one recite the memorized expression.

Like wise, a lot more of babble energy will be required, on top of the babble amount accumulated up to the recitation level, to fully acquire the recited expressions. Also, as the amount of the needed heat energy to change the status of water would vary depending on various variables like amount of water, size of container, etc., so would the amount of the needed babble energy vary depending on individuals, situations, and etc. to improve one's language skills of TL.

However, it is not a disputable fact that the most quick and efficient way of changing ice into distilled water is to apply the strongest possible heat energy from the beginning to the end without a break. Likewise, the most quick and efficient way for one to acquire TL is to exert all efforts of Babble Training with the most powerful energy possible without a break.

The above comparison of the heat energy to the babble energy offers answers to many questions about Babble Training method. The reason that many people do not make much progress in acquiring TL even after spending so many hours every day carrying out Babble Training is because of the lack of the babble energy.

For example, the energy of Babble Training with the audio player while driving, which a lot of people do, would not be sufficient even for memorizing the expressions. Consequently, one would not acquire the expressions with such kind of inactive babble energy. Others would do the babble while resting in falling asleep as they would listen to relaxing music. This type of Babble Training is so inactive that there is almost no energy of babbling. Here, inactive babble means various babble efforts from listening only to mimicking without clear voice heard.

With inactive babble energy, one cannot memorize the expressions as memorization not only includes the sentence component but also the muscle and nerve system to produce the sounds. So, such inactive babble effort would be the babble to listen not to talk TL. Consequently, it is very natural for one who did Babble Training for listening comprehension only not to be able to speak TL fluently.

After all, for FLE educators, to figure out the language skill status of students on given TL expressions, and to prescribe and supervise necessary Babble Training agenda to support the students to acquire them successfully are very important.

4

Sentence Memorization, Recitation, Speaking, Listening, Reading, and Writing Methods vs. BTM

Earlier, I introduced detail comparisons of Direct Method vs. BTM, and SM vs. BTM. Then, what relations are there between BTM and all the other FLE methods which have been applied at the teacher's own wills? Even though so many varieties of FLE methods have been introduced so far, it is not easy to find any method which systematically describes the teaching methods based on the overall process of language acquisition process.

There are some problems that are commonly shared by the FLE methods introduced so far. The first problem is that all of the methods are heavily sided with particular area of language skills such as speaking, listening, writing, or reading. They seem to assume that once students acquire the particular language skills of TL, the students can acquire the remaining skills naturally. For example, the educators who strongly believe in the Grammar Translation Method seem to believe that students can acquire all of the language skills quite easily once they conquer the grammar of TL.

Second, as the methods heavily focus on a particular area of the language skills, they don't provide systematic education process of the other areas. For example, the listening method, which directs students to solely focus on listening to audio media until they acquire the listening comprehension skill, does not offer concrete methods for students to tackle the speaking, reading, and other skills of TL. Consequently, students cannot acquire the language skills of TL through such methods.

Third, most of the methods are more oriented toward the methods for students to teach TL to themselves rather than for educators to teach the students. In other words, strictly speaking, they are not FL teaching methods but FL studying methods. It would not be a too much exaggeration to say that all of those methods introduced so far are of simple minded ideas for the students who teach FL to themselves. Consequently, even though there have been quite a number of different FLE methods, it is true that such methods, as they have not been designed for the educators, have not been appropriate for FL educators to adopt in teaching FL classes.

Fourth, some of the FLE methods are unrealistic. For example, some methods like Direct Method and Content-Based Method, which require the educator to be a native TL speaker or to acquire TL to a native speaker level, are very unrealistic to most of the public school FL programs except for the FL programs in some specially situated countries like the USA. Also, some other methods like Immersion Method are unrealistic to most of the public FL programs as only rich people could afford the expenses incurring for such methods.

BTM shows a big contrast with those limited and one-sided FLE methods quoted so far in that it resolves all of such problems shown above. The relationship between BTM and all of the other FLE methods quoted so far can be analyzed to the relationship between the systematic construction process which handles the overall process of building a house and the work units which are needed in respective process of the construction. That is, BTM can be analyzed to a systematic FLE process to help students to acquire all the language skill areas of TL; and the methods quoted so far focusing on such limited areas of language skills as memorization, recitation, speaking, reading, listening, and writing can be considered as the education units to be applied in respective TL educational process.

While building a house, it is not even imaginable not to follow the systematic construction process. If such work units as ground digging, setting up the poles, laying the bricks, installing windows, finishing the roof, and decorating interior or exterior would be done arbitrarily by the workers without minding the construction process, the failure of the results is guaranteed. One cannot start preparing to put up the roof first because it is rainy; and one cannot insist on laying the brick before setting up the poles for the reason of winds. If one would not follow the construction procedure, sometimes the situation can be worsened with no possibility of recovering or undoing the already caused damages.

Likewise, teaching FL at or against the direction of wind blowing without following an assured and systematic educational process can guarantee a failure at the end. One should not do heavy listening only from the beginning as one cannot listen and comprehend TL; and one should not hurry up reading in TL based on the TL grammar just because one does not know how to read TL. Also, memorizing any sentences popping up would not help either. Further, reciting a lot of fancy sentences and poems from the beginning, when one actually need to pick up the expressions which are needed right away, would not help one to acquire the TL either. BTM provides the systematic FL education process which is needed for effective FLE program.

5

The Language vs. The Piano

Now that I have pointed out that the traditional FLE methods have failed to produce fluent speakers of TL, let me further show how those methods could not be successful in producing fluent speakers of TL. In an earlier article, I pointed out that language is missing from school language classes. For those who still cannot understand my point of saying that language is missing from school language class, I will apply an analogy to the piano education.

Let's assume that the piano teachers would insist that the school piano education should focus on teaching students the piano music grammar (theory) for three or four years because the theories of the piano music are the most fundamental knowledge required before playing the piano. This is exactly the same background of what Grammar Translation Method of FLE is based on.

We know that students would not be able to play the piano very well no matter how many years they would study the theories. All of us know that it is not the way we should learn piano. One may argue that knowing the theory still can improve the quality of performance. Yes, but it would not make so much difference in the beginning stage. As a matter of fact, it could cause serious confusions to the students because there are many different theories for one same thing. So, whatever time and resource spent on it in the beginning would be all wasted.

Now let's further assume that, after such intensive piano music grammar education, the piano teachers started teaching the students on how to read the piano music based on the piano music grammar for a couple of years. This would be quite similar to Reading Method of FLE. Yet, there is no end of the theories with new interpretations and arguments evolving every day. As the students apparently seem to do better in reading and analyzing the piano music according to the piano music grammar, the teachers decided to teach the students, as next step, on how to write the piano music.

The students would work hard to get better in writing the piano music applying the music rules. Then, finally, the students became very good with the piano music grammar, reading, and writing in 6 years of hard work. The teachers feel rewarded and instruct the students to start listening to the piano music using the high tech audio and video equipments just like in the Technological Approach of FLE. Also, the teachers would ask the students to memorize a lot of piano music. So, the students do as instructed by listening to the piano music day and night and by memorizing a lot of piano music. After another couple of years like that, the students could listen and sort of understand how to appreciate the music. Some of the smart and hard working students would get very high scores on various types of the piano music tests which do not require the students to play the piano.

It is very clear to all of us except the piano teachers that the students have not learned the piano yet. Only the piano teachers seem to believe that all the methods above are helpful and necessary for the students to be able to play the piano fluently. So far, there has been no piano itself in the piano class at all. Therefore, we know that the students have not even touched the piano yet, and that the students could not play the piano well. However, the piano teachers insist that they have been teaching how to play the piano to the students, and they don't seem to realize that no piano has been introduced to the students yet.

With about 10 years of such hard training, teachers believe that the students have acquired quite strong foundations to play the piano. Therefore, the teachers expect the students to play the piano. Surprisingly, none of the students can even play the very basic and easy music. The teachers would keep expecting the students to continue playing the piano. Students would not be able to command their hands and fingers even though the brain would know what to do very well.

Most of all, with such 10 years spent on studying the theory, reading, writing, and listening to the piano music, most of the students would miss a lot of good opportunities and the best physical condition to learn the piano to the professional level because their muscles and nerves on the hands and fingers have already aged. We all know what aging means to our physical capacity to learn the piano. Lost of opportunities and physical adaptability for excellent performance, because of the aged body, could be the biggest suffering from such kind of absent minded education.

Fortunately, in the real world, we all know the idea of how we should start learn the piano, and, really luckily, all the piano teachers, even though they may have different levels of skills or qualifications, seem to know very well at least the ideas of how to approach for teaching students the piano. I have not known any piano teachers who would start teaching the piano without asking the students to babble the piano for each piano music repeatedly until the students can play each music very fluently. The piano teachers know the difference between memorizing the music and Babble Training (repeated practice for acquisition) the piano for each music.

There are many common features between learning how to speak a language and learning how to play the piano.

For a language, no matter how much one may know about a language, no matter how much one would have read in the language, and mo matter how much one would have listened to the language, one cannot speak the language without the very fluent coordination of the speech organs. The only way for the speech organs to be so fluent is through Babble Training numerous real life expressions repeatedly until the speech organs can produce them semi-instinctively. Language cannot be acquired effectively without very thorough physical trainings of the speech organs using various expressions.

For the piano, one cannot play the piano, regardless of one's tremendous knowledge of the piano music rules, regardless on one's reading experiences in the piano music, and regardless of one's excellent skills in listening to the piano music, without the coordination of very semi-instinct movement of the hands and fingers. The only way for the hands and fingers to be so semi-instinctive is through playing numerous real piano music repeatedly until one's hands and fingers can play them semi-instinctively. The piano cannot be learned effectively without very thorough physical trainings of the hands and fingers using various piano music.

In this sense, I feel it is very unfortunate that majority language teachers do not realize the fundamental ideas of how to approach for teaching FL to the students. Most of the teachers believe so strongly that grammar is an absolute necessity one should know very well before tackling the language.

Further, most of the teachers believe in that, after grammar, we should focus on reading, writing, and listening to the language. Teachers always say things different from each other. Some teachers would say that one could do FL with strong grammar power of the language. Other teachers would ask the students to read loud a lot to pick up the language. Others would recommend listening to and watching the mass media in TL repeatedly as the best way to pick up FL.

However, the fact that those teachers who would argue so strongly for their own respective methods of FLE have not acquired their own TLs through such methods raises a serious problem. There are two groups of such teachers. Most of them have not acquired the TL they are teaching so that they even cannot command the language very well by themselves. These are the ones who have not been to the world of commanding TL fluently. The remaining small group of teachers learned their TLs in a totally unrelated manner from their own teaching methods. Consequently, both groups of teachers should know what is waiting for at the end the FLE based on such methods.

Yet, it is an irony that the teachers still would not yield their position and change for new ideas. Then, the teachers would expect the students to speak the language in a real world, which only frustrates every body, both the teachers and the students. Even most of the teachers cannot distinguish between Babble Training and memorizing of expressions. Babble Training is done through the speech organs, and the memorizing is done through the memory organs.

We should teach our students FL just like the way the piano teachers teach their students piano. Why? Because the language is exactly the same as the piano in that it is required for us to acquire very semi-instinctive skills to produce and control the sounds. Without such semi-instinctive skills, required by TL, of one's speech organs, mostly the tongue, lips, and vocal cords, one cannot command the language fluently. Without such semi-instinctive skills of one's limbs, mostly hands and fingers, one would not be able to play the piano successfully.

We should teach our students that they need to babble the language repeatedly until they could speak the language very well, just like the piano students practice the piano repeatedly until they play the piano very well.

In piano class, starting with the piano music grammar, and proceeding to reading the piano music, writing the piano music, and even listening to the piano music in gradual sequence means huge loss and waste of all kinds of resources. Even after 10 years of the piano classes, one should start over from Babble Training of the piano music because there is no other way to acquire the skills of playing the piano fluently.

In language class, starting with the language grammar, and proceeding to reading the language, writing the language, and even listening to the language in gradual sequence means huge loss and waste of all kinds of resources. Even after 10 years of the language classes, one should start over from Babble Training the language because there is no other way to acquire the skills of speaking the language fluently.

As one builds up musical intuition through successful Babble Training of the piano, one builds up linguistic intuition through successful Babble Training of the language. Intuition is what one needs to be a successful pianist; and that is what one needs to be a successful speaker of a language.

6

How Many Expressions are Needed?

I would like to emphasize once again that, among the 5 levels of BTM, Babble Training is the best way for a student to acquire the three language acquisition factors simultaneously and harmoniously to a strong enough level for effective communications of TL in one's personal life. In a previous article, I have explained why the dialogue based sets of expressions are better than other types of linguistic resources materials. Then, how many expressions would one need to acquire the acquisition factors of TL to such a strong level?

The answer could be different depending on the linguistic distance of one's own language, which was defined in a previous chapter, to TL. If the distance is close enough as for among such languages as English, Spanish, Italian, French, and German, for example, it means that there are a lot of linguistic features shared between the two languages. This again means that the learners can utilize the already acquired acquisition factors for their MT in learning TL.

To learn a language whose linguistic distance is so close to one's MT would be compared to working on a very old and rusty car whose engine is still in good condition but needs replacements of some minor parts. In this case, one does not need to build the engine and the body from the scratch, but simply need to work on the engine to replace some old parts with new ones, on the body to straighten up the indented areas, and on repainting the body.

On the other hand, for those languages with low scores of the linguistic distance between MT and TL such as between the languages of English versus Korean, Japanese, Arabic, and others, for example, those acquisition factors which students have acquired for their MT rather cause barriers and unfavorable influences for them to learn TL. This can be compared to building a car from the scratch in a very unfavorable environment.

Therefore, instead of answering to the question of what is required to acquire the skills to work on a very old and rusty car to make it run, I will try to answer to the question of what is required to overcome the unfavorable environment and acquire the skills of building a new car from scratch. In the same token, through out this book, I am focusing on the FLE of a strange language whose linguistic distance score from learner's MT is quite high.

Accordingly, those who seek for the answers for teaching family languages with very close linguistic distance to TL would need some discretional adjustments to induce proper answers in terms of the amounts and efforts of Babble Training for respective levels of Babble Training based on the linguistic distance.

To answer the questions, let's look at the MT acquisition by the children as a reference. By the age of 40 months, children can speak their languages quite well. They can create and produce expressions on their own. Even though the children have individual differences, they seem to start creating new expressions by the age of 30 months.

On the other hand, Based on PBS Parents website of Child Development Tracker, children of age around 36 months is known to understand around 1,000 vocabularies, most of which are directly related to their daily life. Then, at the age of 48 months, children can understand 2,500-3,000 mostly composed of nouns and modifiers. However, it does not mean that children of that age can command so many vocabularies. They can command much less vocabularies than what they can understand.

Even though the children can understand so many vocabularies, the actual number of independent expressions which the children are exposed to does not seem to be a lot. One can figure this out easily by considering the number of the linguistic expressions for those situations related to the children's daily life activities. The linguistic expressions offered to the children are mostly related to the daily situations like eating, sleeping, washing, crying, smiling, family terms, body parts, going out with care takers, and playing with toys. The care takers mainly use the same or very similar expressions repeatedly for respective situations. Considering this, the number of total independent expressions offered to the children would be less than 150, or 200 at most. Even if one would try to maximize the number of expressions, it would not exceed 300.

The above observation tells that intensive and thorough Babble Training over about 150-200 of daily life expressions would allow one to pick up the three acquisition factors in a quite strong degree: linguistic intuition, physical capacity, and the linguistic resources. One thing that is very important to be understood is that most of the vocabularies and sets of expressions which the children pick up are directly and closely related to their needs and activities in daily life.

On the other hand, based on my experience of teaching Babble Training to talk, it is obvious that after about two semesters of Babble Training courses, most of the hard working students do acquire the three acquisition factors to quite a strong level, and they can produce some of the very basic expressions on their own. Especially, they can say the expressions they babbled very well, but they cannot continue conversations not much beyond what they know because of the restrictions coming mostly from their limited linguistic resources available. I would say though that their level is much higher than that of 30 months old children.

Also, based on my experience, students depending on individual performances can be really creative in commanding TL after 3 semesters of Babble Training to talk. During the 3 semesters in my class, students are expected to be able to utilize, for creative communications in various situations, about 500 colloquial expressions and over 2,500 vocabularies according to the textbooks and the methods I have been using. In other words, students can utilize these linguistic resources to actively involve themselves in dialogues. Yet, their performance is restricted to the span of their vocabulary skills. At this stage, the students obtain the language skills to read and understand the elementary level texts.

Therefore, I would propose a minimum about 500 daily activity related expressions to be targeted as the goal of the completing the 1st level Babble Training before getting into the 2nd level Babble Training. Through systematic and thorough Babble Training on about 500 real expressions selected from different real daily life situations, we can surely help the students to acquire TL at least to the level of a typical 40 month old child. Even though students surely can acquire TL with Babble Training on about 200 expressions, utilizing more expressions in the 1st level Babble Training should be so much more effective for the students to develop over all language skills of TL.

Regarding the vocabularies, around two thousand colloquial vocabularies would be good for the 1st level. The goal for the 1st level is not just simply to introduce such amount of linguistic resources to the students, which would not require any particular teaching ideas or skills, but to have the students babble over those colloquial expressions gradually and repeatedly so that they could eventually carry out the sets of dialogues very fluently as well as maintaining the vocabularies successfully.

With the completion of the 1st level, one could lead the students into the 2nd level, the 3rd level, 4th and the 5th level for different levels of Babble Training in successful sequences. It is very important to have students maintain Babble Training over the expressions acquired previously and continue Babble Training over new sets of expressions. After all, the more number of colloquial expressions for various situations the students would babble and retain, the stronger oral language skills they will obtain. It will also give the students much more powerful linguistic intuition to absorb TL easily through the activities of listening and reading.

So far, I have described about the types and amount of the real expressions needed in Babble Training during the 1st level Babble Training out of total 5 levels of Babble Training. With respect to the types and amount of the expressions which are needed during the following levels of Babble Training to improve students' over all language skills in a most effective way, one should refer to the BTM diagram.

7

Case Introduction: Sentence Memorization

Some years ago, I met an old gentleman, Kim, who started studying English after retirement, and memorized about 1,000 English dialogue sentences. He had previously visited the USA several times and stayed for several months each time. When I met him first, he was visiting his relatives in the USA.

According to him, he collected individual sentences from various sources and produced a dictionary type note book listing all of the sentences in a certain sequence of his own choice. Since he was retired, he was able to spend many hours and efforts every day for a few years on memorizing the sentences. He would read the sentences repeatedly to himself to memorize them. As a result, he could say each of the 1,000 sentences back and forth. He memorized them like one would do the math property table.

As a result, he could communicate in English with people utilizing the sentences in his memory to quite a degree but not in very fluent level. He is not in the level of a solid bilingual speaker to my judgment. Yet, compared to many people of his age or other adults from Korea, who have not memorized any English sentences and lived in the USA for many years, his English speaking was outstanding. He could by himself order foods in restaurants, do shopping, ask people for help with directions, and so on.

As long as the listeners would be patient to listen to him as they would do when listening to young babies, he would be able to continue talking in English quite more. Considering his age when he started memorizing the English sentences, the fact that he could do so much in English by memorizing the sentences was really encouraging.

When he memorized the sentences, he did not listen to any audio materials produced by native speakers, and he did not practice saying the sentences after the native sounds. As a matter of fact, he didn't pay much attention from the beginning on the sounds as he did not realize the importance of building physical capacity to understand and to perform the oral language fluently. That is, as he did not realize the necessity of building the physical capacity, he was simply occupied with the idea that, once he memorizes the sentences, he should be able to understand and speak English. Many people make this kind of mistake by simply assuming that one's speech organ would work without intensive trainings to build the necessary physical capacity.

When I listened to him speak English, however, I could find some issues in his English. First of all, those memorized sentences are saved in so deep and remote place of his brain. Therefore, except for some expressions which are available right on the tip of the tongue by frequent usage, he would have to manually retrieve the expressions he memorized from his memory. It took quite a while for him to retrieve a not very commonly used expression and to say it out. That is, his stream of ideas is not synchronized with his speaking. In other words, most of the sentences are not ready to be used instantaneously with the occurring situation. So, beyond very basic levels of greeting and introducing himself, he really could not be involved in natural and instantaneous communicative interactions with a conversation partner.

Second, his speech organs are not trained very well. Therefore, his pronunciation tends to be very awkward and strange. His articulation is fully influenced by Korean accents and, accordingly, not accurate so that one could not understand him easily. He memorized the sentences with the sounds that he figured by himself by looking at them. So, he was strongly biased with the sets of sounds he made looking at the sentences.

Third, he would have hard time to understand the native English speakers talking to him as he was not familiar with the sounds and speed.

As a result, he can carry out the ordinary daily life communications in English in a slow and relaxed communication mode where he would be given enough time for thinking, repetitions, and self corrections, and that people would pay extra attention. However, the status of the memorized expressions and the physical capacity to carry out them are such that it would delay the speaking process and cause mispronunciations for him even to command the expressions that he memorized.

Kim's case is quite rare in that not many people really do memorize so many sentences to learn TL. It takes very strong commitment and efforts as well as time to memorize that many sentences. It is especially very difficult for the students of FL classes because most of the current FLE in school does not adapt such method, which means that the students would have to do it on their own in addition to what is taught in school. Yet, it is a very significant example which clearly shows that memorizing sentences still helps a lot for verbal communication. Especially, sentence memorization seems to be much more effective at least than memorizing the grammars, and also more effective than simply reading a lot in TL.

8

Case Introduction:
Babble Training 1

I, like many other typical people in Korea, started learning English in the middle school. Even though I was doing good in all subjects including English, I could not really follow the grammar focused English classes. As a student attending a small countryside middle school, I somehow managed to get good grades in English, but it really did not mean anything in terms of my English skills.

In my high school, which was a business school, we had only one English class per week, which is almost nothing compared to the regular high schools offering at least 6-7 class per week (For senior years, the students would receive over 10 English classes per week from the regular and supplementary programs of the school). Even though my school did not focus on those humanities classes including English, I decided to teach myself English.

I purchased an English grammar study reference book and studied hard to go over the book several times front to back, memorizing all of the grammar terms and the vocabularies from the sample English sentences. After each time I finished the book, I would think of some simple expressions in Korean, and ask myself how to say them in English. Each time, I failed. With repeated failures, I purchased another English study reference book, and did the same way. Yet, no improvement I felt. When I was a junior in the high school, the frustration accumulated so much that I decided to give up studying English.

After the high school, I got a job. Then, I started preparing for a national government officer exam in the electric engineering area. However, I found that English was one of the core subjects for the preliminary qualification exam. So, I again had to start teaching myself English. Yet, it was different method this time. I had no idea of how to start it again. It was by accident that I purchased one of the English conversation audio sets with textbooks to start studying English again.

When I listened to the audio tapes for the first time, even the sounds of the slow version for each expression were still way too fast for me to understand even a word. I had to open the book to see what words were in the sentences. I simply could not catch them by listening to the audio. As I had given up English for about two years, I didn't have much of the English grammars other than some of the grammatical terms like 'subject', 'verb', and etc. I also lost most of English words except for very simple basic terms like most of the personal pronouns, and kinship terms.

Without knowing what and how to do, I would simply read the text first to figure out the sentence components, listen to the audio, imitate the sounds, and try hard to retain all of the expressions. Then, while on the ways to work, home, or other places, I would babble the expressions over and over. This is how I started Babble Training in English. Whenever I was done with a lesson, I would visit all the previous lessons up to that point again and make it sure that I still could say the expressions to myself very well before I moved forward to a new lesson. When I completed the first volume of the audio set, which had 50 lessons, in about 4 months, I went over all the lessons again from the lesson 1 through the end before I started tackling the 2nd volume of the audio set.

While doing Babble Training to talk, I felt the first volume was most difficult, and it took the longest time to finish. However, from the 2nd volume, the babble process got easier: Listening was easier and oral repeating of the expressions was easier. From the 4th volume, I was able to listen and understand the normal speed of the audio presentation quite clearly, and did not have to look up the book to find out the sentence components. Verbal repeating after the audio tapes was also easy enough. After finishing the 5th volume, which was the last of the series at that time, I kept listening to the tapes and doing the babble. It took about 15 months to finish the 5 volumes of the audio sets in the above said method.

Yet, I did not know how much I could speak in English as I had no experience of talking to an English speaker by then. I simply was able to rehearse most of the expressions quite fluently by heart. Even though I realized that I still could not say every thing that I can think of, I at the same time clearly felt that I could express myself quite well for daily life matters in English.

Around the time when I started the audio set volume 4 out of total 5 volumes for the first time, I started reading in English against Korean translation (in Korea, there are many books which are designed in such a way that they have English version on one page and Korean version on next page). Babble Training process for reading which I did at that time was first to read the English sentence from the book; then, look for the meanings of new words; try to guess the meaning of the sentence based on the meanings of the words or idioms; and to compare the guessed meaning against the translation.

Then, whenever I found differences between the guessed meaning and the translation, I would try to find where and why the meaning difference occurred, and analyze how I should interpret the particular phrases or sentences to get the correct meaning. Especially, I paid careful attention on maintaining those new words by putting them down on various pages of the book so that I get to write them several times to help myself memorize them.

By doing so, I also get to review those words repeatedly as I read forward. Whenever I turned a page, I would first look for the words that I put down previously and review them before I start reading the page. This helped me a lot with acquiring strong linguistic resources. By the time I completed reading two books through such reading training, the accuracy of my guess on the meanings of various complicated English sentences became close to 100%, and I naturally picked up the English reading skills.

Around the time when I started listening to the whole five sets of the audio tapes for the 3rd time in repetition, I started writing daily journals in English mostly by quoting expressions from the books that I read. It was hard in the beginning, but about a couple months after, it became quite easy to write full pages of the daily journals.

When I entered a college in Korea some years later, I met an English speaking foreigner on the campus for the first time. He was an English instructor of the college. I, as a freshman, started talking to him and I was able to command quite fluent English and had no trouble getting a long with him in English. He was also surprised at my English skills.

9

Case Introduction: Babble Training 2

Many years ago, on a Christmas day, I met a man of mid thirties at an American friend of mine's house, another Mr. Kim. He is also from Korea, and he had been three years in the USA then. As we were all speaking in English, I noticed that he spoke English very well without accents from Korean. No hesitation, no mumbling, no delay of speaking process, and many jokes. Naturally, I got very curious about how he picked up English so well, and asked him questions about how he studied English.

He told me that he was very bad in English through a college. He could not get in a better college because of his poor English grade in the high school. He said the English classes from the middle school were always hard; and he lost interests in English since then until he started studying English again after he was discharged from the army.

Upon coming back to college from the army, he purchased a set of English conversation audios. He listened to the audio tapes and repeated verbally after the audio presentation of each sets of dialogue expressions until he could say the expressions instantaneously to himself fluently (This is what I consider as the process of Babble Training to talk). He would babble the expressions to himself as much as possible whenever he had time.

After about two years of such efforts, he felt quite comfortable with English. He could speak in English quite well whenever he met English speaking foreigners on the campus or on the street. Then, he read many magazines in English, from which he picked up the English vocabularies. He picked up English in Korea that way, and, some years after he graduated from the college, he immigrated to the USA. However, he said he picked up not so much more English after he came to the USA as he had been getting along mostly with Korean people in the Korean community.

I was quite surprised to find out the way he acquired English from Korea by himself was almost identical to my case.

Another case of successful Babble Training to talk is my wife, JW. When I was working as the editor-in-chief for the English newspaper of a college which we attended together, I met JW who joined the campus English newspaper. She was a freshman, and just like every body else, she did not have the proficiency of commanding oral English. At that time, we would have morning meetings every day in English only. But, I had to be the one who mostly spoke to the members in English, who mostly would react to my questions or requests in simple English. One day, I talked to the members about how to study in order to be able to speak English well. I explained how I gave up English in my high school, and how I started again and did teaching English to myself.

JW followed my suggestions. She purchased the same audio tape sets as the one I used; and she did Babble Training by listening to the audio and repeating orally after each expression. She did quite the same way as I did; and she read several books in English. She would wear ear phones while moving around. After a couple of years, she became quite fluent in speaking English.

More cases of babble stories are from the readers of my book. After I published *New TESL Plus* in 2005, which is written in Korean for the students studying English in Korea, many people started studying English following BTM model. Many people are still doing the 1st level of Babble Training to talk.

For the students in Korea, it is not easy for them to focus on BTM as it requires students to study English in dramatically different ways from the ways the school English programs do. In the school, English classes are still mostly of the grammar and of applying the grammars to break down the sentences by the grammatical category. Accordingly, the students are evaluated based on the grammar and reading skills. Also, they have to follow the trends of the national college entrance exam, where the English exam is again not about the comprehensive language skills including speaking skills, but about the grammar, reading, and listening comprehension.

For the students, the school English evaluation and the national exams are so important for their future life so that they really could not focus on BTM, which requires a lot of time for Babble Training to start with, which at least in the beginning does not help them a lot with the grammar based school English program.

Therefore, not many school attending students seem to be involved in following BTM intensively. However, still quite a lot of working people have posted comments or testimonials on the internet café bulletin board. Among the comments are very successful stories about Babble Training. A Mr. Park ("Park"), who did Babble Training for about one year, wrote that he could now attend English speaking business meetings without worrying too much, and he could express his opinions quite well at the meetings.

Some other members say that they became more confident with speaking in English after Babble Training for about one year or so.

On the other hand, some other people expressed the difficulties to carry out Babble Training because of the noise while babbling, which draws the attentions of other people, or seems to bother other people. Over all, people who have done Babble Training consistently about one year strongly believe that Babble Training is really needed to speak TL very well.

10

Case Introduction:
Babble Training 3

Before I came to the USA, I had taught English to students at some private English institutes in Korea for about two years. I mostly taught high school students and college students. For the high school students, I taught English for them to prepare for college entrance English exam. For college students, I taught TOEFL, and advanced level of reading comprehension. Regardless of different levels of the students, what I taught were overwhelmingly focused on the English grammar and grammar based reading skills. I would easily spend many hours simply introducing the different categories of the respective speech parts in English without having to introduce any English sentences to the students. For the period of two years, I had not taught English dialogues a lot to the students. Even though I was sure that it was a wrong to teach the grammar and reading only, I did not have any choice but complying with the curriculums.

During the course of English classes, I didn't expect the students to pick up any oral proficiency as I had not taught how to speak English. None of the students had complained about not being able to speak even one line of English. Nobody cared about the issue of oral proficiency in English. Some of the high school students were very successful in getting very satisfied scores in the English exam at the end of the year. Yet, they didn't seem to care about how much English they could actually speak. The college students I taught were the same in that they didn't care about developing the oral proficiency in English.

I felt very uncomfortable with continuing to teach the students such kind of English. The fact that I had already acquired English and developed the English oral proficiency to a quite high level didn't seem to be helpful to the students as the English classes were oriented to a totally different direction. Even though it has been about 20 years since then, I know that the English classes in Korea have not changed a lot in nature.

Then, about ten years ago, I volunteered to teach English in the USA to the senior members of the Korean American community in Denver. I taught once a week every Saturday for two hours. This time, instead of teaching English grammar, I used an English conversation textbook for the class. I introduced the ideas of Babble Training method and the goals. Then, Babble Training method for teaching was not developed quite well yet. Nonetheless, I solely focused on teaching them how to speak the English language. As I continued the class, I faced a couple of major issues which would diminish the effects of teaching.

The first issue was that the senior students did not have trust on the method. Most of them were over 60 years of age who had not learned what they called the "basic English" before. To them, what I taught was not the "basic English", rather it was quite advanced English. They expected me to start with teaching them the basic grammar of English. Even though I tried to persuade them to understand the definition of the "basic English", they could not get rid of the long time belief in one day.

The second issue was that there was lack of focused performance by the students for many understandable reasons. As it was a once-a-week class, they are required to do most of the study by themselves during their own time through out the week in accordance with my instruction for Babble Training.

However, as it is typical for most of the people regardless of ages, most of them could not focus on thorough Babble Training by themselves to prepare for the class. They also could not maintain the expressions very well either. The lack of such performance was partially caused by the fact that the classes were not intensive enough with one time class meeting per week. Even though some of the students really liked that they could speak simple expressions in English, the motivation and performance were not strong enough for them to continue Babble Training until they could acquire English.

The third issue was that I, as a teacher, had no binding means, other than continuously encouraging them, to enforce the senior students to study hard. No evaluation was required for the students, and attendance was not mandatory for the students either. No restriction was applied to the performance of the students either.

About one and a half years later, I found that it was very unrealistic to successfully accomplish, through such type of program, Babble Training even for the minimum amount of linguistic resources required for the students to acquire English, which I believe to be around 250 expressions and around 2,000 vocabularies closely related to the various situations in one's typical daily life.

To use a metaphor of an airplane, which requires an absolute amount of energy to take off the run way, such a program would give the energy enough to move the airplane around a runway all day long and all year round, but would not produce such strong propelling power enough to take the airplane successfully off the runway.

Another experience of teaching Babble Training was at a continuing education program of a college in the USA. Again, it was once a week two hour evening session.

However, this time, the students were mixed population of multiple generations. The atmosphere and commitments of the students are such that each time I would find the students not performing the babble as much as I would expect for them to retain given expressions. Also, almost all of them would take the course at most for two quarters, and discontinue.

Quite often, I had to spend quite a time to remind the students of how to study to acquire Korean and to encourage them to carry out intensive Babble Training to talk. Even though many students seemed to be happy with the fact that, through a couple of quarter period, they, in addition to being able to read and write Korean, learned some Korean expressions enough to greet people, introduce oneself, and order foods in Korean restaurant, I could not accept it as successful results. After all, it turned out to be that the airplane was pushed around the runway, but the propelling power was not strong enough for the airplane to dash through the runway to take off.

11

Case Introduction: Babble Training 4

It was not until I started teaching Korean at the University of Colorado at Boulder in 2002 that I started to apply systematic Babble Training method for teaching. The university offers five-class-a-week Korean program in three different levels: Beginning, intermediate, and advanced levels. Yet, I have to confess that Babble Training method has been slowly developed from the principal concept into a somewhat structured system based on trials and errors.

During the first couple of years in the 1ˢᵗ year Korean program for Babble Training to talk, in addition to having the students repeat after me and read loud each lesson several times, I offered quite thorough explanations on the components of each sentence in the dialogues for respective sounds, meanings, and occasionally some grammatical functions also.

Then, as a requirement for their performance evaluation, I requested the students to put all the expressions on the tip of the tongue, but it was not required for the students to maintain the dialogue expressions of each lesson beyond respective lessons, which was mainly due to the fact that I, with the lack of experience of applying the babble teaching method, did not know how many expressions would be the proper amount for college students in general to carry out Babble Training through out the semester. That is, I would test them to see if they could speak the dialogues at the end of each lesson, and the midterm and final evaluations were done based on written tests.

Consequently, the students would pick up the languages for rather short time for the sake of the tests and do not pay much attention on the daily efforts of trying to keep the expressions to themselves. Accordingly, the quality of their acquisition is not a satisfactory level.

What I have found from this type of Babble Training was that detail explanation on each sentence does not seem to be so much helpful for students to pick up the required language skills and to develop oral proficiency.

Also, I have found that such during-the-lesson-duration short term based Babble Training, even with quite thorough and intensive trainings, are not effective enough for the students in general to maintain the expressions in real level through out and after the semester. Consequently, most students failed to retain the linguistic resources introduced during the semester.

Then, I made it as a requirement for the students to maintain the dialogues through out the semester by evaluating them on oral performance based on all dialogues introduced to the class up to the point of the evaluation. For example, for a midterm evaluation, I would do both oral and written evaluation for those lessons covered up to the midterm point; and, for the final evaluation, I would do the same for all of the dialogues covered throughout the semester.

After two semesters of such Babble Training, most of the serious students seemed to pick up quite a number of basic personal level expressions which they could utilize when necessary. However, after the first two semesters, the physical capacity to articulate Korean expressions for many students was not strong enough to pronounce new words clearly. Some students even would have difficulties with articulating the expressions introduced during the classes.

Also, most of the students did not seem to have gained the linguistic intuition on the sounds and structures of the language quite well. The lack of physical capacity clearly means that the babble performance by the students was not sufficient enough. The fact that the students have not gained the linguistic intuition on the sounds and the structures means that the babble performance by the students was not strong or intensive enough, and the amount of the linguistic resources acquired by the students was not sufficient for the students to repeatedly recognize the variety linguistic characteristics of Korean. These kinds of issues could be caused by the amount of Babble Training and linguistic resources either being offered insufficiently through the class, or being poorly performed by the students, or both.

Based on such findings, I have added review evaluation to the curriculum. Students are now required to be evaluated any day for their oral proficiency on any of the expressions introduced to the class. For this review evaluation, I would have individual students make oral demonstration for a particular dialogue which I choose among the dialogues which were covered previously. I also help students with pronunciation if necessary.

Also, the students are required to carry out the expressions introduced during the 1st semester over to the following 2nd semester. In other words, the review evaluation in Spring semester would include the dialogues from the Fall semester. This method seems to be quite effective in terms of helping students pick up the speaking skill.

Through this method, after two semesters of 5 hour-per-week intensive program, serious students do pick up the physical capacity to articulate new expressions clearly, and linguistic intuition on the various types of the sentence structures, I would say, to the level of about 3-4 year old kids. They could communicate in productive manner utilizing the expressions they have acquired. However, they would not be able to produce or understand the essential daily life colloquial expressions which are not introduced from the textbooks.

To cope with such problems, I added another session of 'Words of the day' to offer Korean expressions which students want to learn most. For this, I ask students to bring expressions which they want to learn most. Students bring the expressions in English, and I introduce the corresponding Korean expressions. Typically, I take three to six new expressions from the students as the 'Words of the day'. Sometimes, I introduce some expressions by myself which I think are most needed to the students in certain context. These additional expressions are also included for the review evaluation.

This idea of 'Words of the day' helps a lot in many ways. Students get excited to learn what they need right away; it provides a lot of real expressions as well as vocabularies; and it also helps students learn the usage of the expressions when they are coincidently introduced again in the actual dialogues from the textbook. This way, many students even start talking in Korean during the first semester. They enjoy saying those expressions they wanted to learn. Obviously, in two semesters with this method, students pick up much more improved levels of the physical capacity, linguistic intuition, and linguistic resources to speak Korean as well.

In the program, I offer three semesters of Babble Training to talk. In the 3rd semester, I add 'say it Korean' session after each lesson. Students are required to present their own story for about three minutes on the topics of each lesson. Students who finish the 3rd semester with high level of performance can command the Korean language quite well.

Even though the method is still being developed to maximize its power of helping students to gain the linguistic skills and to develop the oral proficiency of TL, I, based on the experience and observation through teaching both Korean and English, have clearly observed that the successful acquisition of the linguistic skills and development of the oral proficiency of TL clearly depends on the quantity, quality, and reality of the linguistic resources of TL which are retained by the students through Babble Training. That is, the more thorough Babble Training to talk on more linguistic resources is required for the students, the better linguistic skills are acquired, and the higher oral proficiency is developed by the students.

CHAPTER 8

How To Teach: BTM Level 1 – Starting Babble Training for Talking

Nothing started without imitation.

1

Ideas for Class Design

As I have pointed out in an earlier article, I believe that language acquisition is achieved through obtaining such acquisition factors as the comprehensive linguistic intuition, the physical capacity, and the linguistic resources of TL. Therefore, the FL educators, who should aim for students to gain the acquisition factors first, should focus on developing a most effective FLE curriculum for students to achieve such acquisition factors.

For students to secure the acquisition factors of TL requires, first of all, a lot of Babble Training to talk, which include repeated efforts of recitation and real practice over variety of various situation based expressions for quite a period, and creative efforts to utilize such recited expressions in real life are required. FL teachers should consider such requirements when designing a class. Looking into the requirements in detail, one can easily find that the requirements are composed of four issues: (1) intensive babblings, (2) variety of expressions, (3) continued efforts to maintain Babble Training for quite a period of time, and (4) efforts to say one's own meaning. Accordingly, FL classes should be designed in such ways as to assure the fulfillment of the requirements.

To fulfill the first issue, the class should be designed in a way to assure that the students repeat Babble Training always; for the second issue, new linguistic resources should be continuously offered to the students; and, for the third issue, students should be led to continue the babble efforts for enough time of duration; and for the last but not least issue, students should be led to speak their own meanings. In other words, the roles of FL teacher as a babble leader and babble coach need to be balanced very well.

The followings are some of the ideas to be considered in designing the level 1 Babble Training class:

For the beginning level, class operations should be led in the official language of the class to start with. This helps the communication between the teacher and the students for effective operation of the class, and it also helps students to understand the process and to focus better on practicing and acquiring linguistic resources being introduced to them. Many people suggest that Direct Methods should be applied from the beginning. However, it would add to the difficulties of learning TL, and delay the real process of acquiring TL. Once students are settled down toward the middle of the first semester, it would be good to start using TL for brief expressions like greetings and directing simple activities such as 'please read', 'please try it again', and etc.

The goal of level 1 Babble Training level should be to help students to acquire TL to the level of a 40 months old child in mother tongue acquisition by acquiring about 500 personal languages[28] successfully. This way, students will establish solid foundation for

---

[28]   I use the term, personal languages, in reference to the colloquial languages spoken by TL speakers in personal activity environments such as greetings, describing one's feelings such as being cold, hot, chilly, smelling, being cool, liking, and disliking, asking questions for clarification or repetition, asking for direction, asking for how to, complaining for pain, watching TV, grocery shopping, reading books, listening to music, cooking, responding to questions or requests, talking about family members, friends, getting up, going to bed, being late to school, time, colors, animals, age, address, email address, phone numbers, home, house, shopping, sizes, prices, money, health, studying, going to school, going to church, vacation, getting driver's license, applying for SSN, going to a post office, meals, weather, season, going to a doctor's appointment, traveling by air plane, train, car, or bike, and etc.

comprehensive linguistic intuition, the physical capacity, and the basic level of linguistic resources with the skill to produce simple expressions to build the oral proficiency.

The time period to complete the level 1 Babble Training varies depending on the student ages, number of students in a class, number of class hours per week, and the class hour. However, for college students with 5 class hours per week, level 1 Babble Training can be completed in about 3 semesters.

Typically, the class time can flexibly be split into three sections respectively for own meaning talk to personalize the expressions acquired through the babble, reviewing previously introduced expressions, and introduction of new linguistic resources.

Special focus should be given for students to obtain each set of expressions to fluent level of performance, and to maintain the acquired expressions through the repetition of the babbling.

Students should be encouraged to personalize the expressions acquired through Babble Training.

Evaluations should be done mainly to test students on the fluency of dialogue performance, successful acquisition and maintenance of the dialogue expressions, and building up a strong resource pool.

For detail references, let me explain some of what I do for my Korean class with a note again that, by introducing some aspects of my classes, I do not mean by any sense that the ways I do to lead the class are the best of all. Depending on various factors such as the students, teachers, time, and students' commitments, many different ways of leading classes are possible.

For the 1st semester of Babble Training to talk, I typically greet students in Korean when entering the classroom. Then as students get used to the class, I start saying some routine simple expressions in Korean. However, for the most effective communication with the students with respect to operating the class, I lead the class mostly in English during the first half of the semester. The major goals of the class are to help students to develop the physical capacity to deal with the phonological sounds, and to acquire those expressions which students can utilize in the basic daily life environments.

The regular class during the first semester is composed of three sessions in somewhat flexible way: review, 'Words of the day', and textbook.

The review session helps students a lot as it gives daily opportunities for students to perform repeatedly over the expressions previously introduced. It also helps students get to know each other. I typically spend the first 15 minutes for 'review' session, where students are asked to practice in groups or with partners over the dialogues from previously introduced chapters. I would assign a couple of particular chapters for them to practice over during the time. Students are encouraged to speak relying solely on the English translation pages, not opening the Korean dialogue pages. Also, they are encouraged to help each other whenever necessary.

This way, they can learn more effectively by helping or teaching their partners. Then, at the end of the review session, I would ask some students to perform conversations between them over the dialogues for evaluation. For this, I present the English lines of the conversation to the screen so that the students can read them and say the Korean expressions corresponding to them.

While I do the evaluation, I correct wrong performances, mostly strong accents and mispronunciations, of the students whenever I find them to be serious. For corrections, I always try to encourage and not to embarrass the students. I let them know that it is very natural to mispronounce foreign languages. Some students work so hard that they tend to be over confident with the pronunciation by saying words too fast. Those students deserve praises and compliments before correction. Typically, I would say the words or expression first, and ask the student to try them again.

The 'Words of the day' session is to introduce some expressions which students want to learn right away. Typically, I introduce 3-4 new expressions daily based on the questions of 2-3 students. This way, I allow the students to choose what they want to learn from the class. Sometimes, I also volunteer some expressions. The extra expressions introduced to the students through are stored into a computer database and simultaneously presented to the students through the screen.

Then, each of the expressions is allotted to respective chapters for the students to study for the purpose of evaluations like daily review, quiz, midterm, and final exams. For example, any extra expressions collected during the progress of chapter 1 will be included to be part of the chapter, and the students will be tested for the expressions from both the textbook and the database as well.

During the textbook session, I introduce the dialogue expressions from the textbook with foci on the phonological sounds of each expression, and the meaning interpretation mostly based on the vocabularies and the particles. I always try to identify the meanings of each word and particles instead of offering grammatical analysis for the meaning interpretation.

The 2nd semester of Babble Training is basically the same as the 1st semester except that the class is more flexible depending on students' responses, and that I gradually increase the use of Korean during the class by starting the class with simple questions like "What did you do last night?" in Korean for students to answer. I let each student answer the question in Korean.

Depending on the responses from the students, I would lead them into another question also to promote or maintain the interest of the class. Whenever new real expressions are introduced during this free talking, I enter them into a database for a presentation to the class, and lead the class to practice those expressions.

The structure of the regular class for the 3rd semester of Babble Training is also basically the same as the 2nd semester except for 'say it in Korean' session at the end of each lesson. For this session, students are required to make a 3 minute presentation of their own stories, or other people's stories they know, in Korean about the topic introduced in each lesson.

By this time, most of the students who have successfully finished the previous two semesters can communicate in Korean quite well based on the physical capacity, linguistic intuition, and the linguistic resources on Korean they have secured so far.

From the 4th semester, Babble Training includes presentation on daily journal and on specific subjects assigned to students in addition to the use of textbooks. The major difference of Babble Training between up to the 3rd semester and from the 4th semester is that, while Babble Training up to the 3rd semester is mainly based on recitation of dialogue expressions on various situations, from the 4th semester it is mainly based on creative speaking of one's own meaning.

2

Ideas for Evaluation Methods

Along with the class design, the design of evaluation methods is very important as the ways and focus of studying for the students are naturally led by the styles of the evaluations. Regardless of how class is taught or managed, students are very sensitive and naturally tuned to adjust themselves to the trends of the evaluations. Accordingly, the evaluation method and the class design should be supportive to each other toward the right direction of TL acquisition.

Unless we, FL teachers, develop good methods of evaluating the students for continuous Babble Training efforts over variety of expressions, we would not be able to offer effective education for students to continue their efforts toward the acquisition of TL. Again, I will introduce the evaluation methods which I have worked so far on my own class. Even though it may not be the best evaluation method for every different situation, I believe it is well worthy of being a good reference to look at.

I design the evaluation of my students mainly with such methods as the review evaluation, quizzes, homework, oral midterm, written midterm, conversation with partners, say it in Korean, daily journals, oral final, and written final, and language copying in such a way with a focus of the students' fluent speaking skills for the expressions introduced by each chapter during the class.

Typically, I do the review evaluation for about two to four students a day depending on the situations. For the evaluation, selected students are asked to perform the roles of each participant in the dialogues of a chapter which is previously introduced to the class.

Depending on the number of students in a class, all of the students are required to have up to 10-15 review evaluations through out the semester. As a management strategy, among all of the evaluation items, I put the most weight on the review evaluation for the final grades. Accordingly, the students understand that the random daily evaluation are very important, and expect any day to be called for the review evaluation. For the beginners, majority portion of students' grades are coming from the review evaluation.

For the review evaluation, I already have explained before what it is and how I do it. Especially, as a way of promoting effective Babble Training for students, the review evaluation for the 1st year continues through out the year, which means that the linguistic resources introduced during the first semester are still being tested partially during the 2nd semester.

That is, the chapter one of the 1st semester would be excluded from the review evaluation upon the beginning of the chapter two of the 2nd semester; and the chapter two of the 1st semester upon the beginning of the chapter three of the 2nd semester; and so on. For effective Babble Training purposes, it would be very desirous to include the linguistic resources introduced during the 2nd semester in the review evaluation of the 3rd semester.

However, it has not been realistic in my program mainly due to the facts that the summer break after the 2nd semester is too long; that not many students continue taking the class for three semesters in a row, and that many of the students in the 3rd semester are new to the class who have not taken the previous Babble Training classes, but learned Korean from somewhere else.

For evaluation purposes, I grade the student's performance based on 15 points: 7 points for recitation of the resources, 5 points for fluency, and 3 points for presentation.

For the quiz evaluation during the 1st semester, I used to adopt dictation type vocabulary quizzes with the emphasis on the ability to write down the vocabulary correctly upon listening. This type of quiz was partially triggered by the fact that the vocabularies offered through the textbooks I have been using were not so many, especially for college students, that I would have enough time to dictate most of them during the class hour.

From the second semester, I put the English words in the quiz so that the students could write down the counter parts in Korean. The scores of the quizzes are graded based on the correct answers.

However, ever since I have been able to provide and control sufficient amount of linguistic resources, apart from the textbook, through the 'words of the day', I have changed the type of the quiz. In the new type of quiz, other than the very first quiz where I apply the dictation type quiz after the 1st lesson of Korean language orientation, I put all the vocabulary questions in Korean so that the students can write down the meanings in English.

This way, the quiz got easier for the students, but I could put a lot more questions on the quiz. As long as the students focus on intensive Babble Training, they should be able to solve most of the quiz questions and, therefore, the quiz should not be an extra burden to them. Consequently, I put more emphasis on the significance of Babble Training over the ability to the character writing skills.

For each quiz questions up to the 4th semester, I always give numeric numbers in Korean, starting with low level numbers in the beginning and going higher gradually, so that the students can be familiar with the number system quickly. I also put default questions for the students to write down in Korean words for each quiz: the year, month, date, day, and the time of the respective quizzes.

Also, included in the default questions are putting down one's own or friend's phone numbers, and one's own or friend's DOB in Korean. The purpose of such default quiz questions each time is to help the students be familiar with the basic usages of the numbers in various contexts in TL, and the students are told that the information does not necessarily need to be accurate.

Depending on the levels of students, oral proficiency tests are given frequently through out the semester through conversation with partners, OMTs (Oran Matching Test) for the midterm and final, language copying, say-it-in Korean sessions, daily-journal-in Korean sessions, or by asking students a series of questions, or asking students to make short and long presentations.

The design of class and the evaluation methods of FLE should be developed in accordance with the education environment and the linguistic characteristics of TL. In this point, what I presented above can be used as a reference. FL teaching environments are all different depending on the students, schools, FL teachers, government policies, TL, and etc. Therefore, FL teachers should study the environments given first, and develop the most effective methods to provide efficient Babble Training of each level with the students.

3

Things to Teach Before Babble Training

Earlier, I pointed out three acquisition factors to be secured for one to be a fluent speaker of a language: linguistic intuition, physical capacity, and linguistic resources. Without these factors all together in harmonious operation, one cannot acquire TL, nor can achieve high level of oral proficiency of TL. Here, being fluent means more like very natural process of commanding TL as opposed to manual or artificial. One could manually force and operate the brain and speech organs in sequence to assemble some expressions and spit them out based on the knowledge of the system and rules of TL.

However, simply being able to manually produce some clumsy expressions is not what we, as FL teachers and FL students, should be satisfied with after multi years of FL classes. Therefore, the goal of FLE should be to offer an education where students can pick up the acquisition factors most effectively. For this, I proposed BTM as the best way to help the students acquire the acquisition factors simultaneously. The first level of BTM is Babble Training to talk.

Then, how much and what do we need to teach before we really start teaching our students Babble Training to talk?

To answer this question, let's first look at the infants' case of starting the babble. The infants do not receive any formal information on their target languages. They are directly exposed to the language, which they don't understand to start with. They are constantly asked same type of questions in numerous repetitions even when they don't understand a word. Then, once they start babbling, they are led to repeat the babble as the care givers really love interact with them. It is not until they reach middle school age that they learn about the rules and system of the language.

Also, young children who start learning a new language in kindergarten or elementary school do not receive formal educations on how the language works. Rather, they are directly exposed to the language. With this direct exposure to the language, the children are challenged to do babbling. They confront situations where they would have to say something, and they start imitating simply what others say in a similar situation. They cannot say creative things for long time, at least for 6 to 12 months. Their pronunciation sounds clumsy in the beginning, but quickly gets better as they repeat the same expression whenever confronting the challenges repeatedly. They do the babble mostly while getting along with the friends by talking the same expressions repeatedly. They also do Babble Training while they are alone by talking to themselves.

Meanwhile, young children who are taught FL in school without being confronted to say expressions in TL by the environment show different aspect of the language acquisition. So far, I have not heard of any school that intensively teaches grammar or the rules of FL to the children of elementary school or younger age.

Instead, the school would teach many different expressions of TL to the students, or tell stories in TL. In this case, the levels of TL acquisition depend on individual's efforts to maintain the expressions through repeated Babble Training to oneself over time. Obviously, compared to the environment where the children are challenged to speak TL in daily life, it takes much longer time for them to acquire TL, and most of them do not make it for many reasons.

Based on these observations, it is clear that one does not necessarily have to know the system and rules of TL to start Babble Training to talk. Instead, it shows that the environment of confronting one to imitate or babble over others' expressions plays very important role in language acquisition.

Therefore, based on the language acquisition cases of infants and young children, providing linguistic resources for the students to babble over, and confronting the students to babble consistently seem to be the key elements for success.

However, depending on the age groups of students, I believe that teaching some of the very basic characteristics of TL could be helpful for students to promote the efficiency of acquisition. For very young students like kindergartners and elementary children, I believe that direct exposure to the babble situation of TL is more appropriate than trying to start teaching them some basic features of TL prior to applying BTM to them. It is because that they are too young to understand those features and would not be able to utilize such basic features appropriately in learning TL.

On the other hand, for the students of above-the-middle-school age, I believe some degree of preceding knowledge of TL is helpful for them to do the babble more efficiently.

Then, to the students of the secondary and above education, how much of what should we teach to help the students do the babble most efficiently?

I believe that, before starting to teach the babble, FL teachers should better teach the students the very basic features of TL which are necessary for the students to read loud and look up the base forms of lexical items in TL dictionary. For this, the alphabet letters and the sound of each letter should be taught.

Also, the basic ways for the letters to form syllables or characters need to be taught so that the student can figure the sound of words based on the individual sound of the letters. Once the students can figure out the sounds by looking at the words, it would help them a lot with maintaining and continuing the babble for themselves.

This way, whoever wishes to continue the babble process can pursue the process by oneself without having to always listening to the sound.

To sum up, one can do the babble and start acquiring TL without having to have any preceding preparation or study of TL before babbling. With no knowledge of the language, students can focus on the babble process more, especially on picking up the sounds and sets of expressions as heard. Students in Babble Training would be less disturbed by having no knowledge of TL. Adult students will benefit if we teach them, before Babble Training process, how to figure out the sounds of words and sentences.

Therefore, if one would insist on teaching students about TL before starting to teach the babble, it should only be so much as necessary to carry out the babble process efficiently. All the rules and system of TL are to be acquired as a part of the linguistic intuition naturally by the students through the babble process.

4

Types of Linguistic Resources

With the revolutionary development of the technology, many different types of FLE materials have emerged. All different varieties of books, audios, videos, and internet materials on foreign languages are out there waiting to be picked up by us and our students.

Many of the books are about the grammar of TL, and many others are of useful expressions for traveling and business trips in TL as well as of useful expression dictionaries. Concerning the audio materials, they are mostly of conversational expressions, famous stories or speeches, and reproduced media materials such as movies, and TV programs. The video materials are quite similar in nature to the audio materials except that it includes graphics. Some of the internet materials offer interactive phonics presentation.

None of them are useless or worthless at all. I believe that they are all great materials when they are used properly. Especially, I believe that all those materials are quite useful and needed for obtaining of TL skills according to the respective acquisition levels. However, if these are used without cautious judgment along with the process of language acquisition, they could cause very serious damages on our students.

Would the high-tech based materials mean to be better resources than those of old style? As FL teachers, what should we consider to choose appropriate resources for our classes? What are we going to recommend to our students for studying our languages?

Before we deal with how to deal with the different types of the FLE materials, I believe we should first think about various types of the linguistic resources which we should teach to the students.

Are we going to ask our beginning students to babble over the resources from famous stories or speeches? Or, are we going to use newspaper articles in TL for our students' babble? What about the scenarios for movies or plays? Can we put our students directly into the world of formal business languages? What if we start with about one or two page rather short articles at a time for the students to do babbling?

To answer these questions, we should consider some important factors including the goals of the respective babble levels. The fundamental goal of teaching the level 1 Babble Training is to help students to simultaneously achieve the three acquisition factors of TL. Among the acquisition factors, the linguistic intuition can be specified into the intuitions on the sound, word/sentence structure, and the usage of TL. Therefore, one should take this fundamental goal as a priority condition to be met when considering picking up a text material for the level 1 Babble Training.

In addition to the goal of babbling, we should seriously consider some practical issues: they should be doable, easy enough, interesting, useful, convenient, effective, and productive. Also, depending on the situations, we should consider the age groups of our students.

For more effective teaching, I hypothesize that most needed expressions can be obtained more quickly than any other less needed ones; that real expressions are acquired more quickly than those non-real expressions; and that simple expressions are secured faster than complicated expressions. The most needed expressions are decided by individual students from time to time.

Therefore, we should always encourage the students to bring questions of 'how to say in TL' for those expressions which they want to learn most. For the real expressions, teachers should consider the social levels of the students as the types of real expressions may differ for different groups of students. For example, none of the adult beginner students of TL would consider such kind of actual babble talk expressions as between a mother and a baby to be practical. That is, no matter how easy an expression would be, it would not be picked up quickly and remain for long time if it would not be practical to students.

Also, simple expressions in the form as well as the meaning of TL should be considered over complicated or sophisticated expressions in choosing the expressions to be introduced to students.

Considering the goal of Babble Training and the hypothesis, the linguistic resources to be introduced to students for the training purposes of Babble Training should be most needed, real, and simple. For this, I propose teaching students Babble Training with the linguistic resources from the daily activity based dialogues. Especially, in the very beginning of Babble Training to talk, the fundamental or survival communicative expressions like on how to make requests, questions, and responses should be taught.

Then, with gradual success based on such start, we can expand the sets of dialogues for various types of social and business situations in the following levels of babbling. Once the students establish basic communicative skills, it would also be good to utilize play scenarios on daily life stories as a source of the linguistic resources for Babble Training to talk.

Utilizing the resources from the daily life based dialogues seems to be very natural and to meet the goals of the babble education as well as the most, if not all, of the foresaid practical issues. The expressions of the dialogues are relatively short and the word/sentence structures therefore are simple and easy enough for the students to take the language naturally without having to rely on the knowledge of the TL grammar.

Of course, because the daily life based dialogue expressions are short and simple structured, the sound features of them are easier for the students to catch. Also, students do not need to rely on grammatical knowledge to figure out the meanings of each expression.

Accordingly, students can do the babble repeatedly with ease by themselves if they are committed to learn the language. The fact that students can utilize the expressions, which they have babbled over the regular process of Babble Training to talk, very conveniently even if they have not acquired the language yet pretty well could be the biggest benefit for using the daily life based dialogues as resources for the babble. That is, by acquiring the useful expressions for various situations through Babble Training process, the students can utilize them when situated to similar situations by visiting or traveling to the TL community.

Compared to the daily life based dialogue expressions as a source for the resources, utilizing other types of sources for the linguistic resources such as news articles, famous speeches and stories, movies, magazines, novels, and etc, could be quite dry, difficult and less effective for most of the students to perform the babble to talk.

Looking at the natural process of language acquisition by children, who do the babble over the daily life based dialogues, starting Babble Training over the resources from the daily life related convenient expressions seem to be quite natural.

Also, based on my own experiences of teaching Korean as FL to my university students, and teaching myself English, and based on the observations on the disappointing results of so many people who studied TL with TV programs, movies, and other general audio medias from the beginning, and others who started learning TL with grammar, reading, or listening from the beginning, I believe Babble Training of daily activity based dialogues is very effective.

Further, many people who read my humble book, whose English title is *New TESL Plus*, which was published in Korean in 2005, and performed the dialogue based BTM along with my suggestions from the book, have sent me messages conforming that it had been working really good for them.

With respect to the types of materials containing the resources, I believe that book and audio set material is most effective for the students to study FL. Video and internet materials, on the other hand, are less effective.

5

Things to Consider Before Choosing Text Materials

As the traditional FLE methods have not really focused on teaching oral proficiency skills, not many text materials have been produced for such purposes. Thousands of reference materials for FLE are designed and published to meet the needs for the traditional FLE methods: mostly various levels of books on grammar, reading materials, and listening comprehension materials, which have been introduced to the market recently. Not many types of sophisticated study materials which are designed for students to successfully complete the natural process of Babble Training to acquire TL have been introduced to FLE field.

Therefore, changing the traditional trends of FLE into Babble Training method could be quite a challenge depending on languages. It is mostly our jobs, as FL teachers, to decide the text materials and the methods of teaching our languages to the students. Or, depending on languages, one may even consider developing some text materials by oneself in case one cannot find appropriate text materials for the students.

In fact, the task of developing textbook materials goes beyond the realm of any particular individual teacher. As FLE requires multiple years of time over different levels of schools, it requires systematic preparations not only for the writers of the text materials but also for FLE program developers across the levels of the schools. Without such systematic designs and links between the levels of schools, it would be quite difficult to maintain the continuity and consistency of FL class for different levels of schools.

The most basic ideas for us, FL teachers, to develop or choose the textbook materials for FL education can be borrowed from the ways of the piano teachers developing or choosing the textbook materials to teach their students. It is because, basically, the language training process for FL should be just like the piano training process.

Now, let's assume that there are various types of reference books for us to use, and think about some issues which we should consider to select text materials to teach students in accordance with Babble Training method.

First, it should match the level of the students' physical capacity to perform TL. For example, for very beginners, each line of the expression sets should be short and easy enough to do babbling.

One of the most important goals in the very beginning level of Babble Training is for students to acquire the intuition on the sound system of TL through the acquisition of very basic expressions. Such intuition is also a part of the physical capacity to carry out the oral language.

Another goal for the beginning level of Babble Training is to acquire the pronunciation skills. The natural recognition of the sound system and the pronunciation skills of TL can be acquired through Babble Training over short and easy expressions. Therefore, choosing text materials with highly complicated dialogue sets for very beginners would not be the best idea.

Second, it should have audio sets available. Especially, the usage of such audio sets is very beneficial for those who would like to teach FL to oneself. It is very inefficient and time consuming for one to do Babble Training by oneself without the pronunciations by native speakers. One also could easily be stuck with incorrect pronunciations. Not only the people who teach FL at schools, but also the people who teach FL to oneself are of course FL teachers.

In addition, those parents who try to teach FL to their children are also FL teachers. Also, the audio sets for the level 1 Babble Training should better include the explanations in one's MT on the meaning of the expressions as well as on the skills of producing some difficult sound of TL. This will make it much easy for students to babble after the expressions by listening to the audio sets only any time and any where. If the audio would contain only TL expressions without detail explanations about the meanings and the pronunciation skills of TL expressions, it would be too much overwhelming for beginning students to listen to and babble over the expressions.

Another reason for the audio sets being so crucial is that students should be able to listen to and babble the expressions any time and any where they want to outside of the classroom. That is, the audio sets are definitely needed to do Babble Training along with the daily activity pattern. This is why audio sets are much more preferred over the video sets or internet media: Audio sets are portable, but the video sets and internet media are not so much portable as the audio sets. This is the key issue of BTM: students should be able to do Babble Training repeatedly as many times as they can.

Also, the audio set is strongly required for the teachers who are not fluent in TL. Non-native teachers who cannot speak TL fluently should recommend the audio sets for students to use for the purpose of Babble Training. Even though it is very rare in the USA for a foreign language to be taught by non-native speaker teachers or teachers who cannot speak TL fluently, it is still very common in other countries that non-native speaker teachers or teachers who cannot speak TL teach TL to the students. This has been possible so far because the FL teachers have been teaching mostly the grammar and reading skills of TL only in the school. The teachers can teach grammar and reading without having to be fluent in TL.

Third, the dialogue expressions should be real for the students to utilize in daily basis. Especially for students in the beginning level, the dialogue sets should be very real so that they could frequently use them after enough Babble Training on them. The beginners should start acquiring as many instrumental expressions[29] as possible of TL rather than quite sophisticated expressions.

One of the merits for BTM is that after Babble Training, students can utilize the expressions learned from schools in real life even without the complete acquisition of TL. Even if students discontinue studying TL after a semester or so, they still should be able to use the real expressions quite fluently when needed. Therefore, the beginning level of Babble Training material especially should introduce as many instrumental expressions as possible so that the students can still use them very effectively even with short period of studying TL.

Fourth, the linguistic resources introduced to the students should be contemporary and standard registry of the language. Languages are very culture specific that no languages are independent from the contemporary cultures of the country. Also, different community groups tend to share different registries of the language. Accordingly, the dialogue expressions should be updated to the contemporary standard registry of TL.

Fifth, it should cover the variety of real life situations and idiomatic expressions as many as possible. The textbook should introduce variety of expressions from various sources that do not linguistically translate well into other languages. Rather than pattern based drilling over a particular type of sentence pattern, it should introduce sentences of various structures and idiomatic expressions so that students can advance further into the language specific features. The pattern focused drill, which in nature is not a productive way of speaking, in a sense would delay the progress of Babble Training.

---

[29]   Instrumental expressions here refer to such expressions as required to continue communications for survival in the TL community.

6

Roles of a BTM Teacher

Level 1 Babble is starting Babble Training to talk, which is the most basic and important step to acquire language. Basically, based on observing the MT acquisition by children, 100% of language acquisition is made through Babble Training only by around 36-40 months. Many kids seem to acquire MT even by around 30 months. No reading, no writing, no listening to radio or watching TV, and no grammar is required for children to acquire MT.

All the linguistic activities such as reading, writing, and watching TV by the children after the acquisition of MT naturally improve their language skills. This language skill improving process through reading hundreds of books, writing so many school journals and reports, watching movies, and studying grammar continues through out one's college. Therefore, Babble Training is very crucial to the acquisition of TL. Those who succeed in Babble Training will be fluent speaker of TL, and those who fail in Babble Training will remain as a reader of TL at most.

Then, how can we be successful in leading the students to start and continue Babble Training to talk? We are very familiar with how the babble interactions take place between the babble leader, care providers, mostly parents, and the baby. The babble leader tends to exaggerate most of the linguistic and non-linguistic features to the baby. Also, the leader would start the interaction with very simple words describing what is being or happening right in front of the baby. No textbooks and no prepared expressions are used. Every thing is very instantaneous. In MT acquisition process, the interactions between the babble leader and the baby are very natural.

However, the milieu for FLE classes is quite different from that for MT learning. Instead of very flexible, one to one, and real life contexts, FLE class is more of restricted, one to many, and artificial contexts. However, the fact that the students have much more developed intelligence and understand better can really overcome the shadow coming from such class environment.

Then, how should we design our language classes for the students to do Babble Training efficiently? Also, should we play the role of the babble leaders in MT acquisition process? Or, should we play the role of Babble Training coach like football coach running a football team? Or, should we play the role of a college professor giving lectures on highly sophisticated subjects?

As FL teachers, we need to understand that the secret of Babble Training is not in being very good for the exam season only with cramming efforts on a couple of nights, but in being adjusted and improved steadily over time through consistent and repetitive efforts. This is because language acquisition is less of being bright, but much more of putting steady and thorough efforts over time. Through the adjustments, students build up the linguistic intuition, physical capacity, and the linguistic resources of TL which are necessary to obtain TL. Therefore, the babble class should be designed in such a way that students are required to perform Babble Training every day through out the semester and the year in and out of the classroom.

Regarding the roles that we should play as FL teachers, good or bad, we should be able to play all of the three roles very well. That is, we should be able to play the roles of a good babble leader, good coach, and professor at a time needed. Yet, I think that the roles of a good babble leader and a good coach are very much needed most of the time to be FL teacher. Especially, designing an effective course plan and managing the students to follow the plan are the most important role I believe.

Now, what would be an effective FL babble class design? How can we manage the students to do Babble Training every day? I will introduce some ideas of teaching FL babble classes mostly from what I have been doing at my Korean classes. It has been updated every year with the things that I have found from the classes of past years. I see it quite effective in the given circumstances of my university.

By quoting some examples from what I have been doing in my classes, I am not saying that what I have been doing is the most effective ways. Classes may be different from each other for many reasons such as student ages, number of students in a class, number of class hours per week, levels of students, students' commitment and efforts, and etc. Rather, I am saying that one should design the babble class in the best possible way for given milieu that students can learn TL most effectively.

7

Roles of a Babble Leader

The very first and fundamental role that FL teachers have to play in Babble Training class is the role of the babble leader. That is, the teacher as a babble leader should present the students with linguistic resources which are composed of dialogue expressions selected from various types of sources.

The detail ways of demonstrating the linguistic resources to students could be different for different ages and levels of the students: elementary, middle school, high school, and college students for beginning level, intermediate level, and advanced level respectively. I would say that the younger the students are, the more visual presentation would be necessary as it could be too boring for them to get the expressions purely from textbooks.

However, for adult students like college students, I would think that plain and simple presentation directly from textbooks would be better for focus purpose. My students have seemed to be fine with such kind of simple presentation so far. Therefore, at least for college students, it seems to be a good way for the teacher to present expressions, during the course of classes, to the students by demonstrating accurate performances of each line, mostly on the sounds and necessary gestures sometimes, on respective resources such as words, idioms, phrases, clauses, and sentences to the students.

If the teacher is not a native or fluent speaker of TL, the teacher may utilize audio or video equipments to present the linguistic resources to the students. Also, if one wishes to teach FL to oneself, one should consider oneself as a non-native and non fluent speaking teacher of TL, and utilize such equipments as a babble leader presenting the resources to oneself.

For beginning level students, for example, the demonstration should start in slower mode for the students to be able to imitate it. Then, once the students pick up the sounds, the students should be introduced to the normal speaking mode for the babble purpose.

Also, intensive training for students to articulate the resources as clearly and fluently as possible is very important at this stage. Depending on necessity, detail explanations and demonstrations of how to articulate difficult sounds should be offered. This is where it may be necessary for FL teacher to exaggerate the sounds and gestures of those words just like the babble leader for a baby would do to help the baby to learn how to make the sound.

After sufficient demonstrations of the resources or the dialogue expressions, typically 2-3 times of repetitions, students will have opportunities to repeat after the teacher's demonstration a couple of times, or more if needed. Then, students are asked to read the expressions under the advices of the teacher who would correct misarticulated sounds, if any. This way, the students would be ready to perform Babble Training on their own efforts outside of the classroom.

While a student reads, the teacher should listen and advise the student to fix the mispronounced sounds, if any, by explaining the reason for the inaccurate sounds, and showing how to fix them. This is the adjustment session for the students to work on adjusting and improving their physical capacity to articulate the words and expressions. Other students in the class should be benefited indirectly also by the explanation and the showing.

The lower level Babble Training is, the more time is needed for this adjustment session. Also, this adjustment session is very important in that repeated Babble Training over wrong pronunciation would lead students to build a strong bad habit of pronouncing the particular sounds incorrectly. It also could cause general weakness of performing the babble more effectively.

After the adjustment session, the teacher offers further meaning based linguistic information on respective sentence components such as morphemes, words, idioms, related expressions, and etc. Most of the particles and conjugations can be explained by offering the meanings for each of them, and no lengthy grammatical explanation is necessary. This way, students will learn the system of rules one by one and case by case at a time during the acquisition process. During the process of Babble Training to talk, systematic grammatical approach to the resources being introduced to the class is not necessary and should be avoided as it could deviate the students' interests into wrong directions.

At the end of each chapter, students should be evaluated for the recitation of the dialogues of the chapter. The review evaluation is not simply to check the memory status of the students but the quality of the resources retained by the students. Depending on the acquisition level of the expressions, the degrees of fluency, speed, the articulations, and the confidence in the recitation vary. Memory based recitation would be obviously notable in that the process of speech gets significantly delayed, quite clumsy articulation of sounds, and lack of confidence.

FL teacher's role as a babble leader as shown above continues. Yet, as the students gain more and more expressions, the role of a babble leader should be flexible and adjusted accordingly just like the parents role as babble leader to the kids changes in accordance to the acquisition level of the kids.

Also, at the end of each chapter, students should be tested on the vocabularies and idiomatic expressions used in the chapter. This way, teacher's role as a babble leader for a chapter or a set of dialogue expression is concluded.

8

Roles of a Babble Coach

As Babble Training makes progress by completing lesson by lesson, the next role for FL teachers to be added on top of the babble leader role is a babble coach's role to lead the students to keep Babble Training over the expressions so that the students maintain and improve the acquisition level of the expressions. The role as a coach is more about coaching the students what to do and how to do outside of the class.

Repeated Babble Training or practices over the expressions contained in respective lessons during the class is not enough for the students to acquire the resources. Depending on the degrees of acquisition, the students' linguistic skills to naturally utilize the expressions in real situations vary.

Also, the more quantity and the higher quality of expressions are retained by students, they will pick up the language quicker and easier. In the same sense, the more Babble Training one does accurately, the more linguistic intuition and physical capacity to perform TL is acquired. Therefore, to manage students to keep Babble Training over the presented linguistic resources which are introduced during the class is one of the most important tasks along with the role of leading the babble as a FL teacher.

As FL class goes on through out the semester and the year, the number of lessons covered during the classes will increase, and so will the amount of linguistic resources to be retained by each student. In the beginning, the burden for the students to obtain the linguistic resources is not much, but it will increase gradually.

If the students would not acquire the resources in time along with the class progress and put it off until later, they could easily be overwhelmed by the accumulated amount of expressions and lose the courage to carry on. Therefore, coaching the students to manage time and efforts in timely manner along with the progress being made during the class is crucial.

I believe that successful coaching for the students to manage their time and efforts begins with the class design and the methods of the evaluations. Depending on the class designs and evaluation methods, the language skills of the students on TL can be drastically different. Especially, regardless of the class designs, the methods and goals of the evaluation dramatically influence on the students' fundamental attitudes of studying.

If the evaluation, for example, would mostly require students to fill in words in parentheses for quizzes and exams, the students would develop their own strategies of studying only to be able to figure out and write in correct words in the parentheses, which is not most effective in terms of picking up TL.

Also, if the evaluations would focus on testing the students about various subjects such as grammar, vocabularies, reading comprehension, and writing, the students would have to diversify their efforts in so many different directions without being able to focus on particular areas. Basically, to the students, the issue of acquiring TL or not cannot be a bigger concern than getting high scores on the exams. In other words, they are more concerned about how to get high scores on the exams than anything else.

Therefore, FL teachers should understand and be careful not to diversify the students' attention into many different areas by implementing inefficient evaluation policy. Rather, all evaluations should be consistent and focused on the most important agenda of the class. For example, for the classes of Babble Training to talk, the evaluations for the lessons, quizzes, midterms, and finals should be developed in a way for students to be able to successfully manage them by exerting efforts focused on Babble Training to talk.

In my case, I evaluate the students in Babble Training class with the recitation of each lesson, review evaluation, midterm recitation, and final recitation as well as with the quizzes for each lesson, midterm and final. Especially, the review evaluation for the first two semesters requires students to be really focused as it includes expressions from the previous semester. Therefore, students whoever work hard to thoroughly acquire the expressions introduced through the class would successfully manage all the evaluations.

Except for the review evaluation after each lesson, students are expected to be tested on all expressions which have been introduced to them through the class by the time of the daily recitation, midterm recitation, and final recitation. This is the same for the quizzes. Thus, I introduce and strongly recommend some ideas for them to efficiently acquire and maintain the ever increasing expressions as well as to improve physical capacity. Also, based on the advice from the coach and based on their own individual environments, the students develop their own strategies to maintain their acquisition of the expressions.

Also, even though it is not a method of evaluation, I always take some time trying to communicate with students utilizing some of the expressions previously introduced to the students. This way, students can get a fresh stimulation. With such fresh stimulation to the students, I push the students to improve their performance level to such a degree as they could use the expressions in real life situations. Also, I lead the students to feel rewarded by the fact that they could communicate with me in Korean in such a short time.

During the process of coaching the babble, I always strongly request for the students to listen repeatedly to all the dialogues introduced from the class back and forth, and to babble the expressions to themselves with the mouth wide open as many times as possible. They would not need to be in a library or in a quiet place to do this. They can do this Babble Training almost anywhere and anytime of the day if they are really committed to learn TL. This will improve their listening and speaking skills with a very high accuracy.

I also recommend that students should not spend time and efforts from the beginning stage on taking the expressions learned from the class as the base patterns for the exercise purpose of replacing some words with new ones to change part of the usage or meaning. Instead, I ask them to do Babble Training for listening and speaking if they have such time. This is because once the students really secure various expressions in high quality, it would be only a matter of vocabularies for them to be able to use them appropriately in somewhat similar situations.

Therefore, to be effective, it is more important to apply their time and efforts for picking up more number of expressions with higher quality rather than for exercising to utilize some of the expressions poorly acquired for different situations. When considering the fact that one of the most important goals for Babble Training is to acquire the physical capacity to perform TL naturally, it is very important to focus on developing such capacity rather than focusing on pattern expanding exercise in a clumsy manner. Focusing on pattern expanding exercise would delay the process of obtaining new sets of dialogues for variety of situations, which would eventually delay the whole process of TL acquisition. Also, pattern expanding exercises can be done easily by individual students. Therefore, during the class, it is better to focus on providing the students with more amounts of linguistic resources with high quality.

In summary, for the teaching of the level 1 Babble Training, the roles of FL teachers including self teachers and the parents of kids learning FL can be summarized as the role of a babble leader and the role of a babble coach. The role of a babble leader is to continuously introduce new linguistic resources in efficient manners so that the students can acquire appropriate language skills; and the role of a babble coach is to design and manage FLE systems for the students to continuously repeat Babble Training process over the new and old resources so that they can successfully acquire the linguistic intuition, physical capacity, and the linguistic resources which are required for the acquisition of TL.

9

Teaching How To
Understand Expressions

To secure TL expressions without understanding the meanings does not make a sense. Students should understand the meaning before acquiring any expressions. Therefore, FL teachers should teach the meanings of each expression. Also, the teachers need to teach the students about how to understand the meanings. This is where the grammarians argue that grammar education is needed for the students' understanding. They don't think that students can understand meanings of expressions without applying the grammar based analysis to the sentence.

However, it is one of the biggest misunderstandings by those people who insist on grammar education in FLE that students cannot understand sentences without grammatical knowledge of TL. Most of daily life based dialogue expressions are simple and easy to understand by nature. They are not highly technical or complex. Thus, during the process of Babble Training to talk, students can easily understand the general linguistic features of TL simply by learning the meanings of each sentence components as well as the meaning of the sentence. Students do not need to go through intensive grammar programs from the beginning.

The following examples will show how easy it is to figure out the meanings of FL expressions without having to rely on grammatical knowledge of TL:

A: AnNyungHaSeYo?
Hi, how are you
Hi how are you?

B: An AnNyungHaSeYo?
Hi how are you?

A: NalSsi-ka   AJu JoChiYo?
Weather-subject marker very   good-rhetorical question
The weather is very good, isn't it?

B: Ye, AJu JoAYo.
Yes very good
Yes, it is very good.

A: MinSu-Ssi ONul JeomSim Mua MokOssOYo?
Minsu-Mr today lunch/noon what eat-past tense
What did you have for the lunch today?

B: Bul-Go-Ki MokOssOYo
Bulgoki eat-past tense
I ate Bulgoki.

A: YiBon JooMal-e HalIl-i   ManAYo?
This week end-at work to do-subject marker a lot
Do you have a lot of things to do coming week end?

B: ANiYo. ByolRo OpsOYo.
No   particularly not exist
No, not thing to do particularly.

A: KuRom, YiBon JooMal-e Mua HalKoYeYo?
Then this week end-at whatwill do
Then, what will you do on coming week end?

B: ORaeGanMan-e Jom Pook ShiGo SipOYo.
In a long time-at sort of deeply rest would like to
I would like to take a deep rest in a long time.

As shown above, by giving detail meanings for the individual words, idioms and particles, the meanings for most of the sentences become quite obvious by themselves. Then, some of the ambiguities of the meanings can be clarified by an explanation of the fact that the pronouns well known to each other can be dropped in Korean just as the English language sometimes drops the clearly understood components of a sentence like "Good luck".

Even though I used some Korean examples here, I believe that all human languages can be approached by the same way. In the examples above, I used some of the grammatical terms like subject marker and past tense for the convenient sake of glossing the particles. However, I did not mean to introduce the grammar to explain the meanings of the expressions. Such terms can be replaced with lay terms to meet the understanding level of the students.

As students collect more and more expressions on various topics, students will learn various types of regular patterns during the process in addition to the expressions which they could use in daily life. As the students find the regular patterns of particular linguistic areas such as tense, number, aspect, honorific usage, case, and etc. depending on the languages, such findings through the collection of various TL expressions will be accumulated case by case toward the linguistic intuition of the students. This way, the students easily figure out the patterns on those linguistic features which are mostly introduced to them such as case, tense, number, and etc.

Toward the end of the first semester, I normally would give a special lecture on some particular types of regularly occurring patterns like tense, case, and particles for honorific speech forms of Korean. Before I give a special lecture on particular type of patterns, I emphasize that what I would present is only to help the students understand some of the regular phenomena; that students would not be tested on the subjects of my special lecture; and that, therefore, students should not worry about not knowing or understanding the phenomena.

I give such a special lecture to the students mainly because the class is composed of college students whose understanding and learning capacity is fully developed, and who, with far less time to study Korean, still need to start from the very beginning level of Babble Training to talk. For this reason, for those young students like in elementary or middle schools, who take FL class based on a long term program, I would not consider giving such a special lecture to them, but purely focus on offering most effective Babble Training possible to the students.

10

Things to Watch For

As it is true for many things in our life, good starting is also very important for both FL teachers and students. I always find that the students who missed the very first class of each semester in my program have hard time to follow the class. They tend to be out of tune with what I am trying to teach in the class.

During the first class of each semester, I, like most of other teachers, always do orientations for the students about my plans for the semester. I tell the class about how I would lead the class; how students should prepare for the class; what I expect from the students; the methods of evaluations; and the things to avoid.

Among the things for the students to avoid especially for the beginning class is forming the habit of glossing the sounds of word with one's own phonetic symbols. Based on my experiences, the students who glossed the sound of words with phonetic symbols always turned out to be the slower readers in the class. Also, their articulation skills are generally weaker than others in the class. It always took much longer time for them to figure out the individual sounds of the letters or characters.

Typically, in my class, students start reading Korean in about 3 weeks. In about 4-5 weeks, students can read Korean smoothly with quite accurate articulations. However, the students who built a habit of glossing the sounds with phonetic symbols took over 8 weeks to be able to read, and some of them still cannot read very well even after the first semester. The sound glossing habit consequently makes student pay less attention on remembering the sounds for respective letters or characters during the class. When the students study, they rely upon the glossing which really cannot reflect the actual sounds. Therefore, they do create different sounds and build bad habits of mispronouncing the words.

Also, among the things for the students to avoid is stopping their efforts at the level of memorizing or reciting the expressions. The difference between the memorizing, reciting, and acquiring expressions is in whether the students do enough Babble Training or not. In between the memorizing and the acquiring of expressions is the recitation of the expressions. If memory is of simple recollection, recitation is of temporal reproduction, and acquisition is of productive communication.

One cannot perform proficiently language based on simple memory or temporal recitation. One can perform language fluently only with the acquired language skills. An efficient way of teaching students to acquire the language skills to talk is to lead the students to do Babble Training continuously over the expressions which are memorized and recited.

One of the ways to find whether a student's babble efforts is in memory, recitation, or acquisition level is the review evaluation. Typically, students cannot say the memorized expressions fluently due to the problems caused by lack of Babble Training such as mispronunciation, lack of confidence, lack of skills, and so on. Also, one can easily see the manual efforts by the students trying to retrieve the expressions from memory. Further, the difference between recited expressions and acquired expressions can be found through repeated review evaluation over time and through natural interaction with the student utilizing the subject expressions.

In addition to the sound glossing and simple memorizing or temporal recitation issues, students doing the babble with incorrect pronunciation should be corrected. If not, they could get stuck with the particular pattern of the sounds, and it will be difficult for them to correct the sounds later.

Also, Babble Training with narrowed mouth with fading voice should be corrected. Students should be encouraged to do Babble Training with widely open mouth and with loud enough voice, which helps a lot with forming accurate articulations. Students should frequently be reminded that the fluency and oral proficiency of one's TL skills would totally depend on the manners of Babble Training to talk.

Some students would insist on their old habits of studying FL relying on grammar reference books, and do not exert lot of efforts on babbling. This is because they believe that accumulating the knowledge on the rules and systems of TL would be most effective for them to learn TL. Those students should be introduced to watch and understand the natural language acquisition process.

For the students who wish to learn FL, there are a couple of very important things the students should always carry with.

First one is a solid, thick, and handy vocabulary notebook. This notebook is to hold the linguistic resources for Babble Training purposes such as sets of expressions, words, idioms, and other useful expressions from various sources which are to be collected.

Whenever new useful expressions are introduced to them during the class or outside of the class, students need to collect and maintain them very well so that they could always babble over the resources for acquisition. Students can use their textbook to keep the record of new linguistic resources. However, as one finishes the book and moves to the next book, it would not be easy for one to revisit the linguistic resources in the old book. I have found that students who maintain the vocabulary notebook well perform better in learning TL.

Second one is a portable audio player ("PAP") for obvious reasons. PAP really helps students to babble over variety sets of expressions. Without a PAP, students would have to rely on the class and the book only for babbling. However, when doing Babble Training after the class, it is not easy to remember the sounds accurately especially for the beginning class. PAP helps a lot to improve Babble Training quality as students can listen to the expressions any time and any where they want to. Also, students who utilized the audio system have shown much better performances in my class than others who do not use the system.

Finally, students should be reminded and encouraged to continue revisiting and repeating the babble on their own wills over all the linguistic resources as frequently as possible. If students would completely stop Babble Training for the breaks like summer vacations, they will lose a lot of linguistic resources quickly and eventually be discouraged to continue learning TL. FL teachers can have direct interactions with students only during the class hours, and would not be able to lead and coach the babble during the break. So, it is very important to remind the students to continue the efforts to obtain TL.

11

Equipments for Babble Training

I cannot emphasize the importance of Babble Training on real expressions too much. It is just like the football coaches who cannot emphasize the importance of the repeated trainings to develop skills and physical toughness for beginning football players. Yet, as FL teachers, we cannot be an all-time babble leader for our students like the mothers or fathers for their kids in natural language acquisition. Therefore, we should recommend the students to utilize the civilization of modern technology to hire any-time babble leader for them.

Among many high-tech based equipments which are used by many FL teachers and students are audio sets, video sets, computer phonics program, phone interactions, internet based visual interactions, cellular phone based services, and etc.

Then, what kinds of equipments would be most effective for Babble Training purpose. The answer may be different depending on the ages and levels of students. However, for adult students like high school and college students, I believe the audio sets are the most effective babble equipments for many reasons. I also believe that audio sets can still be most effective for most of young students as long as the students are willing to utilize such equipment.

Students should be recommended to babble over real expressions while listening repeatedly to the audio set, which, for the beginners, should be able to play both slow and normal modes of the language. This would help the students a lot to build the physical capacity to produce fluent pronunciations and to build very strong listening comprehension skill. If students would simply rely on FL class, and do the babble by reading the books, it would be harder and take much longer time to produce correct sounds. Also, students would not build the listening comprehension skills.

Babble Training with an audio set of the dialogues has clear advantages over Babble Training with the book or with a video set. The merit of an audio set is in that students are required to focus on getting the information only through ears, which really develops strong ear attention. This way, students can build up strong listening comprehension skills quickly.

Also, it makes it easier for one to focus on Babble Training as one can concentrate only on listening and imitating the expressions. Also, it is much easy for one to carry out the audio set with oneself and, therefore, to do Babble Training any time and any where one wishes to. It can easily be an all-time anywhere babble leader. It takes as little as one ear and the mouth so that one can do Babble Training easily always even on the move. Especially, for the students who take FL classes, and, therefore, receive helps from FL teacher on how to articulate particular sounds, the audio set can be a very ideal babble leader.

Most of people tend to consider that the video sets as the best material to use for learning FL simply because student can listen and watch at the same time. However, in the beginning level, Babble Training with a video set can deviate student's attention easily. First of all, more attention gets focused on the eyes to get the information. It also occupies all of the eyes, ears, and the mouth to babble over the video set.

Therefore, the ears do not get the 100% of the attention to figure out what is going on, which, I believe, should delay the process of building listening comprehension skills. For the same reason, the babble energy gets deviated. Most of all, as it is very difficult to take the video set with oneself around (even if one could, because it occupies the eyes, one really could not do it on the move) Babble Training practice gets restricted to a certain time and place of the day.

Therefore, it cannot be an all-time around babble leader. Some people would point that the video set would help for the beginning self-teachers without FL teacher to learn the process of articulating some difficult sounds. Yet, one can do it by listening to how to make the sounds also. There are not many sounds that cannot be learned by intensive listening to the sounds and with verbal explanations on how to make such sounds also.

Utilizing other technologies such as phone interactions, or internet based visual interactions raise too much restrictions in terms of time, place, and cost so that it cannot be an all time anywhere babble leader. Most of all, the fact that such technologies always require another party to participate in prove that they are not really practical means.

CHAPTER 9

How To Teach: BTM
Level 2 - Adding Babble
Training for Reading

1

Ideas for Class Design

Upon successful completion of the level 1 babble course, students can be expected at least to be involved in conversations on daily matters. In other words, students can communicate on their own based on the expressions they have acquired through the babble. They would be able to reproduce the expressions by replacing parts of the expressions with the words they need to put in to deliver a message. In this level, students would be able to produce a lot of expressions if they would have a large amount of TL vocabularies, linguistic resources.

However, even though they could speak TL to a degree, they would seriously suffer from the lack of linguistic resources. Therefore, the students' communicative performance will be seriously restricted due to insufficient amount of linguistic resources available instantaneously.

At the same time, students still need to acquire a lot more of new set of expressions to enhance their capacity to command higher level of TL expressions. On top of the daily activity based expressions, they also need to learn the communication skills for social or business activities in TL.

The followings are some of the ideas to be considered in designing the level 2 Babble Training class:

1. If possible, somewhat flexible direct method should be applied to leading the class. Somewhat flexible direct method means almost always in TL only. Some of the difficult and abstract concepts can be explained in students' MT.

2. The time span for required level 2 babble also varies depending on the student ages, number of students in a class, number of classes per week, and other environment issues. For college students with five class hours per week, it would take about one to two semesters.

3. The goals for Babble Training level 2 are: To continue Babble Training to help students to acquire about 200 social languages[30]; and to have students read about 2-3 books of 150-200 pages in TL with back translation into source language, and to encourage students to build up strong linguistic resources to increase the oral proficiency.

4. Students should be encouraged to utilize the expressions previously acquired. Students should be emphasized to be productive to speak own meaning.

5. The goal amount of reading for adult students in level 2 babble is about 1-2 books of 150-200 pages.

6. Students, especially for young age students who cannot follow their own agenda by themselves, can rely on the

---

[30] I use the term, social languages, in reference to the colloquial languages spoken by TL speakers in social activity environments such as meeting friends, introducing oneself and others, making phone calls, showing directions, going to restaurants with friends, talking about past or coming weekend events, visiting friend's homes, going to parties, emailing, inviting people, setting up plans for group activities, commenting on one's appearance, encouraging friends, sharing sadness together, complimenting, offering gifts, condoling, and talking about news, hobbies, favorite issues, pot locks, religion, hiking, schools, one's feeling, playing golf, going to movie theater, holidays, going to concert, dating, making proposal, arrangement of schedules, accidents, and etc.

method of story telling by the teachers or by video/audio presentation instead of reading the books by themselves.

7. Teaching Babble Training to read should solely be based on the individual meanings of the morphemes, words, and idiomatic expressions in relation to the context rather than grammatical analysis of sentences.

8. Evaluations should be focused, among others, on students' capability to use the acquired expressions for own meaning speaking; on the reading comprehension as well as the vocabularies from the reading.

When considering level 2 babble classes, there are some important things to be kept in mind. The first thing to be kept in mind clearly is that even though Babble Training to read is added in level II, the main focus of level 2 is still on Babble Training to talk. In other words, Babble Training should be the main part of level II, and Babble Training to read should be the supplementary to the efforts of picking up the speaking skills. The most important thing in Babble Training is always picking up new expressions in very fluent manner so that students can utilize them when they confront the same or similar type of situations.

Second thing to be kept in mind is that, from the level 2 babble, Babble Training should be focused on acquiring social activity related expressions. Students should always be encouraged and asked to participate in active talking activities among the students during the class. In this level, students can clearly listen and understand most of the daily routine dialogues. They also can talk about daily routine activities utilizing the expressions they acquired previously. Providing opportunities for active talks between the teacher and the students or among the students would motivate the students to utilize the expressions and try to create new ones.

Third thing one should keep in mind is that Babble Training to read does not need grammatical approach to the sentences. Once the door to the grammar is open, the door will be wide open to all different types of grammar classes, which will definitely kill a lot of precious times for both the teacher and the students with not much rewarding. Teachers should rather focus on helping students read with correct sounds, and with guessing the meanings of given sentences based on the meanings of each sentence component.

Also, Babble Training to read is to provide trainings for students to acquire the reading skills, which enable students to understand the written languages. However, without the power of vocabularies, the reading skills only are not so much meaningful. It is like a language robot without linguistic resources. Therefore, even after acquiring the reading skills, students should focus on continuous reading to build the vocabularies power.

Accordingly, depending on the schools' individual circumstances and students' capabilities, the level 2 babble can be expanded as much as necessary.

2

Adding Babble Training to Read

The successful completion of the level 1 babble with around 500 independent expressions can be likened to the completion of developing a language robot which can utilize around 500 different types of linguistic forms to speak and listen. If someone has successfully completed the level 1 babble with 600 independent expressions, it would be just like to have successfully developed a language robot with the capacity of utilizing 600 different types of linguistic forms for effective two way communications, which is much more smooth and efficient than the other robot. Having such language robot developed successfully cannot but be very rewarding. Depending on Babble Training materials used for the class, such successful completion of level 1 with the 500 different forms of expressions would produce students with intermediate high level of proficiency according to the proficiency guidelines.

However, even such an amazing language robot would not be worth of so much without plenty of linguistic resources available always in its database. Without the supports of ample linguistic resources on various industry fields, even the language robot would have no choice but being restricted only to using those initially built expressions repeatedly for particular sets of situations, neither recognizing new expressions nor being productive for creative meanings for new situations.

The level 2 education in BTM is composed of Babble Training and to read. Ideally, students are expected to have acquired and be able to command freely about 500 daily activity related expressions as part of the linguistic resources. At the end of level 1 with so many linguistic resources, students should have quite strong linguistic intuition as well as very high level of physical capacity. With such intuitions and physical capacity, students should be able to command TL even for new situations quite fluently as long as the linguistic resources are available at handy.

Therefore, one of the goals of the level 2 is to help students to be really fluent and productive with the daily activity related expressions obtained previously, and to improve the capacity and quality of the language robot or students to handle social activity related linguistic resources up to about 200 independent expressions or more. The other goal is to support students to secure as many as linguistic resources to be used as linguistic resources for them. Of course, having the students experience various types of sentence structures is another goal of the level 2 of BTM.

One of the most important goals of reading in FL acquisition training is to collect the various types of linguistic resources to be used by the students. Of course, one can collect the resources from other than reading like talking to people or watching movies. However, among many different methods of collecting linguistic resources, the most effective way of collecting the linguistic resources is, I believe, through reading for many reasons.

First, one can read in one's own agenda. It also does not require a 2nd party to talk to. Therefore, one can control the progress in reading. When more time is needed to understand, one can take more time and think about whatever makes it difficult to understand. Being able to do things in one's own agenda brings about a lot of benefits to one.

Second, one can maintain the linguistic resources effectively. Whenever new expressions or words are introduced, one can put them down in one's vocabulary notebook, and revisit them later to acquire them. As one of the most important goals of reading in FLE is to collect the various types of linguistic resources, it is always important to put down new resources in a place so that one can revisit them as many times as one wishes to.

However, linguistic resources collecting from reading has a couple of big risks. The first risk is the fact that one does not get all linguistic information on how to say the expressions from one's own reading. That is, when reading, one cannot pick up the native speaker's pronunciations from the book because one has to rely on the linguistic information coming through one's eyes. By looking at the resources, one can easily invite the risks of getting the bad habits of creating incorrect pronunciation patterns. Many linguistic resources acquired without the real sounds could cause difficulties in actual communications due to mispronunciations.

Another risk is that students can easily be infected with the grammar virus. In other words, when faced with difficult sentences, students would try to find out the grammars applied to the sentences. This is especially true with the students who have not acquired TL through the level 1. Without thorough efforts for the level 1, one would not acquire the linguistic intuition of TL on the sounds, structure, and usage of the linguistic resources. Without the supports coming from one's strong linguistic intuition, one naturally tends to rely on grammatical analysis of the sentences while reading.

This is one of the main reasons for students to do intensive Babble Training in level 1, and Babble Training to read in level 2. If one has acquired about 500 independent expressions through level 1, one should have acquired quite strong level of linguistic intuition enough to be able to figure out the sentence structures, and gradually be familiar with the sophisticated sentence structures of TL. Accordingly, for those who have acquired FL to the degree of the level 1, to start reading comprehension is not so much difficult deal as long as they can figure out how to recognize the written words.

Students in general seem to pick up linguistic intuition on the various types of sentence structures of TL during the process of the level 1, which, depending on linguistic distance to TL and respective FLE agenda, could be as little as 1 semester and as many as 4 semesters or more. Therefore, to begin reading after the level 1 can be done very smoothly. However, for those languages which do not use alphabetical writing systems, like Chinese for example, it would require quite extra efforts and time to go through Babble Training to read.

Beginning to read after acquiring the colloquial forms of TL is the same route as the children take during the course of learning and developing the MT. In natural language acquisition process, reading does not come until the learner completely learns the MT. By the age of around 36-40 months, children become fluent in their ML. Their linguistic intuitions on MT are strongly obtained; their physical capacities are quite fully developed except for some particularly difficult resources; their linguistic resources are plenty enough to carry out the daily verbal interactions with others; and they can speak MT productively on their own.

Also, there are still millions of adults who can speak their languages fluently but cannot read and write their languages. This tells us that language surely can be acquired only by Babble Training, and that reading or writing is not required to obtain fluent language speaking skills. In other words, language itself can be fully acquired by BTM level 1, Babble Training to talk, only. Yet, in the modern society, sometimes, the communication through written material is much more crucial in our life that we should obtain very good skills of reading comprehension. BTM level II is designed, in addition to continue developing the oral communication skills of TL, to develop the reading comprehension skills for such purpose.

3

Textbook vs. Workbook

Before adding Babble Training to read on top of Babble Training to talk, choosing and recommending proper books to read needs to be done first. In doing so, there are several issues to be considered. However, just as in approaching Babble Training to talk, the basic concept for approaching to Babble Training to read is to follow the reading process which has been successfully applied to all language learners in the natural language acquisition, and to utilize the increased brain capacities of the students to be more effective.

Basically, Babble Training to read is to train for the students to learn the skills to guess the meanings of sentences accurately based on the meanings of the individual sentence components. After all, it is a concrete process of finding the meanings of each sentence component first, and, then, demonstrating to the students about how to induce correct meaning of the sentence based on such findings.

However, as the students, through BTM level 1, have developed some strong degree of the intuitive guessing skills to figure out the basic sentence structures and the meaning interpretation patterns of TL, they can also tackle those of somewhat sophisticated sentences without much difficulty. Consequently, the students would not need intensive classes on how to interpret TL sentences, but they need systematic curriculum to follow to perform the babble to read training by themselves. This type of training to read is really different from what the translation method does to train the students for reading.

As the level 2 combines Babble Training for social activities and to read, the most ideal textbook for beginning level 2 would be the one which combines sets of various social life activity related dialogues and short stories in relation to the topics of the dialogues. The length of the story can be gradually increased. This way, students can start reading with ease, and it will also help students to pick up the linguistic resources closely related to the given topics.

However, as the development of the skills to talk in TL is still the top priority matter in BTM level 2, it is not so much effective for the teachers to spend so much time to cover the required amount of reading materials during the class. Therefore, as a way of promoting effective reading training for the students, the teachers should consider utilizing workbooks in addition to the textbook for the class. That is, the textbook should be designed for intensive Babble Training on social life activities and for demonstrating how to interpret meanings.

On the other hand, the workbooks for Babble Training to read should be utilized as part of the curriculum so that the students can perform the required amount of reading by themselves. It is very important that the curriculum should include appropriate evaluation method for students to maintain the linguistic resources collected from the readings.

Now, let's consider ideas for choosing efficient workbooks for the students to do Babble Training for reading required by a systematic class curriculum.

First, choose for an easy start. The goal of Babble Training to read is to acquire intuitions on the structures of TL and the usage of expressions, especially written expressions. Therefore, the contents of the textbook don't have to be difficult at all. It should be rather interesting and easy to understand.

Also, it should be matching to the understanding level of the students. Obviously, using kindergarten level story books as text materials for grown up students would be inadequate. Also, even if the students are grown up professional people, using highly professional industrial magazine as text materials for the beginning level Babble Training to read would be not effective either. The beginning level text materials should be of daily and social life related stories on various subject matters.

With respect to the format of the text materials, I would recommend solid and somewhat thick books of about 150 to 200 pages rather than temporary types of hand outs, prints, or flyers. Later, I will explain the reason why I prefer solid and somewhat thick books as a text material. I don't necessarily mean that the stories need to be so long. Stories can be as short as 2 pages or even 1 page. The length of stories does not matter.

Second, choose for easy going. The workbooks for the reading should better be edited in bilingual mode of both languages of TL and MT. It would be ideal to have the each of the MT pages following right after the respective corresponding pages of TL. This way, students can compare easily what they think the meanings of TL expressions would be with what they actually are as said in their MT in the next page.

Not only the bilingual mode of the workbooks, but also important is that the workbook should have glossaries for key words and idiomatic expressions used in each page on the bottom of the page. For beginners of especially a strange language, the students would encounter numerous new lexical items on every single page. For them to look up a dictionary each time for all of those items would not be an easy job. Further, some of the idiomatic expressions would not be easy to find in dictionaries.

Also, it would be really time consuming. Students would need to look up dictionaries anyway to find the meanings of some words which are not glossed. But, still the glossary would save a lot of time for the students. Therefore, instant accessibility to the meanings of each new word would help students continue reading a lot. This will make it much easier for the students to make progress in reading. It will save time and efforts of the students, and help the students to maintain the focused concentration.

The bilingual mode and the glossaries for key words are very important as they allow the students to study by themselves away from the class. They also are effective as students can save much time and efforts. I will discuss later in detail how students can use the bilingual mode and key word glossaries.

Third, choose for fun. The efforts of choosing workbooks in bilingual mode with glossaries for key words or idiomatic expression can be much more rewarded by looking for the workbooks with interesting or stories very well known to the students. This would help especially for the beginning students as they would face more difficulties understanding some complicated sentences in TL. For example, many stories from Aesop's Falbes are well known to most of the people. Therefore, if one could find Aesop's Fables as the workbook for Babble Training to read, it would help the students to read and understand the stories in TL better than the unfamiliar culture specific stories.

4

Reading Skills and Vocabulary Building

During the past decade or so, a lot of discussions and gatherings have occurred among FL teachers and the professions of FLE in relation to the new FL evaluation methods such as the OPI and the iBT TOEFL, which can be seen as revolutionary changes of directions from the traditional methods of evaluations. Yet, I still find that the reality of the FLE has not changed so much. This is because the teachers have not changed.

I believe the biggest cause for the failure of the traditional FL classes to produce solid bilingual speakers is the grammar translation method oriented approach. Grammar is not needed at least to be fluent speaker, reader, and writer of a language. It is not simply that grammar is not needed to learn language, but that grammar causes serious problems with the acquisition of language or FL. Grammar takes most of the precious time away from students and do not leave any time for them to try something different.

By the time they realize that grammar does not work, it is too late for most of the students as they have to graduate from the schools. Also, grammar builds a horrible habit of having to rearrange the incoming and outgoing information to be processed properly, which delays the process of linguistic perception and production. This is especially so for processing the languages which have quite high linguistic distance scores on the phonetic features to each other. It also causes significant problems with the pronunciation issues. Due to lack of repeated babblings and/or due to repeated Babble Training over wrong sounds, it forms a strong habit of poor pronunciation. Yet, teachers do not acknowledge these types of problems.

Some people asked me how students could read TL without knowing the grammar. When I say to them that students can read FL mostly by looking up for the meanings of the morphemes, words, and idioms which are used in a given sentence, they would not buy it. Instead, they say it would be much more effective and accurate to read TL with grammatical understanding of sentences. Even though I vehemently tell them it is not necessarily so, they don't want to be bothered. They truly believe that because that is the only way they learned how to read TL.

To build reading skills without grammar is simple and clear. If one can speak TL, the person very naturally can read in TL without grammar. So, that is why it is so important for the students to conclude BTM level 1 training process successfully. However, it does not work the other way.

When students read complicated sentences, we should let them figure out the meanings by conjecturing first, and verify their figured meaning against the authentic meaning from FL teachers or from the MT version of the story. Based on the linguistic intuition on TL acquired from the level 1 babble, the students can perform quite accurate reading comprehension on most of simple sentences. When dealing with complicated sentences with conjectures, students will develop the necessary linguistic intuition from their own error correcting processes with the help of the teachers or the MT version of the story.

Once students start reading after successful achievement of the level 1 babble, the collection of vast amount linguistic resources becomes the most important and critical power in furthering one's TL acquisition level. It will expedite the process of improving such skills as speaking, reading, listening, and writing. Therefore, successful vocabulary building practice is very crucial for the success of TL acquisition.

Many people have relied upon various types of efforts to maintain the words and idioms they gather from reading. Many of them choose the method of writing each of them many times on a piece of paper like 10 or 20 times in a row.

Some people would read books continuously without really singling out the words or idioms from the text for extra special exercise to memorize them. They would look up a dictionary for the meaning, and continue reading. Some other people don't even bother to look up a dictionary to get the meanings of new words. They believe that the meanings would come naturally from the context in the continued process of reading a lot.

However, to be most effective, I believe that the efforts to memorize linguistic resources should be done repeatedly over time to make them available to be used in speech.

For the reasons above, I recommend rather thick volume books than thin volume books as workbooks for reading. Thick books have a lot of pages in it, and these pages can provide a lot of clean space for students to write down the words and idioms found during the process of reading. This is an idea which I personally utilized when I taught English to myself in Korea. Whenever new words or idioms were found, I would write them down a total of about 6 to 7 times: About six times on six different places of the book with about 10 to 20 pages apart from each other, and one last time on my vocabulary book. This way, almost all blank spaces of the book would be full of the words and idioms hand written by me.

Then, whenever I turn over a page and before I start reading the page, I would read and try to keep in memory the words or idioms that I put down on the page previously. If I found some words or idioms to be so strange as if they were new items, I would write them about 6-7 times in the same manner as shown above. So, this way, the lexical items are to be repeated for memory.

Also, when I am not reading and have some time, then I would look at the vocabulary book to review all the vocabularies I gathered so far. This way, even after I am done with particular books, I would still have the vocabularies in a place under my frequent reviews. This was always very helpful for me to learn many English vocabularies. Also, in my notes, I would keep all kinds of important information which I learned from my own error correcting process so that I didn't have to repeat the same errors.

FL teachers should emphasize the importance of the vocabularies and recommend students to develop their own best methods of keeping the vocabularies of TL in memories always available. It is very obvious that a book volume amount of grammar knowledge would only impede developing the oral proficiency of TL. On the other hand, collection of a book volume of the TL words and idioms would surely speed up the acquisition of TL.

CHAPTER 10

How To Teach: BTM Level 3 – Adding Babble For Listening Comprehension

1

Ideas for Class Design

Upon the completion of the level 2 babble course, students can be expected to be fluent in oral languages related to personal and social life activities. Students should be able to say own meanings utilizing the expressions and lexical items acquired in previous level studies. In other words, they can be quite talkative in TL if they wish to.

However, even though they could be quite talkative about their personal and social life activities, students will be challenged by lack of expressions to deal with the business world. Also, they will be challenged by the media languages[31], which was not a concern yet during the previous levels as they would feel themselves too far away from such languages.

To be able to listen to the media languages and to be able to understand them are two different things. To be able to listen to the media languages means that one can clearly listen and single out the individual forms of words and structures of expressions used in the media languages. In other words, it refers to the listening comprehension skill, which clearly requires a lot of trainings to be acquired.

---

[31] I use the term, media languages, in reference to such types of languages spoken by TL speakers in the mass media environment such as the radios and TVs.

Yet, to understand or comprehend the media languages one clearly heard requires the power of vocabularies. Without knowing or being able to figure out the meanings of the words based on the contexts, one simply cannot understand them. From this stage on, the power of vocabularies means every thing in one's proficiency of TL.

The level 3 Babble Training is composed of such babbles as for talking, reading, and listening. The followings are some of the ideas to be considered in designing the class:

1. Class instructions should be done by direct method so that students can be fully committed to speak TL.
2. Babble Training should aim to have students acquire about 200 business languages[32].
3. The main focus of the class should always be given on Babble Training for the business activity related expressions, and on improving the speaking skills of own meaning.
4. Babble Training to read should aim to have students read about 2-3 books in TL with successful maintenance of the lexical items collected from the readings.
5. Babble Training for listening comprehension should aim to have students acquire the listening comprehension

---

[32] I use the term, business languages, in reference to the colloquial languages spoken by TL speakers in business activity environments such as opening bank accounts, reporting to the police, contacting government agents, participating in business meetings, dry cleaning, setting up appointments, going to business trips, talking to the police on the street, job interview meeting, parents meeting at school, buying insurance policies, buying a computer, buying flowers, buying tickets, breakfast meeting, car trading, car repairing, buying a car, loan application, closing, meeting with an attorney, at a gas station, showing ID, getting a traffic ticket, ordering foods at a restaurant, greetings at work, meeting with a boss, meeting with an employee, making business phone calls, meeting with customers, inviting customers, responding to complaints by customers, asking for excuses, attending business parties, recommending people, and etc.

skills of the standard media languages in TL such as TV, movie, and radio.

6. The time span for required level 3 babble also varies depending on the student ages, number of students in a class, number of classes per week, and other environment issues. For college students with five class hours per week, it would take about one to two semesters.

7. Students should be encouraged to utilize the expressions previously acquired. Students should be emphasized to be productive to speak own meaning.

8. Teaching Babble Training for listening comprehension should solely be based on the individual meanings of the morphemes, words, and idiomatic expressions in relation to the context rather than grammatical analysis of sentences.

9. Evaluations should be focused, among others, on students' capability to use the acquired expressions for own meaning speaking; on the reading comprehension as well as the vocabularies from the reading; and on the listening comprehension skills.

Students' listening comprehension skills of TL are most strongly influenced by their speaking skills of TL. If they can speak TL fluently with clear articulation, it will certainly boost up their listening comprehension skills. Any expressions they can say fluently, the students will have no problems with listening and understanding them no matter how fast the media languages of TL would be. However, if students are poor with their own skills of speaking with clear articulations, the students will have hard time of listening to media languages even with much slower pace.

Therefore, the students' success in mastering over the minimum required expressions in previous levels of the babble is the key to the initial success of acquiring the listening comprehension skills.

Consequently, moving forward without accomplishing the strong foundations from the previous levels would not be effective. Accordingly, for young and relying-on-teacher students, it would be more effective to take enough time and build strong foundations in the lower level babbles before tackling the higher level babbles.

Even though the level 3 babble adds the trainings to acquire the listening comprehension skills, it does not mean that students can comprehend all the media languages of TL at all. It requires a lot more supports from one's power of vocabularies on top of the training to acquire the listening comprehension skills. For this, continuous reading to collect and maintain a lot more of the linguistic resources becomes more important.

One's power of vocabularies based on the reading volumes from the level 2 and 3 babbles are very limited, and it would be quite overwhelming for students to challenge the media languages. It would require the power of vocabularies from a minimum of 20 volumes of books to be able to comprehend the media languages in general topics. Accordingly, students should continuously focus on building up the strongest possible power of vocabularies by reading continuously in TL.

2

Adding Babble Training for Listening Comprehension

Students should be able to listen and comprehend the oral languages of TL with the completion of the level 2 babble. The intensive trainings to talk with the help of native speakers or native speaker level teachers would lead student to acquire the skills of not only speaking but also listening to TL. Also, based on my own experiences, students who teach themselves with the help of the audio technology should also develop these skills.

Babble Training to build the listening comprehension skills can be done quite effectively in the beginning level by using the audio versions, if available, of the babble-for-reading workbooks use in previous levels. Of course, it would be better if the audio version include the texts spoken in different speeds.

One of the merits of utilizing the audio versions of the babble-for-reading workbooks is that it would offer easier start as the students would still remember the story they read before. As the story and the vocabularies are familiar, it is much easier for the students to focus on listening to the story.

Also, students will have opportunities to learn the pronunciations of the words whose sounds are difficult to learn for them.

In addition to that, students will have opportunities to brush up the vocabularies they studied before. Once students establish solid foundation of listening comprehension skills this way, students can now challenge the TL mass media to enhance the listening comprehension skills.

If the audio versions of the babble-for-reading workbooks are not available, the TL mass media can be used from the beginning stage. One thing that overwhelms the students when exposed to the media languages is the speed and length of the language.

Also, students tend to be discouraged by the vast amount of vocabularies in the medial languages. The feelings of being overwhelmed and discouraged are very natural in the beginning. However, depending individual achievements, some students may feel very proud and confident with such finding that being able to listen to the media languages is not so much difficult.

Even though the speed and length of the media languages seem to be threatening in the beginning stages, students soon find that it is not the speed or the length of the languages but the levels of vocabularies that really challenges them. They easily realize how it is important for them to retain vocabularies. Getting used to the speed of the media languages is rather easy.

It is very obvious that the vocabularies one collects through up to the level 2 babble would not be sufficient to cover the various events occurring in every field of the industry. Depending on the materials used, the number of vocabularies would vary.

However, considering the target volumes for each of the babble level, one could roughly get an idea of the amount of the vocabularies acquired by then: about 2,000 very basic level vocabularies from the level 1 babble target of about 500 individual daily life activity related independent expressions; and, depending on the number of books read by each students, about 1,500 to 3,000 vocabularies from the level 2 babble target of about 200 social activity related independent expressions, and about two to three 100-150 page books.

Even if the students acquire and maintain all of the vocabularies, which would not be the case for most of the students except for those who are strongly committed to acquire TL, the total number of vocabularies acquired after the level 2 babble would be around 5,000 vocabularies. However, as many of the vocabularies are of such narrow environment situations as personal daily life situations, students cannot be expected to be familiar with the languages used by the media. Accordingly, students should be understood of this new challenging situation, and should not be discouraged at all.

The first step of challenging the media languages of TL starts with producing the study materials by recording portions of the media languages. When recording the media languages, it would help students to have very clearly articulated speeches with no background noise. The length of the recording could be around 5 minutes or so at a time. If possible, it would be an ideal for the beginners to have the recording done in different speeds.

Instead of manually recording the media languages, teachers can use the audio materials produced by commercial entities for similar purposes. For example, the collection of famous presidential speeches in TL can be a good candidate as a babble text to develop listening comprehension skills. Also, audio copies of media languages professionally recorded can be conveniently used.

Now, the training to pick up the listening comprehension skills should begin. It is a good idea to let students listen to the normal speed several times first. This way, students would locate the places where they have difficulties to understand. Then, students can listen to the slower version so that they could figure out the elements of the expressions. Once they could figure out the components of those difficult arrears to listen in normal speed, then students can listen to the normal speed again.

Once students become familiar with the speed of the media languages, students should be encouraged to keep listening to such languages continuously as a part of daily life.

3

Maintaining Efficient Balances

As students make progresses into higher levels of the babble, effective management of the class requires teachers to be more sophisticated in designing the classes. I would say that the success of teaching TL to students in this level relies upon the effective managing of the different areas of Babble Training.

Considering the reality of the contemporary FLE, it could be only a nominal goal for most of the school FL programs to lead students into the acquisition of TL. Even though almost all schools profess to have FL programs to promote the oral proficiency, it may not be an exaggeration to say that many of them have not been successful to substantiate such statements.

Some of the main reasons are that they have not adopted proper FLE methods; and that even if they have, they have not maintained the systematic balances between the different areas of skills to be developed through out the programs. When FLE programs are not oriented properly, the student factors do not matter for the success of a FLE program.

Students getting into the level 3 babble should be able to feel comfortable with commanding the personal and social languages of TL. They should be able to continue communications in TL with teachers using such skills as asking questions for clarification of difficult words and idiomatic expressions as well as requesting for repeats or paraphrasing unclear expressions. In other words, students can take the initiative in communication to control the stream of incoming and outgoing meanings.

Yet, it is still obvious that students in this level can command those expressions similar to or made up based on the expressions they acquired through the babbles much more fluently than those new expressions which students would need to come up with on their own. This indirectly tells how it is important for students to acquire as many expressions as possible during the process of Babble Training to talk.

Therefore, it is much more effective for students during the early stage of learning TL to be introduced to the proper expressions to be acquired rather than to be forced to come up with their own ways of expressions. Accordingly, teachers should always offer new useful expressions during the class.

For the level 3 babble class, the class should be instructed in TL. The new expressions to be introduced in the level 3 babble are of the real expressions in the business activity related situations. As the students already have obtained the speaking skills on such daily life environment situations as the personal and social life activities, it is relatively much easier for them to collect new expressions introduced to them.

That is, the students, who previously would need to repeat listening and rely on the textbook to figure out the sentence elements and meanings of new expressions, from now on can listen and comprehend the expressions without having to replay the audio or ask for the expressions to be repeated. Also, students can recite and pick up the expressions with less efforts of babbling. Depending on the individual skills of TL, some students may be able to acquire new expressions by simply listening to them a few times.

Even though students may seem to be well versed in engaging themselves to speaking in TL for the narrow environment subjects, they still would not produce idiomatic expressions which they have not heard of or read before. Thus, students should continuously be introduced to wider environment subject expressions gradually.

Therefore, introducing business environment expressions should better start with the ones which are more realistic to the students, and then continue with the ones which are possibly realistic in the future. The best way to find out the business expressions which are most needed to the students is to ask the students.

Students who teach TL to themselves would not have such regular class environments. This would delay TL acquisition process for such students. However, continuously focusing on Babble Training tracks to talk with the audio equipments, Babble Training to read, listen, and write, which is BTM level 4 babble will lead them to acquire TL.

To maintain efficient balance of teaching between the babble areas to talk, read, and listen in operating BTM level 3 classes, FL teachers would need to design the class activities to the most effective ways considering the students ages, given class hours per week, and the length of the program. Yet, the main focus of the class should be on helping students acquire higher level of speaking skills based on the new expressions introduced to them through the respective areas of babbling.

For example, teachers can rotate the classes for the babbles of different areas of trainings like talking, reading, and listening comprehension: Mondays for talking, Tuesdays for reading, Wednesdays for listening comprehension, Thursdays for review of talking, reading, and writing, and Fridays for evaluation, for example.

Also, the weekly class hours for each area of the babbles can be assigned like 2, 2, and 1 hours respectively for the babble for talking, reading, and listening comprehension.

For the reading class, as students build the skill to read without much difficulty on their own efforts, teachers can utilize new words and idioms from the reading materials to introduce new expressions for students to acquire. For the listening class, teachers would need to explain in detail the phonological phenomena occurring to particular morphemes, words, and phrases in given chunks of sounds so that students can understand and acquire them effectively.

Once the students get familiar with the sound phenomena, teachers can lead the classes into higher level such as asking the students to shadow the media languages. Shadowing the media languages will help students to acquire the rhythms of the formal languages of TL.

CHAPTER 11

How To Teach: BTM Level 4 – Adding Babble Training for Writing

1

Ideas for Class Design

The primary goal of up to the level 3 babble courses was to help students build the oral proficiency of the colloquial forms. The whole process of the trainings has been focused on building linguistic intuition, developing the physical capacity not only for speaking skill but also for listening comprehension skill, and accumulating linguistic resources of TL. Through the intuition developed, flow of the incoming and outgoing meanings has become very natural: students don't have to rely on knowledges of TL or analytical skills to process the meanings. Through the well developed physical capacity, the performance of articulating and listening to the expressions acquired or newly created has become quite fluent. With the linguistic resources accumulated so far, expressions needed in particular situations can be easily retrieved and used from the resource pool.

The 4th level babble adds the training to write. Writing is oriented to build the creative skills of both colloquial and non-colloquial forms of TL. Also, writing babble is to introduce various writing styles of TL to the students. Another new concept added to this level of Babble Training is professional languages[33] as opposed

---

[33] I use the term, professional languages, in reference to the non colloquial languages spoken by TL speakers in such environments as presentations, lectures, and speeches to a group of people.

to such colloquial languages as the personal languages, social languages, and business languages which were introduced previously. Professional languages are not colloquial but speech, presentation or lecture style languages to present ideas or information. The trainings for writing will support the training for the babble of professional languages.

Level 4 Babble Training is composed of such babbles as to learn talking for professional languages, reading, listening, and writing. The followings are some of the ideas to be considered in designing the class:

1. Class instructions should be done by direct method so that students can be fully committed to speak TL.

2. Babble Training should aim to offer students opportunities to make about 10 minute presentations in TL on various ideas or products about 30 times. After the presentations, students should be invited for discussions and comments.

3. The main focus of the class should always be given on Babble Training for professional languages, and on improving the speaking skills of own meaning.

4. Babble Training to read should aim to have students read about 3-4 books in TL with successful maintenance of the lexical items collected from the readings.

5. Babble Training for listening comprehension should continue to have students build the listening comprehension skills of the standard media languages in TL such as TV, movie, and radio. Also, the audio versions of the workbooks can be used for improving the listening comprehension skills.

6. Babble Training to write should start with writing personal daily journals. After personal journals, students should be introduced to various types of sample business

documents in TL to help students practice writing business documents.

7. Students should be encouraged to use the styles and skills of the sample documents. Also, students should be encouraged to feel free to quote languages from the sample documents as well as the reading materials.

8. The time span required for level 4 babble varies depending on the student ages, number of students in a class, number of classes per week, and other environment issues. For college students with five class hours per week, it would take about one to two semesters.

9. Evaluations should be focused, among others, on students' capability to use the acquired expressions for own meaning speaking; presentation; reading comprehension as well as the vocabularies from reading; the listening comprehension skills; and creative writing skills.

2

Adding Babble Training to Write

For students who have successfully obtained the oral proficiency with the colloquial forms of the personal, social, and business languages with quite strong linguistic resources available, the training to write in TL will be much easier. Students would not need any grammatical approach to start writing in TL. In the beginning, it would be a simple matter of putting down one's own meanings instead of saying them in TL. It will not take long before they find themselves writing pages in TL as if they are writing in their own languages. However, without the success of the trainings required in the previous levels, efforts to build up the writing skills would be not effective.

Teachers can start the training by asking students to write daily journals about a half page to start with. This way, students will write very basic activities of each day without adding much of the emotional or descriptive languages.

Then, in a month or so, teachers can ask them to write a full page. By increasing the amount of daily journal, students would need to be more specific or details in describing apparently similar or routine daily activities by using the descriptive or emotional languages. For students in higher grades, teachers still can increase the amount of the daily journal to one and half to two pages in accordance with the progress made by the students. Then, students would need to write not only about the physical activities but also about the emotional activities of the day to meet the quantity required.

To expedite the progress and save time, teachers can offer sample daily journals written in TL so that students can get ideas of how to begin, and continue the journal in TL. Also, students should be encouraged to utilize all the materials that they have used to reach to the current level: the textbooks used in each level of the babble. It will make the students revisit the books in search for the vocabularies and expressions they might still remember or which are fading away from the memories of the students.

By revisiting the textbooks or materials uses before, it will help them to refresh their memory of the story as well as the vocabularies they collected, some of which they might have lost from memory. The performance of the students' writing may vary depending on the linguistic foundations which each individual has established in the previous steps of respective trainings.

Encouraging students to feel free to quote the sample expressions in part or whole depending on the degree of the sample expressions fitting into one's situation will also help students learn error free writing skills. By imitating or quoting the error free expressions to convey one's own meaning, one will build the habit and intuition of writing error free sentences.

Sometimes, students will face situations where they cannot find example sentences and do not know how to put particular meanings in writing. For such a case, teachers can show them how to put them down in TL, or ask the students to look up dictionaries for clear meanings and examples, if any. Then, even if they could not find samples for proper writings of such meanings, students will remember that when they get hints or find answers to the issue later. Writing daily journals as said above will help students speak TL in a narrative form. Students can describe verbally what they did, saw, and how they felt.

As students get familiar with describing their daily activities, students should be introduced to the babble for professional business writing. Of course, students should be encouraged to continue writing daily journals as they could write them very quickly and easily.

People tend to feel much burden to produce business documents such as business letters, invitation cards, notices, request for sponsorship, curriculum vitae, self promotion letter, advertisements, complaints, affidavits, minutes of meeting, and etc. Even many native speaker people with higher education feel uncomfortable to produce such types of documents. The reason they don't feel comfortable is not because they don't know how to put down their opinions in writing, but because they are just not familiar with the styles of such documents.

Yet, it is still important for students to babble on those types of professional documents. Once the students get exposed to various types of professional documents, and have opportunities to train themselves by imitating or quoting those types of sample documents, students will gain much more confidence of handling such matters by themselves or with the help of others.

3

Maintaining Balances

Level 4 babble is actually the last step to build the language skills because the next level is the beginning step of improving the oral proficiency to the advanced level s or even to the superior level based on the language skills. Upon successful completion of this level, students are expected to perform personal, social, and business life activities in TL community smoothly. All of the intensive interactions in TL during the course of the babbles are to help students achieve such practical goals of being able to mingle with the community members of TL.

The level 1 Babble Training is most important in obtaining TL as the success with the level 1 secures a very solid foundation of the acquisition factors: linguistic intuition, physical capacity, linguistic resources, and productive capacity. Therefore, in the beginning, it is far more important for students to be able to figure out the sound phenomena, structures, and usage of TL expressions, to be able to articulate sounds of TL fluently, to be able to maintain the expressions acquired, and to be able to utilize such expressions in similar environments than for them to be able to understand the systematic rules of TL, and to be able to read and write in TL.

As the level 1 is so crucial to one's success in the learning TL, no students can be expected to be successful in acquiring TL without success with the level 1 Babble Training. Therefore, whoever is successful with securing the basic acquisition factors will be able to manage through the life in TL community.

Then, the second prerequisite to acquire TL is successful maintenance of the linguistic resources. The resource maintenance requires steady and consistent commitments to revisit them regularly. Without this, successes with the higher level will not be sustained for long. They will go away quickly with time. Temporary grasping of the resources as passing through the higher levels of the babbles will not lead to a successful acquisition. The fact that even the people who have used their native languages for decades in their whole lives could lose their languages by not maintaining them for many years clearly tells how crucial it is to maintain the resources frequently and consistently.

Therefore, the primary concept of balance through out Babble Training stages should be understood in terms of the balance between oral performance and the resource maintenance. No writing, reading, or listening comprehension skills can excuse insufficient oral proficiency. The skills of writing, reading, and listening can only be recognized with full credits only when the oral proficiency is fully recognized.

So, it is important to encourage and push sometimes the students to do the babbles of talking, reading, listening comprehension, and writing without failure in each individual area. However, it is far more important for us to come up with ideas and plans to do so effectively with the focus on strengthening the improvement of the acquisition factors and the dynamic pool of the linguistic resources. We need to design the classes in such a way that students should demonstrate what they have earned from the respective levels of acquisition training always through well balanced performances of the oral proficiency. In other words, all the efforts for the babbles of talking, reading, listening, and writing should converge into achieving high level oral proficiency.

CHAPTER 12

How To Teach: BTM Level 5 – Adding Babble Training for Comprehensive Oral Proficiency

1

Ideas for Class Design

With successful completion of up to the level 4 Babble Training, students can be considered as having acquired TL to the advanced level of oral proficiency. There are three most important factors to achieve high levels of the oral proficiency: quality of the physical capacity, amount of linguistic resources, and the ability to understand the culture. If the quality of acquisition is poor, the poor habit may continue through out one's life in performing TL.

For example, if the physical capacity is very poor due to lack of sufficient practices, chances are that such poor articulation will not go away. Insufficient linguistic resources would directly affect one's oral proficiency as one may not make effective communications. Lack of understanding the culture makes one unable to process some of the culturally sensitive incoming meanings, which consequently causes improper process of the outgoing meanings too.

This level is the final course of the oral proficiency-oriented BTM. As the final course, it focuses on expanding the vocabulary power and the cultural experiences of the students to maximize students' oral proficiency. This level is characterized as the comprehensive oral proficiency training level. High level oral proficiency is not achieved simply by the pure linguistic performance of understanding incoming lexical meaning and producing outgoing lexical forms. It requires the understanding of not only the surface meanings but also the background meanings related to the culture of the TL country. It also requires extensive understanding of the TL society's political as well as historical backgrounds on top of the culture. The more one knows about the TL country, the higher oral proficiency one can achieve.

A new concept which is added to this final stage of Babble Training is cultural languages[34] which are distinguished from the types of languages introduced to the earlier levels of Babble Training.

Level 5 Babble Training is composed of such babbles as to learn talking for cultural languages, reading, listening, and writing. The followings are some of the ideas to be considered in designing the class:

1. The comprehensive oral proficiency training should aim to invite students to flexible and creative discussions on wide range areas of interests. Also, students should be encouraged to be familiar with the culture specific languages such as proverbs, useful sayings, jokes, and direct quotes from the speech of the famous people of the TL community. Students should be invited for discussions and comments also with quotes from the cultural languages.

2. The operation of class should not be restricted to the formality and to certain regularized patterns. Rather, the class operation should be very flexible depending on the students' excitements, interests, responses, and desires about on going subjects or topics.

---

[34] I use the term, cultural languages, in reference to the idiomatic or proverbial languages spoken by TL speakers as metaphoric instruments to deliver implicit meanings. I also use the term to mean the culture specific languages which are based on the tradition and history of the TL community.

3. Continuous efforts to upgrade the vocabularies used by students and to introduce new useful terms by teachers are important.

4. The main focus of the class should always be given on the oral proficiency trainings around the cultural languages.

5. Students should be encouraged to familiarize themselves with the detail aspects of TL culture, especially with the contrasting cultures to their own.

6. The workbooks for Babble Training to read don't have to include the translation any more. Students should be able to read books and magazines in TL only with accurate understanding. Students should be encouraged to read about the history, tradition, and other culture related books so that they could use what they learn from the reading for the oral proficiency training.

7. Students should be encouraged to listen to the radio, or to watch TV of TL looking for cultural languages. Also, students should be encouraged to share the news, ideas, and information with others for discussions or debates.

8. Time span: One to two semesters.

9. Evaluations should be focused, among others, on students' capability to use the cultural languages for own meaning speaking; on the reading comprehension as well as the vocabularies from the reading; on the listening comprehension skills; and creative writing skills. No evaluations should focus on the grammatical errors.

2

Babble Training For Comprehensive Oral Proficiency

Students who have put serious efforts for going through all of the previous Babble Training would have achieved advanced level oral proficiency by now. They now can face the real world of TL and immerse into the community smoothly without much difficulty. They should be able to perform business activities including getting a job which does not specialize in the professional usage of TL. At this level of successful babbling, students, may choose to face the real life in TL community, and upgrade the oral proficiency.

Once students successfully reach this high level of Babble Training, every thing that matters is the power of vocabularies. After all, one can say that language training starts with the babble to talk, but it ends with the power of vocabulary. That is, one would not acquire TL without the babble to talk, and one would not achieve the oral proficiency without the power of the vocabularies. Consequently, one who fails in the first level of Babble Training will fail to acquire TL, which in consequence leads to further failure in the efforts of achieving the oral proficiency.

Even if one would succeed to achieve advanced level of TL through relatively short period of intensive programs, the status of acquired TL would yet to be solid and very vulnerable as the age of TL with one's tongue is very young. Such a young aged language to one's tongue without proper maintenance can easily be rusted in a short period of time. Therefore, efforts to make TL as a solid language are always required.

While the students are in FL classes, it would not be so much of an issue to maintain TL as they will get to participate in various talking activities. Students should be led to choose topics or subjects for debates or discussions. FL teachers should try to maintain the balance among the class members so that every body gets somewhat equal opportunities and exercises to speak TL.

For students to participate in live talks actively, choosing topics of students' interests is very important. As one of the ways to choosing topics for discussions, teachers can pick up topics, which students might be already talking about among themselves before the class starts. The only thing that the teacher needs to do in such a case is to invite the students to change the language mode to TL instead, and provide supports for the discussion to be continued. Then, the teacher can be a coordinator of the discussion distributing fairly equal opportunities to every body.

Based on my experience, this has been the most effective way to choose a topic. It typically works much better than relying on preplanned topics. I have almost always been successful with this kind of method. So, when I enter the classroom, I always pay attention to what topics, if any, the students were talking about to each other before my entrance. Students enjoy continue talking on the same subject; the class hour is always not enough; they really pay attention to each other's words; and they get very serious about what they learn. As a coordinator, I, with care not to interrupt or break the flow of exciting discussion and attentions of the students, would help students by offering better vocabularies and useful expressions which fit to the context. I also naturally become a member in the discussion giving my views and thinking.

A typical method of choosing topics for discussions is by assigning topics in advance so that students can prepare for discussions in advance. Depending on creative coordination by the teacher, students can be led to have active discussions. However, the atmosphere typically tends to be dry and appears to be sort of turn-taking presentation instead of every body being eager to jump on the discussion. No matter how interesting topics I would offer to the students for preparation, the instant hot topics, which students naturally bring into the class room, have always been more successful in leading the students to be involved in excited talking.

Successful completion of this level should allow students to be able to attend college classes in TL community. Students should be equipped very well with the TL skills of speaking, reading, listening, and writing for college training. Even though all the focus and outputs of the trainings for reading, listening, and writing have been thoroughly dedicated to the enhancement of the oral proficiency, such skills will always remain as very useful byproducts available anytime to be served as alternative proficiencies.

However, completing the 5th level Babble Training cannot be the end of learning TL. It is only the end of the program through which students acquired and polished the oral proficiency of TL to the skillful performance level. Yet, it requires constant and consistent efforts of maintenance. Here in this level of the training, it includes some real activities to actively maintain and continuously grow one's TL skills.

For those teachers who teach themselves, now is the time to look for TL speaking partners to experience being immersed into TL community. Up to the previous level, they could follow BTM trainings for themselves with the help of audio equipments. They could acquire personal, social, business, and professional languages through Babble Training after such languages produced by the audio equipments. Of course, depending on the situation of available BTM textbooks for each level and on the individual capabilities of the teachers, the linguistic resources offered for each level of BTM may not be so systematically sorted well into such different of types. In other words, even though it is not so easy, self teaching teachers can do Babble Training for themselves up to the previous level without babble leaders and coaches. They could acquire, and improve the oral proficiency of TL quite well. However, in order to finalize their TL skills before challenging the real world of TL, they would need to mingle with TL speakers and face the real flow of language.

In order to maintain newly acquired TL, students need to live in TL at least for some times every day either by talking, reading, writing, or watching TV programs in TL. Of course, the best way is to be involved in talking activities every day.

3

Trainings To Be Culturally Correct

It is well understood by everybody that language and culture are inseparable from each other. Language clearly reflects the culture of the people. Therefore, without understanding the culture, one would face many situations of misunderstanding or offending other people.

As one gains higher oral proficiency of TL, the significance of speaking culturally correct expressions becomes greater because people expect one's cultural behavior to match somewhat similar level of their language skills. If one's language skills are poor, people would be quite generous about the person's lack of cultural etiquette, and even be happy to teach the person to be culturally adjusted in the community.

However, if one speaks TL very well, but commits culturally unacceptable acts for lack of cultural understanding, people would feel offended and, depending on the degree of the offense, not even give the person a chance to clarify the mistakes. Therefore, it is very important for students who achieved high levels of oral proficiency in TL to acquire the cultural features of the TL community.

After all, one can say that the judgment criteria of being culturally correct is based on the level of one's oral proficiency. Anyone with high oral proficiency level would be expected more to be culturally correct than ones whose oral proficiency is in a low level.

Also, the cultural distance between any two cultures could be measured, I believe, in proportion to the linguistic distance of the two languages used in the communities. Thus, there would be less cultural distance between the cultures of two language communities whose linguistic distance to each other is lower. Obviously, two cultures with less distance to each other would bring about less cultural shock to the new comers.

Trainings to be culturally correct does not only mean to learn the culture of the TL community, but also it means not to carry over one's own culture into the TL community. However, even though acts based on one's own culture may bring about misunderstandings or offenses to people, it is not easy to intentionally disobey one's own culture. This is why being culturally correct is not easy.

The purpose of cultural training is not just to avoid unknowingly caused mistakes. Sometimes, understanding the culture of TL correctly becomes a matter of innocent people's fate. Let me take an example, many years ago, I read an article of an incident where a child was killed by a TV set which fell from a drawer on to the child. At that time, the mother was at work. However, the mother with a breaking heart for losing the child lamented saying 'I killed my baby' in Korean repeatedly out loudly.

To abridge a long story, the mother's such saying was taken by the people as confessing to have killed her won baby. Consequently, she was charged with a murder. I do not know the truth of the case, and I am not making an argument for the prosecutors' side or for the mother's side. What the article was trying to make an issue of was the interpretation of the mother's language: it was not a confession to the acts of killing her own child.

In other words, it was purely cultural language which had nothing to do with the acts of killing. The circumstance according to the article was clear that the mother was at work. However, just because the mother said so, the prosecutors considered it as the mother preplanned on the killing and put her in jail. Even though she later changed her saying that she did not kill the baby, the prosecutors did not trust her any more.

In Korean culture, most of the parents would have indefinite sense of responsibility or guilty for any types of serious problems including death of their children. I believe this is based on the Korean people's traditional beliefs on retribution or karma. Therefore, in a situation like above, many Korean parents do say that they are the ones to be punished even though they did not cause such problems to their children.

If the incident was really an accident, what the prosecutors did to the mother based on her such saying is the result of misunderstanding of the Korean cultural language. Had the mother understood the culture of the USA, she would have not said such culturally misleading statements, which would have made the prosecutors and the investigators think it different ways.

Also, had the prosecutors and the authority people understood the culture of how typical parents from Korea would say and react to such a situation, they might have taken different approaches from the beginning.

The way the Korean kids use the word of 'to kill' also causes many troubles both to the kids as well as to the others. One time, I helped a relatively new immigrant family whose middle school boy was suspended from the school for threatening other student to kill, which sounds to be very serious threatening. However, the word 'to kill' in Korean language culture commonly means to give a hard time, or to give physical blows. However, such kind of threat mostly does not mean the action of killing someone.

Again, if the Korean student understood the seriousness of using such kind of language in the USA, he might have not used the same language. Also, if the other kid had known what it typically means when the Korean people say such language, he might have not been so scared.

Another story I heard from a man from Korea is also an example of happenings due to lack of understanding cultural languages. Not long after he came to the USA, he met a blonde lady at work. She was so beautiful that he would daydream about dating her. One day, dream came true. He met her for lunch one day. He met her more often for lunch as he treated her lunch each time.

Now, he started daydreaming about getting married to her. One day, he met her for dinner; and gave a ride to her home. As she got off the car, she thanked him for dinner, and told him, "I will give you a ring tomorrow", and ran into house. She looked sort of shy saying so. Finally, dream came true again. She made a proposal to him, and would give him a ring as a token!!! He was so excited that he could not sleep well that night. The next day, she called him, but did not talk anything about the ring. He waited for days in vain.

Tired of waiting, he finally asked her about the ring, which, of course, she denied to have told him to give such kind of a ring. Finally, she figured out what caused such a misunderstanding, and explained to him what she meant by telling him that she would give him a ring. She also told him that she had a boy friend.

Even though many of the TL expressions learned during the processes of Babble Training may be culture related languages, it would not cover the wide areas of the TL culture. Therefore, offering language trainings specifically featured for the cultural aspects of TL would be one of the most effective teachings for students to increase their language skills.

For those languages with specific sets of registries for social hierarchy like Korean and Japanese, for example, it would be helpful to review those different sets of registries after students become fluent in speaking such languages. If one would try to introduce the variety levels of registries all together, it would make the students very confused, and dissuade the students from continuing the class. Accordingly, during the training process for TL acquisition and oral proficiency, the teachers should lead the students as easily as possible by focusing on one general registry.

Cultural trainings on TL should be done through the natural way of the comprehensive oral proficiency trainings. The discussion topics for the cultural trainings should include among many others such features as religions, beliefs, traditional values, ways of thinking, taboos, social value, superstitions, man and women relationships, family lives, home etiquettes, ceremonial occasions, holiday events, human relations, marriage life, child education, body gestures, social structures and hierarchy, foods, proverbial expressions which represents the values and ways of people's life, political backgrounds, history, geography, entertaining tradition, and etc.

CHAPTER 13

How To Teach: BTM Level 6 – Adding Babble for Grammar

1

What is Grammar?

Depending on the sources, the definition of grammar varies widely. Some of the definitions I found from a few sources are (1) the study of the formal features of a language as the sounds, morphemes, words, or sentences; (2) knowledge or usage of the preferred or prescribed forms in speaking or writing; and (3) the accepted rules by which words are formed and combined into sentences. According to *A Dictionary of Linguistics and Phonetics* by David Crystal, the definitions of grammar are subdivided by the types of grammars.

One of the grammar types is descriptive grammar, which is defined as a systematic description of a language as found in a sample of speech or writing. Another type of grammar in contrast to the descriptive grammar is called prescriptive grammar. It lays down rules of correctness as to how language should be used, and aims to preserve imagined standards by insisting on norms of usage and criticizing departures from these norms.

With all of such varieties of definitions, what do we really mean when we say we should or should not teach grammar to begin with? I believe that the generic common meaning of grammar is more like the accepted rules by which words are formed and combined into sentences.

Then, who make such rules and how? The descriptive grammar provides the answer. That is, the systematic description of a language based on sample speeches or writing becomes the accepted rules. The rules are of the sounds, morphemes, words, sentences, and meaning interpretations of a language. Then, people apply the concept of prescriptive grammar in judging other people's language skills.

Then, the concept of being accepted is very subjective, and it is very vague to draw a clear line between being accepted and unaccepted. Let's think about the two forms of *'He has no good friends'* and *'He don't have no good friends'*. Based on the prescriptive grammar approach, people are educated that the one is accepted or acceptable, and the other is not accepted or unacceptable. People take the other with a couple of blue underlines under the words of *'don't'* and *'no'*. That is what exactly the intelligent computer programs do to let us know some problems when we write using a computer. However, as many people do say such double negation expressions, it becomes less unacceptable, and eventually turns out to be acceptable.

People say that such kind of double negation is used particularly by the people with low education, which is not really true. In addition to such double negation issues, one can easily find many real life examples of languages, which are unacceptable languages according to the prescriptive grammar view point, turning into being acceptable. One of them is *'me'* replacing *'I'* as in *"Me don't like it"* instead of *"I don't like it"*; *"It's me"* instead of *"It is I"*; and *"Me either"* instead of *"I either"*.

What is my point?

First of all, I am trying to persuade the teachers and the students of FLE to understand that language is a live animal. It always changes and grows up. Language changes over time, people, and geographical locations. That is how the one human language from God has gotten divided into thousands of local languages. We should not insist that there should be one such thing as one and one only standard of being grammatical or acceptable.

Second of all, I am trying to make it understood clearly that grammar does not represent a language itself. So, it is a misunderstanding for one to believe that they are teaching TL by actually teaching the grammar to the students. Also, the belief that grammar education offers the basis for students to learn TL is an outdated belief. In old time, the primary goal of FLE was to teach the techniques for students to read and comprehend the written form of TL.

However, the primary and ultimate goal of contemporary FLE is to teach the students to acquire the oral proficiency of TL. Even if we would start with teaching how to speak TL from the first class of the beginning FL program, we may not have sufficient time to teach the students to acquire the desired level of the oral proficiency during the school FL program. Accordingly, we should not spend years of time just to teach students how to read and comprehend TL.

Also, it is not a subject which can be properly handled by the FL teachers and by the FL students. It is very complicated research objects for grammarians. Grammar is the products of the highly educated research professional people. They are fluent speakers of the languages before being grammarians.

Yet, even those people do not always agree on describing some phenomena of a language. Therefore, failure of learning the grammar by the students with no acquisition and oral proficiency of the language is very well expected result.

Third of all, I want to point out that we would not be able to help students effectively to catch the flying TL by teaching the grammar or the paper language. Teaching a book volume of the grammar on the morphemes, words, and sentence structures written on paper would not result in the acquisition of TL and the achievement of high oral proficiency for students. Also, it would not lay a solid foundation for the acquisition and oral proficiency of TL either.

After all, based on the nature of grammar, teaching the grammar of a dialect to the students who wish to learn a dialect of one's own language would help the students to pick up the dialect because a dialect would not require whole new sets of the acquisition factors to be acquired from scratch. A dialect would have very minimal or near zero linguistic distance from the standard dialect. So, simply understanding some particular features would make one acquire the dialect and achieve high oral proficiency. However, teaching a language, especially a language with a drastic linguistic distance from one's own language, with grammar would not work as it has been proven to be ineffective through out the centuries of FLE history. My point is that grammar-oriented FLE should be discouraged.

2

Why Do People Think Grammar First?

Do you believe that the secondary and the post secondary students should start with grammar to learn FL? If so, why? Have you ever thought seriously about the reason?

It does not take so much speculation to figure out how the concern about FLE in public schools started to spread widely. With the appearance of the industrialization in the 18th century, the countries in the world were awakened and got busy to enjoy what the industrialization could bring to their countries. They started to put spurs to the revolutionary development of their new industry. As the trades with oversea countries kept increasing, they soon realized the urgency of being able to make effective communications with the trading partners.

I don't mean to trace back to the origination of FLE. I just want to speculate about how a systematic FLE was started. We know for sure that FLE by native speakers in the schools was not feasible in the early time of the industrialization mainly due to lack of transportations to bring native speakers from hundreds, if not thousands, of miles away. We also know that the audio devices and radios were not available to the public until the mid of the 20th century.

Accordingly, the FLE before the 20th century must have been done through books with no actual sounds of the languages. Also, it was not so much crucial as nowadays for the people to be able to communicate verbally so well. As long as they could read and understand the letters or documents written in TL by taking time as needed and using dictionaries, they were OK for the business. They just needed to know how to write business documents in TL, in response to the business letters, for successful business trades.

In other words, they were in the document based communication mode with plenty of time in between. For this, they had plenty of time to work on responding in TL. It was not like nowadays when we are required to make simultaneous verbal interactions with the other parties. Therefore, they didn't have to speak the language semi-instinctively. In other words, they were OK to produce expressions with plenty of time through the step-by-step assembly process based on their grammar knowledge of TL.

This fact based on speculation would not require many arguments among us to agree. Also, when they studied FL, chances are that they would teach the languages of the neighbor countries to the students because the trades at that time were mainly among the countries with relatively convenient transportation. Also, the languages of the neighborhood countries are more likely members of the same linguistic group, which means a lot of common or quite similar linguistic features are shared such as the spellings, sounds, vocabularies, sentence structures, word structures, and etc.

Then, as the international trades increased rather rapidly, the necessity of mass FLE in the school was raised. Therefore, ideas for systematic FLE were introduced so that the students can learn FL more effectively. The ideas were to help the students understand FL in written forms very well, and also to help the students write business letters and documents in TL.

For this, linguists got together and analyzed the linguistic phenomena of FL such as the sentence structures, word structures, sound patterns, and finally introduced the grammar showing how the sentence elements are to be interpreted.

For the reasons said above, I believe, the Grammar Translation method was developed as the first generation FLE method. Also, we can see that it was almost the only possible FLE method at that time. That is, they could not think of other methods due to the limited resources at that time.

The grammar apparently helped a lot the students with analyzing the sentences and assembling the meanings. Few people have raised objection to teaching grammar first in schools as the basics to start learning a language for centuries. Therefore, the schools started teaching the grammar as the very basic for the students to be able to read and write documents in FL.

As such foreign language education system has passed down to generations after generations, our fathers, grand fathers, great grand fathers, and great great grand fathers started learning FL the same way: starting with the grammar. Not only that, our great great grand fathers also advised and taught our great grand fathers to study FL the same way.

Also, the language teachers who learned from our ancestors taught their students exactly the same way as they were taught in the past. Finally, such kind of systematic education became a strong tradition. The tradition continued down to generation after generation and finally to us. We trust our parents and grand parents, as our parents and grand parents trusted their parents and grand parents, as they would give us the best advice from their experiences.

We also trust our teachers to teach us the best based on their experiences. We think that our teachers would understand clearly what grammar is, and how it works to help us acquire the language. Therefore, we didn't ask them what grammar is, and how it is supposed to work to help us be a solid bilingual speaker. We just took their lessons and worked hard following their instructions. However, our teachers did exactly the same to their teachers as we did to ours.

So, without knowing the true reason, we believe that the grammar is the one we should start with to learn FL.

Is this the same answer that you have about why you believe we should start grammar first to learn a language? I know many people to whom it is true. Let me give you one episode as a good example why people think of grammar first when they think about FLE.

Some years ago, I received a phone call from a Korean lady. It happened to be around the same time that I received a phone call from the American lady who has a son in Montana.

"Would you please let me know what kind of grammar book you use for your class?", she somehow already knew that I was teaching at a university.

"I have many of them in my office, but I do not use grammar books in my class", I said.

"Then, could you recommend one for me please?", she asked.

"Why would you need a grammar book?", I asked out of curiosity.

"I need it to teach Korean at my church because I became a Korean teacher of my church."

"Why would you teach the Korean grammar to the students?", I continued asking.

"Just because. How else can I teach the basics of the Korean language?", she answered with no hesitation.

"Who told you that grammar is the basic to start first?"

"No, nobody. But, that was how we were taught English in school in Korea, so I think I should teach the Korean grammar to start with", I knew where she is approaching from, but I continued asking.

"So, did you learn English at school that way?"

"No."

"Then, can you speak English now?", I asked her.

"Yes."

"How?"

"I got married to my husband, who is an American, and I learned English living with him after I came to the America."

"If you didn't learn English from the grammar in school, do you expect your students to learn Korean from the grammar you teach?"

"No, but what can I do?", she really sounded not to have any idea of what else she could do.

3

Misunderstanding on the Basics for FL Learning

Many years ago, I volunteered to teach English to the Korean community members in Denver for a little bit over one year. It was once a week session for 2 hours on Saturday afternoons. Not many students gathered: only about 15. Most of them were senior members who have difficulties with articulating the English sounds after numerous repeated exercises.

I knew that it was not an ideal agenda for the members to pick up English because it is very hard and almost impossible for anybody to pick up FL through a two hour session a week. However, I had ideas to help them study through out the week for themselves. Therefore, I ran the English class for about one year. Some of the members were able to use basic expressions for daily life. However, none of them picked the linguistic intuition I believe from the class. So, I see it as not successful. There are many obvious reasons for the unsuccessful results I can think of.

Instead of illustrating all the reasons, I will introduce one of the unsolved conflicts between the students and myself. It was about the concept of the basics to learn English. Most of the students had different expectations from the class. When the words went out to the community about the English class, many people called and asked me if I would start teaching the basics. Even though I was well aware of what they meant by the "basics", which is completely different from my concept of basics, I would say 'yes'. Otherwise, I knew that I would have to argue or give a lecture over the phone to each individual who called me for the same question.

When they came to the class, I could see that they were disappointing right away. Every Saturday, I would check the babble homework that I gave to the members previous week. Then, I would introduce new chapters for them to babble repeatedly over the next week. Of course, I would explain the meanings of the new expressions, and words. I would also explain how to articulate new words individually and what the actual sounds of those words or phrases would be in a real world speaking.

However, after the class, the students would say to me that what I was doing was way too high level for them. They would confront me that I told them I would start from teaching the basics. Knowing what they meant by it, I still asked them what they mean by the basics. As I expected, they would insist that the basics are the grammar and reading.

Then, I would explain that the very basic for learning any language is doing the babble over the daily survival expressions for various situations to be able to use them. However, their responses were how you would do such things without knowing the grammar and without being able to read it. Their tone was so strong, and they believed I was wrong. I would explain again about the way all of us acquired a language from the time when we were born, and I would tell them that, fundamentally, it should not be different for us to learn FL. We, as adults with fully developed brains, could apply intensive efforts and some skills to shorten the time period of the language acquisition process.

When so many people believed in the grammar and the reading skills as the basics of a language, and still were strongly pursuing it, my lonely cries were not strong enough to overcome the big shadow.

Such belief in the grammar as the very basic of learning FL is not only prevailing to the Korean people. Not to the senior people only either. It is a worldwidely prevailing belief regardless of ages, genders, education levels, or professions.

A few years ago when I was working on my first book, *New TESL Plus,* which was published in Korean in 2005, I received a phone call from a lady. Somehow, she found out that I was teaching Korean at the University of Colorado at Boulder.

She introduced herself first and asked me.

"I was wondering whether you would be able to recommend a Korean grammar book", she was very gentle and polite asking the question.

"Why would you need it?", I asked her with surprise.

"I have a son going to a university in Montana. He met a girl friend from the school, who is Korean. My son loves her so much, and he wants to learn Korean. I am very excited that he wants to learn Korean. So, I am looking for a Korean grammar book for his birthday gift", she sounded quite excited as she said.

"Why do you think a grammar book would help him?", I asked.

"Because my son does not have any background of the Korean language. I would assume that is what he should start with."

I thought she was lucky to call me for my opinions. Otherwise, I am quite sure that his son would end up wasting a lot of time and finally give it up with nothing gained after all.

I talked to her about an hour of how we acquired our mother tongue, and why she would believe we should do it different ways to learn FL from the ways we learned our mother tongue. Of course, I talked to her about the strong requirement of Babble Training over various types of daily life expressions to start with. I also corrected her misunderstanding about the concept of the grammar. The grammar of any language is not the basics of the language in a true sense of language skills. It is one of the highest level research areas for professional linguists.

It is not surprising at all to find out many professional language teachers consider the grammar as the very basic also. Matter of fact, I have not met any language teachers who deny the grammar as the very basic to start with to learn FL. I was very surprised when I found from the homepage of a famous author of English conversation textbook that the author emphasized, as the very basic element, the importance of quite thorough knowledge of the grammar to learn FL.

Why grammar should not be the basic of FL? It is because grammar is too difficult even for native speakers; and because one can pick up FL without having to know the grammar just like every body picks up the mother tongue without knowing the grammar. Also, strong habits of grammatical approaches to FL structure interfere with the natural process of performing FL fluently.

Why do people believe that grammar is the basics to learn FL? It is because, I believe, of the popular FLE method: Grammar Translation method, which has become an undisputed tradition for generations after generations. If the first generation FLE people had started with BTM, which I am proposing here, I am quite sure that people would believe the babble, which I am going to introduce in detail later, as the very basics to learn FL. Unfortunately, it didn't start that way.

Then, what should be the basic of learning FL? I believe Babble Training over easy and simple daily life dialogue expressions should be the basics to start with. It is much easier to perform compared to the grammar; it gives one the abilities to talk in FL to deal with the common daily situations; and, as a learner accumulates those expressions, one would get the linguistic intuition on FL structure, sounds, meaning, and usages.

4

Why am I Opposed to Grammar-oriented FLE?

I have talked to many people that I believe the schools should not put its FLE focus on grammar at least to begin with, if not forever. Among those people are FL teachers and FL students. It is especially difficult to sell such belief to FL teachers. Typically they would strongly rebut my arguments insisting that grammar is very necessary in the beginning because it helps the students understand systematically the linguistic features of TL such as the word structures, sentence structures, tenses, and etc. Furthermore, they would question me how the students would produce TL sentences without knowing the grammar.

The reason I am opposed to grammar based FLE is very simple and clear. Based on the testimonies and long time observation of those who have received intensive grammar focused FL educations for many years, I believe that grammar focused education hurts or at least delays seriously the acquisition process of TL.

Among the people who show concerns on the traditional grammar focused FLE, different groups of people argue in different ways about the necessity of the grammar education. Some people argue that grammar focused education is not necessary at all. Some other people say that the amount of grammar education should be reduced significantly. Also, other people say that the very minimal grammar education is necessary to teach FL.

The fact that grammar education is not necessary or required to acquire language simply has been proven over the human history by the people in the world who have acquired the MT naturally. Also, it has been proven by tens of thousands, if not millions, of people who have become bilinguals without going through the grammar based language classes. Based on their own experiences of having learned or taught MT to the kids, people can easily understand the foundation for the argument that grammar education is not necessity for learning language.

For the same reason, all FLE teachers also know these facts very well. Yet, they still insist on teaching grammars in FL classes. The only belief for them to do so seems to be that grammar education would help students learning TL in some way. However, the multi year grammar focused FLE has failed for a couple of hundred years to produce solid bilingual speakers.

The people who advocate the grammar based FLE argue that without the grammar knowledge of TL students would not be able to read and understand TL very well. For example, one of my readers recently sent me an email from Korea saying that how can one understand such a sentence as "I should go to school to study English" without knowing the grammar on the word order and the functions of the to-infinitive verb. He wrote that he truly believed in Babble Training to acquire language skills. Yet, he still believed that basic grammar should be taught together with babbling.

The question above was of the necessity of grammar education for students to understand the meaning of the sentence. My answer to his question was that anybody could easily guess the meaning of the example sentence by simply matching the meanings of each word of the sentence. Even for more complicated sentences, it would be the same. Also, the functions of the to-infinitives can be naturally learned one by one as one acquires each expression through Babble Training. Such kinds of grammatical features can be acquired together with the expressions as a part of linguistic intuition on sentence structures and the usage of the lexical items. This is easily proven by the natural language process. Therefore, no particularly grammar based teaching is necessary.

On the other hand, people do not easily understand my arguments that grammar is a pool of harmful viruses and, therefore, should not be taught as it has been in the traditional methods because it hurts or delays the process of language acquisition. Most frequent and harmful habitual grammar viruses are of very strong pattern of accents or incorrect pronunciations of words, applying the grammar as a screen to filter through between MT and TL while speaking or listening to TL, which causes delay or incorrectness in speaking and listening to TL; serious concerns on grammatical errors; and serious time delay in speaking TL. All these types of problems are caused due to heavily focused attention mainly to the grammar without understanding the significance of the special trainings required to articulate and produce TL expressions.

Once people get used to and stuck with the harmful viruses of the grammar through very intensive grammar education, it consequently severely interferes with the acquisition process. Typically, people believe that grammar is very difficult to conquer, but, once conquered, it should be of help for one to learn TL. However, many people who have gone through very intensive grammar education for many years can understand very well exactly what my arguments about the problems of intensive grammar education mean.

So far, I have pointed out the un-necessity as well as harmful virus functions of grammar in FLE. Now, let me show further in detail, to help the understanding of readers, why I am strongly against for FLE to teach the grammar to begin with, and to continue focusing on the grammar.

I don't recommend, a grammar session, if one insists, in the beginning for one or two hour orientation to show the linguistic differences between one's mother tongue and TL. I am opposing to what they call the Grammar Translation method type of FLE or somewhat similar to it, which is still worldwidely prevailing method, where the schools offer multi year intensive grammar focused FL classes.

First and most important reason for me to oppose to the grammar based FLE is that grammar is not the language itself at all. No structural grammar focuses on introducing what and how people actually say in real life situations. Grammar may show the principles of how to combine words, but does not show the proper usages of words and expressions in real life situations. Any grammatical combination of believed-to-be relevant words does not make an effective communication. That is why students with strong background of grammar do not know what and how to say in real life situations.

Depending on the views, grammar could be defined in many different ways. However, in any sense, the nature of grammar and that of language cannot be defined as the same. They are not the same, and cannot be the same.

Therefore, no matter how long we would teach grammar to students, and no matter how well they would learn the grammar, it would not make the students pick up the TL itself. It could only help the students obtain the knowledge about how TL is structured at most. Insisting on teaching the rules or linguistic features of TL is no better than insisting on teaching the rules or musical features of music. Such knowledge does not offer realistic help to the students with, most importantly among others, acquiring the physical capacities required to perform the language or the music.

Secondly, the traditional Grammar Translation method spends too much time to teach or learn the grammar. Typically, the secondary schools would spend about 3 years for the Grammar Translation method. For example, the schools in the Asian countries like Korea,

Japan, and China offer the grammar intensive FLE to its middle and high school students, which means 6 years. Even though the high schools in Korea lately introduced English listening classes to prepare the national examination for college admission, it really does not appear that the schools have changed the philosophy of FLE method.

Consequently, I believe that such grammar based FLE really takes away the opportunities for the students to pick up the language itself. They would spend all of their times in their school ages to study grammar, and they would graduate with no real language skills of TL. I don't like the school spending the whole time not on TL but on the grammar of TL.

Thirdly, as grammar is not the language itself, it is not necessary for one to teach TL. That is, one can teach TL without having to teach the grammar. FL teachers would say to me that knowing the language would help one pick up TL better, which I don't agree with. In fact, it rather seems to interfere with the natural language learning process than helping it. This is true because one would pick up a bad habit, from the intensive grammar classes, of always, whenever reading, listening or speaking TL expression, trying to apply the grammar one knows to every single expression. Therefore, when the grammar one has cannot verify some particular expressions, one has to find ways to figure it out before accepting them. This kind of process is a very bad habit in developing FL skills.

Fourthly, no grammar is complete. There are exceptions, to which regular grammar rules do not apply, everywhere in TL. Not many people can get the complete sets of grammar knowledge. Therefore, one cannot find out all the grammars that match the real life expressions. However, even with very trivial amount of grammar knowledge, one would always stop first and try to apply one's grammar to screen the structures before performing the language.

Last but still very importantly, as the history of FLE methods shows for the Grammar Translation method, the goal of intensive grammar focused education is for the students to be able to translate TL into one's language and vice versa. It does not serve the goals of FLE required in modern era.

In the modern era, students are required to prove oral proficiency in TL. They need to perform TL verbally with high efficiency. Students need to pick up TL just like our own mother tongue. Once they pick up TL fluently, they could do the translation without having to go through the grammar education.

Let me get back to FL teachers' question of how the students would produce the words and sentences without knowing the grammar. My answer to them is 'look at the 36-40 month old babies'. If they could do it with only about 30 months of babbling, we, with fully developed brains and athletic senses, should be able to do it much better than what they do.

5

Training To Be Grammatically Correct

It is my belief that intensive grammar education of TL should not be offered to the students until they pick up high level oral proficiency for many reasons. However, it does not mean that I do not care about the students being grammatically incorrect from the beginning at all. Yes, it is important to teach for the students to be grammatically correct as much as possible from the beginning. Then, how can we teach students to be grammatically correct?

One of the most important reasons I have found for people to believe in grammar-oriented FLE is that one cannot avoid making grammatical mistakes without learning the grammar. I am sure that this is a totally wrong understanding. Also, the belief that one can avoid making grammatical mistakes by studying grammar is a very clear misunderstanding.

Additionally, being grammatically incorrect does not necessarily occur only to the foreign language speakers. Most of the grammatical errors occur not because people did not learn the grammar but because they did not learn the correct languages. Sometimes, grammatical errors can occur because of the grammar being outdated. In other words, based on the criteria of old grammar, any new phenomena of the language can be considered as ungrammatical. Also, most of the grammatical errors are of speech errors rather than of the speaker's ignorance of the grammar.

I know many people from many different countries who received near 100% in the English grammar test. However, most of them still make grammatical mistakes so much in speaking and writing in English. Not only that, I also have found the native speakers of English who lived their whole life in the USA make grammatical mistakes in their speeches and writings. I also claim that I have quite high level of English grammar knowledge. However, even after over 17 years of residing in the USA, I still find myself making what they call grammatical errors in speaking and writing in English.

As a matter of fact, I also make grammatical mistakes in speaking and writing in my own mother language, Korean, sometimes. Some of the reasons for my mistakes in speaking or writing Korean are that some of the grammars which I learned when I was young are changed by the authorities; that I knowingly insist on my way of using ungrammatical expressions as I don't like the supposedly grammatical forms; and that I would rely on my intuition just because I am confused with the rule. After all, grammar of a language can vary depending on individual speaker's preferences. This is just like we acknowledge that different musicians can write their music in different patterns.

What do we need to do to teach students to be grammatically correct as much as possible without having to start with a grammar book? We already know the answer. We should teach them to acquire correct languages from the beginning. It is that simple. In order to teach the students to pick up correct languages from the beginning, the FL teachers do not have to be fluent like the native speakers of TL thanks to the technology. Of course, it would be more ideal to have native speakers teach the students. However, providing native speaker teachers do not necessarily resolve the problems of the inefficient FLE problems.

If the native speaker teachers would follow the traditional grammar translation methods, the students would fail to acquire and develop the oral proficiency of the language anyway. Also, if the native speaker teachers would have to deal with many students at a time only for certain amount of time per week, they would not be able to serve efficiently as models whom the students can learn from.

To teach students to learn correct languages from the beginning, the FL teachers' job is to lead and coordinate Babble Training of the students with the correct forms. For this, it would be great if the school could provide sufficient number of teachers who could always lead the individual Babble Training in person by offering model languages to the students just like the parents would do to their child.

The best babble leader model we can find would be a mother or father like human model. So, finding an ideal home stay host for students would be a good way to provide a babble leader. However, these types of babble leaders are not what the FL teachers can find for the students. Instead, the teachers should find the best babble leaders available to given circumstances. I have suggested using the audio equipments as one of the most effective and available babble leader which can provide model forms of TL.

While it is important for the FL teachers to teach students with correct expressions, providing realistic expressions to the class so that students feel interested in the language is very important job also. Through BTM model, I have suggested sets of correct language models such as personal languages, social languages, business languages, professional languages, and cultural languages to the increasing levels of the students.

The role of the teachers should not be teaching the grammar or any kind of skills for evaluations, but be managing and directing the students consistently to acquire and develop the oral proficiency of TL successfully after the model languages. For these roles of FL teachers, they don't have to be native speakers of TL. Correct understandings of how language is acquired and of the FL teaching process is much more important than being a native speaker FL teacher.

Students who acquire and develop the oral proficiency of TL through the correct model languages will develop such natural linguistic intuitions that they would be grammatically correct. No particular sessions of grammar classes are necessary. This is just like how children develop the intuitions to be grammatically correct. Then, any grammatically incorrect performances of the students should be corrected by the teachers case by case, which will again help students to build correct intuitions on the language.

Once students achieve high level of oral proficiency of TL, they will have acquired most of the grammar by heart. Yet, they may not be able to explain the grammatical features using the grammatical terms, which is not a problem at all in making successful communications. Unlike the grammar crammed into one's brain through multi year intensive FL programs which mostly end without acquiring TL, the grammar acquired naturally like this will not interfere with the natural and meaningful process of incoming and outgoing meanings. Therefore, the language process between MT and TL will be very natural without any artificial filter or screen in between the two languages.

Even though the respective fields of the grammar can be acquired through the process of developing oral proficiency, not all of the individual features may be acquired by the students during such process.

In other words, even after students achieved high level of the oral proficiency, students still may not have developed sufficient intuitions on particular features of TL mostly because those features are not pattern based but independent characteristics, which have not occurred frequently enough during the acquisition process.

For example, the Korean language has numerous number of sentence ending markers, most of which are not commonly used. Only several of them are frequently used typically. Students who acquired Korean as TL should know about the grammatical category of such sentence ending markers. They should also know the general function of the markers. That is, the markers do not change the proposition but simply denote the modalities. However, it is highly unlikely for them to know the respective modalities represented by each of the markers which they have not read or been told before.

Also, it is true that students may still be confused with some of the grammatical features either because they have not had enough opportunities to acquire them or because the grammatical features are quite complicated. Typically, students will acquire them with enough time and experience. However, students can be benefited a lot from a series of grammar sessions as they now know what they don't know and what confuses them.

Accordingly, once students acquired and developed the oral proficiency of TL, offering a series of grammar summary sessions can be helpful to mature the students' understanding of TL. Also, the grammar summary sessions will not be so dry and hard to the students as they can feel and understand how the grammar is processed. It would not take so long time for the students to understand the grammar. Depending on the students' proficiency levels, and depending on the depths of the grammar being taught, it may take as less as a couple of weeks or a month based on 5 class hours per week. Then, students will be much more confident about being grammatically correct.

We do not need to spend years of time, in the beginning, to teach the grammar which would help students to develop the reading proficiency at most.

CHAPTER 14

Ideas for Successful Self BTM

Ideas suggested here is a guideline for a short-term basic level program model.

Intensive Babble Training is the only way to overcome the accent of one's mother tongue, and to make it easy to acquire TL.

To enhance oral proficiency for higher levels, a lot more of intensive Babble Training over extended amount of Real Input is strongly recommended before one starts the 2nd level Babble Training to read.

Real Input of 500 ~ 1000 expressions for talking is quite minimum level for the 1st level Babble Training. For better performance, I strongly recommend 2,000 ~ 3000 expressions or even more of real input for talking because it is the only best and fastest way to acquire language to higher level of oral proficiency.

The higher amount of Real Input expressions for talking is acquired, the higher native-like oral proficiency would be achieved.

Students who already have acquired the reading and listening skills through the traditional methods would want to heavily focus on Babble Training for a maximum number of expressions to learn the variety of as-is useful expressions and become fluent in ones daily, social, professional activities.

1

Hurdles To Employ BTM
for Public Programs

What I wrote in this book is mainly to introduce the concept of BTM and show how to apply BTM to the public language programs in general. So, some specific ideas I proposed in terms of the quantity of real input and the duration of the program may need to be adjusted to accommodate the actual environments of individual programs.

The language programs whether in public or private schools, and whether for elementary schools or colleges, have all kinds of hurdles to overcome for successful application of BTM to their programs.

Among the many hurdles I have experienced as a language teacher, I believe that the most critical challenge to employ BTM for the public language programs is with the authorities and the teachers who have led the language programs for centuries. They need to realize the crucial facts that the long-lasting conventional programs have completely failed to help students acquire the target languages; that intensive grammar programs before acquisition are absolutely harmful in many aspects and seriously interfere with acquisition; and that language is acquired in one and only way through repeated

Babble Training over real input, which I call BTM, just like how the babies acquire their mother tongues.

Without their recognition of those crucial facts, no meaningful changes can be expected in the public language programs. Just like it was very hard for mankind to accept the sun-centered universe for long time, it would be quite challenging for most of the authorities and teachers to realize those crucial facts and change their minds completely away from the conventional programs.

Even if they would find the effectiveness of BTM, they would not give up the conventional program for long time. Instead, they might want to combine BTM and the conventional methods, and see how BTM works, which would significantly compromise the efficiency of BTM for many reasons.

I have tested BTM not only in the college programs I ran to teach Korean, but also in the private programs I ran to teach English for small groups of immigrants from Korea for many years. I learned about some serious challenges to run the programs successfully.

For the college program, the most serious problem is the fact that the curriculum does not secure a minimum of two years which, I believe, is required to acquire a language to the elementary level. Students needed to take only 3 semesters of a language program to meet the requirement, and, yet, very few students would complete even three semesters to go through a rather demanding BTM program (for a language neither so popular, at least back then, nor so easy to learn) compared to the less demanding conventional programs. In the college programs, classes not meeting the required minimum number of students would be canceled.

However, I saw significant success for students to talk fluently using the expressions they learned through BTM program. Unfortunately though, I knew that they would lose the expressions soon when they do not keep Babble Training over the expressions for at least two years. Based on my own experience of English acquisition and observation of language acquisition of others, I would say that each expression would take repeated Babble Training or practice efforts for at least two years to stay in the long term memory and be contributed toward the acquisition.

For the private programs, the students were adults with full time jobs between 40s and 50s, which, based on my input-output hypothesis, means that they have the strongest level of linguistic resistance to overcome. Most of the students did well. Yet, the biggest problem was again that the programs could not last more than a year. Students had to quit the program for various personal reasons related to their jobs, health, and family issues. So, even though they would pick up about 800 ~ 1000 independent expressions during the time, they would lose those expressions soon unless they keep Babble Training over them at least for another year or so until those expressions get processed repeatedly in their LAD enough for them to acquire the needed acquisition factors such as the linguistic intuition, physical capacity, and the linguistic resource.

As I pointed out above, the public or private programs have various types of hurdles and difficulties to meet an individual's goals to acquire a language. Therefore, a student may consider applying BTM to his or her own self-study.

2

Employing BTM for Self-Study

Before one starts self-learning, learner should know that (prescriptive) grammar is not only not needed but also very harmful to acquisition. This will be a quite challenging fact for a learner to accept. Just relax and be assured that one would be much more successful to acquire a language without the interference of grammar. Should one have a strong background of grammar already, sorry, it's a bad luck. One with strong background of grammar skills will have much longer and tougher time to go through the tunnel of acquisition. Grammar which mostly serves as a rule to control the expressions and the logic of thinking is basically a pool of bad habits built during the process and as a result of learning grammar. So, get rid of grammar. Stay away from grammar as much as you can. Start with BTM, and grammar will be acquired naturally during the process and as a result of acquisition.

Learner also should know that no skills of reading, listening, or writing are required to acquire language. As long as one has the skills to listen to, repeat after, recite, and mimic expressions, one would need no other skills at all to acquire language. Yet, it would be of great help if one can recognize the sounds of letters, characters, or alphabets of the target language.

To start self learning with BTM, one needs to find textbooks composed of real input or personal expressions which one can use in one's daily activities. Also, the textbook should come with audio sets produced with native speaker's voice. Also, ideal textbooks would be in a bilingual form between the two languages so that the student can easily understand the expressions.

These textbooks are for Babble Training to talk. To acquire the target language to the beginner's level, one would need a minimum of about one thousand real expressions. The more real expressions one would pick up, the more fluent and advanced level of acquisition will be achieved.

3

Self Babble Training to Talk

Once one found or obtained textbooks utilizing real input, he or she can do Babble Training as follows:

1. Spend about one to two intensive hours or as needed every day to listen, repeat after the audio to memorize, and practice new expressions; and to build a pool of real input in their Language Acquisition Device. Ten to fifteen expressions a day or as much as one can afford will be good. It can be quite challenging to pick up 10-15 expressions in one to two hours in the beginning. However, as one gets familiar with the language and depending on individual skills, one would need only about 30 minutes or so to pick up 10-15 expressions.

2. Spend about one to two relax hours or as needed every day to practice the expressions acquired during the past 7 days. The relax hours here means those time when one can listen and repeat after, or recite those expression in multi task mode like driving, resting, biking, riding bus, exercising, and etc.

3. Spend about one to two relax hours or as needed every week to practice the expressions acquired during the past 15 days.

4. Spend about one to two relax hours or as needed every month to practice the expressions acquired during the past month.

5. When a book is done, take time as needed to repeat the book two more times before starting a new book. For this book review, start from the last scenario of the book going backward.

6. When the book was reviewed twice successfully, start a new book following the above steps 1 through 5.

7. While following the steps 1 through 5, take time as much as needed every three months to repeat all the books or expressions acquired in the past.

The whole process of Babble Training will lead learners to strong levels of mental immersion in the target language, and increase the efficiency of acquisition.

If a leaner can fluently acquire about two thousand real expressions this way, one can say the learner has acquired the language to the elementary level. This way, learners can acquire a language to the elementary level in two to three years. If one would continue Babble Training for additional amount of real expressions, one can advance the acquisition to higher levels. This way, one can acquire the language to an advanced level, which an adult may not achieve through the physical immersion in the country of the target language for the same period of time.

4

Self Babble Training to Read

With successful Babble Training to pick up about 500-1000 (or more as desired) expressions of real input, and while keeping Babble Training for more amount and higher level of real input, one can add Babble Training to read. The Babble Training textbook to read should include audio sets with native speaker's voice for the purpose of Babble Training to listen as well.

Ideal textbooks for Babble Training to read would be in a bilingual form between the two languages so that students can save time and efforts to understand the sentences. Also, the bilingual form will enable students to compare their own understanding of sentences against the translation, and correct their mistakes in understanding of any particular words and/or sentences. One can choose books of one's own interested subjects.

Also, one would need notebooks to keep the vocabularies one gets during Babble Training to read.

1. Spend about one to two intensive hours or as needed every day to study vocabulary; guess the meaning of the sentences purely based on the meaning of the respective words in the sentence; compare the meaning against the translation; and to correct the problems which had led one to misunderstand the sentence. In the very beginning,

one may be able to read only several sentences during the one to two intensive hours. Yet, it will pickup the speed as one makes progress gradually.

2.   Write down new vocabularies in the notebook. Then, put each vocabulary item on four or five different pages to come in the book with increasing number of interval pages like 5 pages, 10 pages, 15 pages, and 20 pages ahead respectively. This way, one will get to repeat memorizing the vocabulary items as one goes on reading the book.

3.   Use spare times every day to visit the vocabulary notebook to review the lexical items entered in the notebook previously.

4.   Once a book is completed for reading, read the book three or four more times before one starts reading a new book following the steps 1 through 3 above. As one repeats the book, one will be able to build strong intuition to understand the sentences of the target language. Also, one will obtain expressions one could use in creative talking and in Babble Training to write later.

5

Self Babble Training to Listen

When Babble Training to read on the book #1 gets successfully repeated three or four times, one can add Babble Training to listen by starting listening to the audio version of the same book #1. One can start listening practice for 5 to 10 minutes, covering 2 ~ 3 pages or so at a time, and repeat it as many times as one can in a day.

Then, complete repeating three or more times of listening to the book #1 before starting Babble Training to read on the book #2. This is the end of Babble Training to read and listen to the book #1.

Babble Training to listen by listening to the same textbooks for reading, which one already is familiar with through repeated Babble Trainings to read, will help one improve the listening skills very effectively. Not only that, by repeating the same book for a total of six or 8 times through reading and listening, one's vocabularies and sentences will become very rich and be easily deployed in real talking.

Through this method of training to listen, one will find that it is much easier and more effective compared to trying to listen to the TV programs, movies, or radio programs.

One would need Babble Training to read and listen for five or six books, or more as one desires. This would surely enable one to acquire reading and listening skills.

6

Self Babble Training to Write

While one successfully follows the self Babble Training to talk, read, and listen as described above, one can add Babble Training to write by starting to write daily journal. Writing daily journal does not have to be creative writing. One can copy sentences from the textbooks one used to learn talking and reading/listening. Or, one can make minor changes from those sentences by replacing words here and there as needed to write one's own meaning in the journal. Writing the first journal will be most challenging. However, it will get faster and easier as one keeps writing every day.

7

Self Babble Training to Learn Grammar

Once the student successfully reached to the level of Babble Training to write, he or she will have acquired a very strong level of the intuitive grammar skills. Studying the systematic grammar is not necessary. One can easily go through the grammar book and find that he or she has acquired most of the grammar skills already.

However, going through a thorough study of grammar at this state will help one with handling grammatically complicated expressions. While studying grammar, one will have many 'aha' moments.

8

Completion of BTM
for Self-Study

The whole process of the accumulated Babble Training to talk, read, listen, and write can take at least good three or four years, if not more, depending on the variables of the individual's desire and contributions to the program.

At the end of successful Babble Training, one will have very strong and solid acquisition of such acquisition factors as the linguistic intuition, physical capacity, and linguistic resources to command the speaking, reading, and writing the target language.

REFERENCES

Bloom, Paul (1994) Language Acquisition. The MIT Press.

Bragger, Jeannette D. (1986) "Teaching For Proficiency: Are we ready?".

ADFL Bulletin 18, no. 1 (September 1986): 11-14.

Crystal, David. (1991) A Dictionary of Linguistics and Phonetics. Blackwell Publishers Ltd.

Freed, Barbara F. (1989) "Perspectives on the Future of Proficiency-Based Teaching and Testing". ADFL Bulletin 20, no. 2 (January 1989): 52-57.

Hudson, Mutsuko Endo. (2007) "Workshop on Proficiency-oriented Language Instruction".

Lee, Cheol Beom. (2005) New TESL Plus. Chonghap Press.

Phillips, June K. (1985) "Outcomes And Expectancies In A Proficiency-oriented Program: Toward Realistic Objectives". ADFL Bulletin 16, no. 3 (April 1985): 9-12.

Slobin, Dan Isaac (1979) Pshcholinguistics. Scott, Foresman and Company.

Univ. of Idaho on line. (2007) "Teaching Methods and Correlation to Learning in the Language Classroom". http://ivc.uidaho.edu/flbrain/learning.htm.

Stephen Krashen (Oct. 15, 2010), Stephen Krashen on Language Acquisition (https://www.google.com/search?q=krashen&rlz=1C-1CHBD_enUS851US851&sxsrf=ALiCzsYuNsyxIYdBbfHt-D2xZZnUj37B5eQ:1670791715029&source=lnms&tbm=vid&sa=X&ved=2ahUKEwjw0auVuPL7AhXRIDQI-Hf3eCK8Q0pQJegQIBRAG&biw=1600&bih=757&dpr=1#fpstate=ive&vld=cid:9baca7e6,vid:NiTsduRreug)

Stephen Krashen (Dec 26, 2019), Optimal Input (https://www.google.com/search?q=optimal+input&rlz=1C1CHBD_enUS851US851&biw=1600&bih=757&tbm=vid&sxsrf=ALiCzsbJLhEpiMtsdSoiAgN4z-7tImJIArw%3A1670791723672&ei=K0KWY_POKIGB0PEPo4mp6Ac&oq=op&gs_lcp=Cg1nd3Mt-d2l6LXZpZGVvEAEYADIECAAQQzIFCAAQgAQy-CAgAEIAEELEDMgsIABCABBCxAxCDATIL-CAAQgAQQsQMQgwEyCwgAEIAEELEDEIMBMMg-gIABCxAxCDATIFCAAQgAQyBQgAEIAEMgsIAB-CABBCxAxCDAToECCMQJ1CnFFiKF2DqLWgC-cAB4AIABmgGIAeACkgEDMS4ymAEAoAEBwAEB&s-client=gws-wiz-video#fpstate=ive&vld=cid:7cebafee,vid:S_j4JELf8DA)

www.ingramcontent.com/pod-product-compliance
Lightning Source LLC
Chambersburg PA
CBHW071659120626
46550CB00001B/44